Power Query for
Power BI and Excel

Chris Webb

Apress®

ISBN-13 (pbk): 978-1-4302-6691-4

ISBN-13 (electronic): 978-1-4302-6692-1

Publisher: Heinz Weinheimer
Lead Editor: Jonathan Gennick
Technical Reviewer: Jen Underwood
Editorial Board: Steve Anglin, Mark Beckner, Ewan Buckingham, Gary Cornell, Louise Corrigan, Jim DeWolf, Jonathan Gennick, Jonathan Hassell, Robert Hutchinson, Michelle Lowman, James Markham, Matthew Moodie, Jeff Olson, Jeffrey Pepper, Douglas Pundick, Ben Renow-Clarke, Dominic Shakeshaft, Gwenan Spearing, Matt Wade, Steve Weiss
Coordinating Editor: Jill Balzano
Copy Editors: Ann Dickson and James Fraleigh
Compositor: SPi Global
Indexer: SPi Global
Artist: SPi Global
Cover Designer: Anna Ishchenko

Distributed to the book trade worldwide by Springer Science+Business Media New York, 233 Spring Street, 6th Floor, New York, NY 10013. Phone 1-800-SPRINGER, fax (201) 348-4505, e-mail orders-ny@springer-sbm.com, or visit www.springeronline.com. Apress Media, LLC is a California LLC and the sole member (owner) is Springer Science + Business Media Finance Inc (SSBM Finance Inc). SSBM Finance Inc is a Delaware corporation.

For information on translations, please e-mail rights@apress.com, or visit www.apress.com.

Apress and friends of ED books may be purchased in bulk for academic, corporate, or promotional use. eBook versions and licenses are also available for most titles. For more information, reference our Special Bulk Sales–eBook Licensing web page at www.apress.com/bulk-sales.

Any source code or other supplementary material referenced by the author in this text is available to readers at www.apress.com. For detailed information about how to locate your book's source code, go to www.apress.com/source-code/.

To Helen, Natasha, and Mimi. YAVNANSB!

Contents at a Glance

About the Author xv

About the Technical Reviewer xvii

Acknowledgments xix

Preface xxi

■Chapter 1: Introducing Power Query 1

■Chapter 2: Power Query Data Sources.. 17

■Chapter 3: Transforming Data with Power Query 63

■Chapter 4: Data Destinations.. 99

■Chapter 5: Introduction to M 115

■Chapter 6: Working with Multiple Queries.. 149

■Chapter 7: Power Query and Power BI for Office 365.............................. 167

■Chapter 8: Power Query Recipes 189

Index..243

Contents

About the Author xv

About the Technical Reviewer xvii

Acknowledgments xix

Preface xxi

■Chapter 1: Introducing Power Query 1

Power Query and Power BI 1

    Power BI Components 1

    Power Query and Power BI Licensing 5

    Installing Power Query 6

Power Query Concepts 6

Power Query Walkthrough 7

    Creating a Simple Query 7

    Editing an Existing Query 9

    Why Use Power Query? 13

Summary 15

■Chapter 2: Power Query Data Sources 17

Querying Relational Databases 17

    Connecting to SQL Server 17

    Navigating through a Database in the Query Editor 22

    Connecting to Other Databases 26

Extracting Data from Files 26

    Working with CSV Files 27

    Working with Text Files 28

Working with XML Files 29

Working with JSON Files 30

Working with Excel Files..31

Working with Folders and Multiple Files 32

Working with Data from the Windows File System...32

Combining Data from Multiple Text Files 33

Working with Data from the Current Excel Workbook 34

Working with Data from the Web 35

Scraping Data from Web Pages 35

Calling a Web Service 38

Finding Data Using Power Query Online Search...38

Using Other Queries as Data Sources 43

Referencing Entire Queries..43

Duplicating Queries 45

Using Individual Values from Queries 45

OData Data Sources 46

Working with Generic OData Web Services 46

Working with Data from Excel Workbooks Stored in SharePoint..47

Working with Data from SharePoint Lists 48

Working with Data from the Windows Azure Marketplace 49

Working with Data from Windows Azure Blob Storage and Table Storage 52

Working with Data from HDFS and HDInsight 52

Working with Active Directory Data..53

Working with Data from Microsoft Exchange 53

Working with Data from Facebook 54

Working with Data from SAP BusinessObjects..55

Reusing Recent Data Sources 56

Managing Credentials 57

The Importance of Locale...58

Setting a Default Locale 59

CSV Files and Code Pages 60

Summary 61

■**Chapter 3: Transforming Data with Power Query** 63

Queries and Steps 63

Working with Columns 65

Naming Columns 65

Moving Columns 66

Removing Columns 66

Splitting Columns 66

Merging Columns 69

Setting the Data Type of a Column 70

Changing Data Types and Locales 72

Filtering Rows 72

Filtering Rows Using Auto-Filter 72

Filtering Rows Using Number, Text, and Date Filters 73

Filtering Rows by Range 76

Removing Duplicate Values 78

Filtering Out Rows with Errors 79

Sorting a Table 79

Changing Values in a Table 80

Replacing Values with Other Values 80

Text Transforms 81

Number Transforms 83

Date/Time/Duration Transforms 84

Filling Up and Down to Replace Missing Values 86

Aggregating Values 88

Unpivoting Columns to Rows 91

Transposing a Table 93

Creating Custom Columns 94

    Built-in Custom Columns 94

    Custom Columns with M Calculations 97

Summary 98

■Chapter 4: Data Destinations 99

Choosing a Destination for Your Data 99

Loading Data to the Worksheet 100

    Using the Default Excel Table Output 101

    Loading Data to Your Own Excel Tables 101

Loading Data to the Excel Data Model 103

    Viewing Tables in the Excel Data Model 103

    Advantages of Using the Excel Data Model 106

    Power Query and Table Relationships 107

    Breaking Changes 110

Refreshing Queries 110

    Refreshing Queries Manually 111

    Automating Data Refresh 112

Summary 114

■Chapter 5: Introduction to M 115

Writing M in the Query Editor 115

    The Formula Bar 115

    The Advanced Editor Window 116

    Creating a Blank Query 117

M Language Concepts 118

    Expressions, Values, and Let statements 118

    Writing M 119

Lists, Records, and Tables 123

    Lists 123

    Records..126

    Tables 127

    Selections and Projections 135

Functions..138

    Defining Functions Inside a Query..138

    each Expressions 139

    Queries As Functions 140

    let Expressions in Function Definitions 142

    Recursive Functions 143

    Functions Imported from Data Sources...143

Working with Web Services...143

Query Folding 145

    Monitoring Query Folding in SQL Server 145

    Preventing Query Folding in Code 146

    Other Operations That May Prevent Query Folding..147

Summary...148

■Chapter 6: Working with Multiple Queries..149

Using One Query as a Source for Another 149

    Referencing Queries in Code 149

    Creating Parameterized Queries...150

Working with Data from Different, External Data Sources 152

    Data Privacy Settings...152

    The Formula Firewall..154

    The Fast Combine Option..156

Appending Data from One Query onto Another 157

    Appending Queries in the User Interface...158

    Appending in M...160

Merging Two Queries..161

Merging Queries in the User Interface 161

Merging in M 164

Summary 166

Chapter 7: Power Query and Power BI for Office 365 167

Sharing and Using Shared Queries in Power Query 167

Sharing queries 167

Consuming Shared Queries 171

Updating Queries That Have Been Shared 172

Managing Shared Queries in the Power BI Data Catalog 172

Finding Your My Power BI page 172

Viewing Shared Queries 173

Viewing Usage Analytics 174

Managing data sources 175

The Data Steward 177

Who Is the Data Steward? 177

Certifying Queries 178

Which Queries Should Be Shared? 179

Sharing Functions 180

Power BI for Office 365 Data Refresh 180

Supported Data Sources 180

Enabling Scheduled Refresh 181

Summary 187

Chapter 8: Power Query Recipes 189

Calculations 189

Percentage Share of Grand Total 189

Percentage Growth in Sales from the Previous Day 193

Tied Ranks 199

Counting the Number of Distinct Customers 202

Table Transformations 205

    Converting a Single-Column Table to a Multiple-Column Table...205

    Finding New, Lost, and Returning Customers...210

    Generating a Date Table...217

    How Long Was a Stock Price Above a Given Value? 223

Working with Data from the Web 230

    Web-Scraping Weather Forecast Data...230

    Finding the Driving Distance Between Two Locations Using the Bing Maps Route Web Service......238

Summary..242

Index...243

About the Author

Chris Webb is an independent consultant and trainer based in the UK. He has over 15 years' experience with the Microsoft BI stack and has worked in a variety of roles (including several years with Microsoft Consulting Services) across a wide range of industries. A regular speaker at user groups and conferences around the world, such as the PASS Summit and the PASS Business Analytics Conference, he is also one of the organizers of the SQLBits conference in the UK and has received Microsoft's Most Valuable Professional award for nine years running. He is the co-author of several books such as *MDX Solutions, Expert Cube Development with SQL Server Analysis Services,* and *SQL Server Analysis Services 2012: The BISM Tabular Model,* and he blogs about Microsoft BI at http://cwebbbi.wordpress.com. More information about his consultancy can be found at www.crossjoin.co.uk and about his training courses at www.technitrain.com.

About the Technical Reviewer

Jen Underwood has almost 20 years of hands-on experience in the data warehousing, business intelligence, reporting, and predictive analytics industry. Prior to launching Impact Analytix, she was a Microsoft Global Business Intelligence Technical Product Manager responsible for technical product marketing and field readiness for a $10+ billion market suite of analytics offerings spanning across Microsoft SQL Server, Office, and SharePoint. She also held roles as an Enterprise Data Platform Specialist, Tableau Technology Evangelist, and a Business Intelligence Consultant for Big 4 Systems Integration firms. Throughout most of her career she has been researching, designing, and implementing analytic solutions across a variety of open source, niche, and enterprise vendor landscapes including Microsoft, Oracle, IBM, and SAP.

As a seasoned industry analyst, presenter, author, blogger, and trainer, Jen is quite active in the global technical community. Recently she was honored with a Boulder BI Brain Trust (BBBT) membership, a Tableau Zen Master (MVP) award, a Worldwide PASS Excel BI Chapter leadership role, and a Dun & Bradstreet MVP. She writes articles for BeyeNetwork, SQL Server Pro, and other industry media channels.

Jen holds a Bachelor of Business Administration degree from the University of Wisconsin, Milwaukee and a postgraduate certificate in Computer Science—Data Mining from the University of California, San Diego.

Acknowledgments

I would like to thank the following people for their help (either directly or indirectly) in learning Power Query and writing this book: Jen Underwood, Melissa Coates, Andrea Uggetti, Faisal Mohamood, Miguel Llopis, Reza Rad, Douglas Day, Ron Pihlgren, Steve Wright, Matt Masson, Theresa Palmer-Boroski, Steven Peters, Jimmy Haley, Bob Phillips, John White, Lee Hawthorne, Curt Hagenlocher, Oliver Engels, Matthew Roche, Kasper de Jonge, Jamie Thomson, Andrew Fox, Zafar Abbas, and Marco Russo.

Preface

It's easy to create amazing demos with Microsoft's new Power BI suite of tools. If you've bought this book you've probably already seen more than your fair share: See millions of values summed up in a second using Power Pivot! Watch bubbles bounce around a chart with Power View! Zoom over a 3D landscape with Power Map! Talk to your data with Q&A! Quite often Power Query is only shown for a few seconds, if it's shown at all. And yet... anyone who tries to do any real work with Power BI soon realizes that Power Query is the real star of the stack. I fell in love with it as soon as I saw the first experimental versions, back when it was called Data Explorer, and I've watched it grow up into an immensely capable tool - one that is both easy-to-use for the novice analyst and extremely flexible for the experienced BI consultant. I expect that the millions of Excel users who have already embraced Power Pivot will find Power Query just as useful.

One of the best things about Power Query, however, presents a big problem for this book. Over the last year development team have been releasing new versions of Power Query nearly every month: new functionality has been added, the user interface has been altered and improved, and bugs have been fixed. This book was written in the first few months of 2014 and uses the May 2014 release (version 2.11.3660.141) as its baseline. However by the time you read this it is certain that further versions of Power Query will have appeared and as a result some parts of this book will be out of date. This is the unavoidable consequence of Microsoft's new policy of accelerated release cycles and I hope it does not spoil your enjoyment of this book. Even if new features have been added and the user interface has changed, I expect the core functionality of Power Query to stay the same.

This book is structured as follows. Chapter 1 provides an overview of Power Query, what it does and how it fits into the wider Power BI stack; it also introduces the Power Query user interface. Chapters 2, 3 and 4 then go into more detail about the functionality available from the user interface, covering how to extract data from all of the supported data sources, transforming that data, and loading that data into the worksheet or the Excel Data Model. Put together these chapters deal with almost all of the functionality that the casual Power Query user will ever need. Chapter 5 has a more technical focus: it deals with the M language that underpins Power Query. Learning M is necessary if you want to go beyond the basics of Power Query but if you are not comfortable with programming then you may want to skim over this chapter. Chapter 6 looks at how to work with multiple queries, and while it has a certain amount of M code in it you do not need a deep understanding of M for many of the subjects it discusses. Chapter 7 shows how to share Power Query queries via a Power BI site and is only relevant if you have purchased a Power BI subscription. Finally, chapter 8 consists of a series of step-by-step examples showing how you can solve common business problems using Power Query and is recommended for all readers.

■ ■ ■

CHAPTER 1

Introducing Power Query

This book is for people who spend a lot of time working with Excel building reports and dashboards. More specifically, this book is for people who work with Excel building reports and dashboards and who are bored with copying and pasting data into worksheets, bored with clicking the same sequence of buttons every month to clean and shape that data, and bored with fixing the problems associated with complex formulas, dirty data, and the errors that are inevitable when you have to follow the same procedures over and over and over again. The good news is that Power Query is here to free you from these dull, repetitive tasks and give you time to concentrate on what's important: analyzing your data and gaining insights from it. Even better, Power Query is easy to use and lots of fun to learn (so long as you're the kind of person who thinks that playing with data can be fun—no need to feel ashamed if you do) and, as a result, it will make you more efficient, more productive, and, hopefully, less bored.

Power Query and Power BI

Power Query is an Excel add-in developed by Microsoft, and its purpose is to make it easier to load data into Excel from external data sources. It's part of the Power BI suite of tools and, as such, it's just one tool out of many that you can use when developing what are called "self-service Business Intelligence solutions" in Excel. What is "self-service Business Intelligence?" I hear you ask. Well, it's just a fancy term for those reports and dashboards that you build as part of your job. The aim of a Business Intelligence (usually shortened to "BI") solution is to make business information accessible to people so that they can use it to make informed decisions about how to do their job; other terms you may have heard include "management information systems" and "decision support systems". The whole process is referred to as "self-service" because the people who want to use this data, the analysts, the accountants, the managers and so on, are also the people who are building the reports—they do not have to rely on help from the IT department to do so. Of course, this has always been one of the most popular uses for Excel but, with Power BI, Microsoft has focused on making it even easier to do this. By doing so, Microsoft has reaffirmed Excel's position as the tool of choice for anyone who works with data as part of their job.

Given that Power Query is just one part of the Power BI suite, it's important to look at all of the components of Power BI so you can put Power Query in context, understand what it does, understand when you should use it and when another tool is more appropriate.

Power BI Components

The components of Power BI divide up into two groups: Excel add-ins and the cloud services that are available via Power BI for Office 365. Following are the Excel add-ins:

- Power Query
- Power Pivot
- Power View
- Power Map

And following are the cloud services available via Power BI for Office 365:

- Power BI Sites
- Q&A
- Power BI Data Catalog
- Mobile BI app

Now, let's look at each one of them in a bit more detail, in the order that you are likely to use them, so that you can see what their roles are.

Power Query

Conveniently enough for this book, Power Query is going to be the first component in the Power BI suite that you use when building a new BI solution. That's because the first step in creating any kind of report or dashboard is to get hold of the source data for it. Power Query allows you to connect to a wide variety of different data sources, extract data from them quickly and easily, and define a series of repeatable steps to clean, filter, and otherwise transform your data before it gets loaded into Excel. Power Query gives you the option of loading data directly into the worksheet or, if you are using Excel 2013, into the new Excel Data Model. Obviously, this is a greatly simplified account of what Power Query is capable of, and the rest of the book will go into a lot more detail!

Power Pivot and the Excel 2013 Data Model

The Excel Data Model is an in-memory database engine that runs inside Excel and that allows you to load very large amounts of data (much larger than you could ever fit on a single worksheet—it can handle millions, even tens of millions of rows of data) for analysis purposes. In a traditional Excel BI solution, you might be used to loading your raw data onto a hidden worksheet and then using VLOOKUPs to move values from this hidden worksheet into a report, or using PivotTables to slice and dice your data. The Excel Data Model gives you a better way of doing both of these things. If you load your data into the Excel Data Model, you no longer have to use a hidden worksheet to store your data; once the data is in the Excel Data Model, you can create PivotTables directly from it and you can use Excel's Cube Formulas to import individual values into cells in the worksheet.

The Excel Data Model is, in fact, the database engine behind the Power Pivot add-in, first released for Excel 2010. In Excel 2010, Power Pivot was a self-contained unit: the add-in consisted of a user interface as well as a database engine. In Excel 2013, it was split in two and the database engine was built directly into Excel. The Power Pivot add-in still remains but only as a user interface. You have to use the Power Pivot add-in to be able to use certain, more advanced functionality, but you do not need it if you only want to perform basic tasks. The split between Power Pivot and the Excel Data Model in Excel 2013 has confused many people and, as a result, you will find plenty of books and articles that still refer to both as Power Pivot.

Apart from the ability to work with very large data volumes, loading data into the Excel Data Model has many other advantages over the "hidden sheet" method including the following:

- Multiple tables of data can be loaded into it. After you've loaded the tables of data, you can create relationships between those tables similar to those that you can create in Access or other relational databases. Once relationships have been created, you can create PivotTables that include data from all of these tables—traditional PivotTables are limited to just one source table.

- Complex calculations can be written in DAX, the language of Power Pivot. These include time series calculations, percentage shares, and many other types of calculations that are difficult to implement in regular Excel formulas.

- The Excel Data Model compresses data very efficiently so loading your data into it, instead of into the worksheet, can drastically reduce the size of your workbooks. This is particularly important if you intend to upload your workbook to a Power BI site because there are limits on the size of workbooks that can be uploaded, as you'll soon find out.

- You can add features such as hierarchies, which allow your users to drill down through your data following a predefined path, and KPIs, which are special calculations that help users track business performance.

Power Pivot and the Excel Data Model are together a gigantic topic and deserve a book to themselves; indeed many excellent books, white papers, and blog posts are already out there. If you are serious about building BI solutions in Excel, then you owe it to yourself to learn more about this topic.

Power View

Power View is a new feature of Excel 2013 that allows you to create attractive, interactive dashboards as new worksheets inside your workbook. It is very closely related to, but not to be confused with, a stand-alone application that is also called Power View but that is only available in SharePoint. Power View in Excel takes data stored in a worksheet or from the Excel Data Model as its starting point, and then, using drag and drop, it allows you to create tables, charts, and maps that can be easily filtered and sliced. Even if you can already build dashboards and reports in a regular worksheet with PivotTables or PivotCharts, Power View gives you more options for visualizing your data, it is easy to use, and the end product is more visually appealing.

Power Map

Power Map is an Excel add-in that allows you to overlay geographic data onto 3-D maps. For example, if you work with retail data, you can use Power Map to plot sales of all of your stores on a map. At the location of each store, you can use it to show a bar graph of sales within that store. Once you've done this, you can explore these maps, panning and zooming in, and even record "tours" that show data for many different locations. Like Power View, its main strength is its "wow" factor—swooping low over a city and seeing hundreds of tiny graphs appear over a neighborhood you know makes for a very impressive spectacle.

SharePoint and Power BI for Office 365

Having loaded your data into Excel using Power Query, created PivotTables and reports using Power Pivot and the Excel Data Model, and created dashboards and visualizations using Power View and Power Map, the next thing you are likely to want to do is share the fruits of your labor with your colleagues. There's nothing stopping you from e-mailing your workbook to them, but there is a better way: SharePoint.

The on-premises version of SharePoint is used by many organizations to manage documents. SharePoint Enterprise Edition includes Excel Services, which allows Excel workbooks to be viewed and edited in a browser. Excel Services does not support all Excel desktop functionality, but it does have very good support for Excel's BI features: PivotTables, Excel Cube Formulas, and Power View sheets can all be viewed in a browser. This makes SharePoint and Excel Services a great way to make your reports available to your coworkers.

An increasing number of organizations are now moving to SharePoint Online, Microsoft's cloud-hosted version of SharePoint, which is available as part of Office 365. If your organization has moved to Office 365 and uses SharePoint Online, you can publish your workbooks to a SharePoint Online document library, share them with other people, and interact with them in a browser via Excel Services. For simple scenarios, this may be sufficient for your reports and dashboards.

3

If you purchase an additional Power BI for Office 365 subscription, you get several very useful features in addition to what is available with a regular Office 365 subscription:

- While SharePoint Online allows you to upload documents of up to 2GB in size, if you want to be able to view your BI workbooks using Excel Services in a browser, you are limited to workbooks of only 10MB. Power BI for Office 365 allows you to increase this limit by distinguishing between the size of the data in the Excel Data Model (which can be anything up to 250MB at the time of writing) and the rest of the workbook (which is still limited to 10MB).

- Data held in the Excel Data Model of workbooks can be refreshed on a schedule, even if the data sources are not themselves in the cloud. Installing the Data Management Gateway component on-premises allows Power BI for Office 365 to connect your workbook in the cloud with your organization's SQL Server and Oracle databases.

- The Power BI Data Catalog allows administrators to provide access to a variety of public and corporate data sources through a Power BI site by exposing them as OData data feeds.

- Power Query users can also share their work with their colleagues via the Power BI Data Catalog. (This will be explained in more detail in Chapter 7.)

- Power BI sites provide a smarter, more businesslike way to organize your reports and dashboards than a regular SharePoint Online document library.

- Power BI sites also provide management dashboards that allow you to track which workbooks your colleagues have been using and when.

- Q&A is a feature of Power BI for Office 365 that allows users to query the data held in the Excel Data Model of workbooks using English language queries and then see the results of these queries displayed in a Power View report. While Q&A only speaks English at the moment, other languages may be supported in the future.

Mobile BI

The final component of the Power BI suite is the Mobile BI app. If you have uploaded a workbook to a Power BI site, you have the ability to see parts of it—tables, charts, named ranges, PivotTables, PivotCharts, and Power View dashboards—via the Mobile BI app. This is a Windows 8.1 app designed to allow users of Windows tablets to access BI data while they are away from their desktops. Similar apps for other mobile platforms such as iOS will be released in the future.

Workflow Summary

In summary, then, the Power BI workflow is:

1. load data from external data sources into Excel using Power Query

2. model data in the Excel Data Model and add calculations using Power Pivot

3. build reports and dashboards on this data using PivotTables, Excel Cube Formulas, Power View, and Power Map

4. publish your workbook to a Power BI site in SharePoint Online so other users can access the reports in it

Figure 1-1 shows the workflow in more detail.

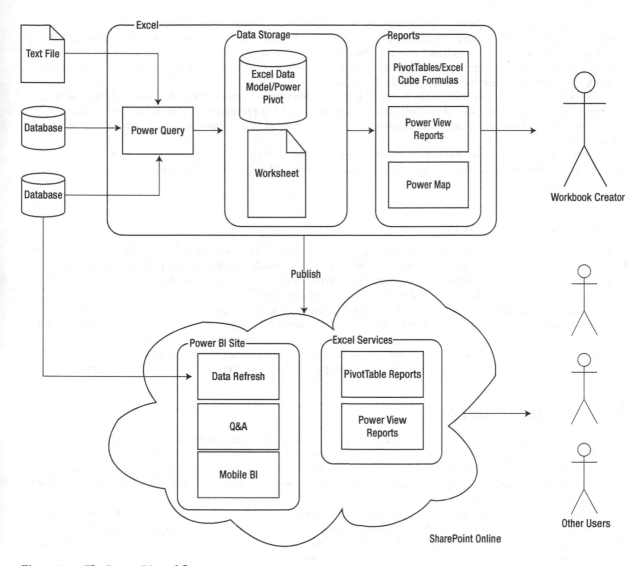

Figure 1-1. *The Power BI workflow*

Power Query and Power BI Licensing

The licensing model for Power Query and Power BI for Office 365 is not straightforward and requires some explanation. For Excel 2013 users, Power Query is licensed in exactly the same way as Power Pivot and Power View (though not Power Map, which is only available if you have an Office 365 subscription), and it is available as for free if you have bought one of the following:

- the stand-alone version of Excel 2013

- an Office 2013 Professional Plus license for your desktop

- an Office 365 subscription that gives you access to the Office 2013 Professional Plus desktop tools. There are a large number of subscription SKUs, but the Office 365 ProPlus, E3, and E4 SKUs all include the right version of Excel.

If you have Excel 2010, the only edition that supports Power Query is Office Professional Plus Service Pack 1. Power View and Power Map are not available for Excel 2010, but Power Pivot is available for all SKUs of Excel 2010.

The ability to view Excel workbooks stored in the on-premises version of SharePoint in a web browser is only available in SharePoint Enterprise Edition, and the functionality works best if you have SharePoint 2013. In addition, you will need to have Power Pivot for SharePoint installed.

The cloud-based services included in Power BI for Office 365 (Power BI Sites, Q&A, the Power BI Data Catalog, and the Mobile BI app), are covered by a separate subscription model. A prerequisite of using these services is an Office 365 subscription that includes SharePoint Online; you then need to purchase an extra subscription to use the services themselves.

Full licensing details, as well as links to install the various Power BI components, can be found at `http://www.microsoft.com/powerbi`. None of the Power BI Excel add-ins are available in the Apple Mac or Windows RT versions of Excel.

Installing Power Query

Power Query must be downloaded and installed separately after Excel has been installed; if you do not see the Power Query tab in the ribbon after you have installed it, you may need to enable the add-in manually. It requires Windows Vista or greater, if you are installing it on a desktop PC, or Windows 2008 or greater if you are installing it on a server. It also requires .NET 3.5 Service Pack 1 and Internet Explorer 9 or greater.

There are 32-bit and 64-bit versions of Power Query available. If you have the 32-bit version of Excel installed, you must install the 32-bit version of Power Query; if you have the 64-bit version of Excel, you must install the 64-bit version of Power Query. The 64-bit version is recommended if you are going to be working with large amounts of data.

New versions of Power Query are released on a regular basis and these can include significant new functionality. The Update version on the Power Query tab in Excel will light up when a new version is available to download.

Power Query Concepts

Now that you have seen where Power Query fits in the Power BI suite, it's time to start looking at it in more detail. A good place to start is by defining some of the concepts and terminology you'll encounter when working with Power Query. Luckily, there isn't much terminology to define. (If you find it easier to learn by seeing rather than reading, you may prefer to skim over this section and then move onto the next one, where you'll find the same concepts described by means of a worked example.)

The most important concept in Power Query is that of a *query*. (Unfortunately, this means you have to talk about "Power Query queries.") A query is a job that imports data from one or more data sources, optionally does something to the data such as filter it or aggregate it, and then loads it into Excel. Queries are stored inside an Excel workbook, and one workbook can contain multiple queries. Queries themselves can be used as data sources for other queries; two queries may also be merged together rather like one table can be joined to another in SQL, and a query can be appended onto the end of another.

A query is composed of one or more *steps* that are arranged in a specific order. A step may connect to a data source to retrieve data (usually the first step in a query does this, but subsequent steps may do this, too), or it may take the data returned by a preceding step and apply some kind of transformation to it. The last step in a query returns the output of the query as a whole. Steps are defined in Power Query's own expression language, "M," which sadly bears no resemblance to Excel formula language or VBA and is, in fact, a functional language like F#. When you create a new step in the Power Query user interface, Power Query will generate the M code necessary for that step automatically. If you are a confident programmer, you can edit the code behind each step yourself or create new steps by writing your own M code. However, in the majority of cases, this is not necessary.

Although Power Query steps may connect to external data sources, there is no concept of a connection to a data source as a separate object, and Power Query cannot use connections defined elsewhere in Excel (that's to say, the connections that can be found on the Data tab in the ribbon). However, the output of a Power Query query does become a traditional Excel connection and can be used just like any other connection. This allows Power Query to be able to output results to a table in a worksheet, for example.

Power Query Walkthrough

This section illustrates the concepts described above by walking through the creation and editing of a simple Power Query query. It also acts as a brief guided tour of the Power Query user interface. As you start to use Power Query, you'll find that all kinds of extra menus, panes, and tabs appear depending on what you're doing. In the following chapters, as you learn more about Power Query functionality, you'll become more familiar with the details of the user interface.

Creating a Simple Query

The starting point for all of your Power Query work will be the Power Query tab on Excel's ribbon menu, shown in Figure 1-2.

Figure 1-2. *The Power Query tab*

On the left-hand side of the Power Query tab, in the Get External Data section, you can see the options to import data from different types of data sources, while in the Excel Data section you can see a button to import data from an Excel table in the current workbook. Elsewhere in the Power Query tab, you can see options for combining data from different queries as well as various other administrative options that will be covered later in this book.

Click the From File button. On the drop-down menu click on the From CSV option as shown in Figure 1-3.

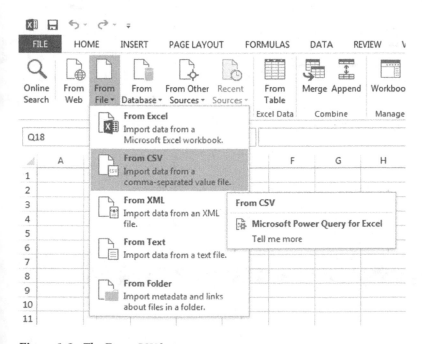

Figure 1-3. *The From CSV button*

A dialog box will appear. You should select the file 01_01_SimpleSales.csv from the sample files for this chapter. When you do this, the Power Query Query Editor window will appear as shown in Figure 1-4. The five main areas of the Query Editor window, marked in Figure 1-4, are the following:

1. **The Query Editor toolbar.** This is a ribbon menu containing all of the options for creating new steps in your query.

2. **The Formula Bar.** This is where you can edit the M expression for each step in the query.

3. **The Navigator pane.** This collapsible pane allows you to navigate through certain types of data sources such as XML files so you can find the particular data you are looking for.

4. **The Results pane.** This is where you can see the data returned by the currently selected step.

5. **The Query Settings pane.** This pane displays the name of the query you are editing, a description, a list of all of the steps in the query in the Applied Steps section, and two check boxes that control where the output of your query will be sent to in the Load Settings section.

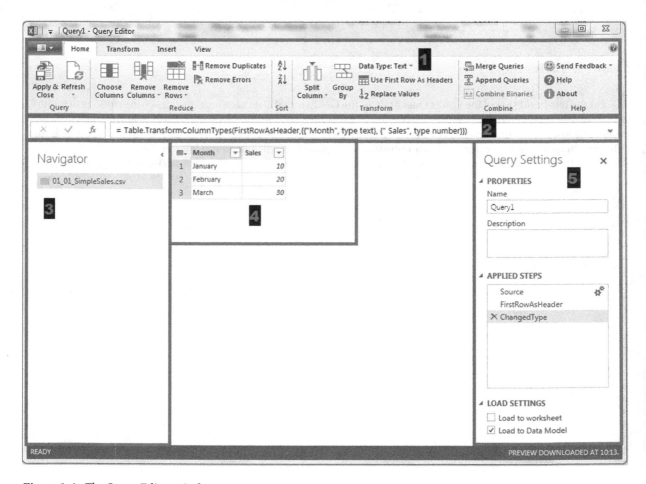

Figure 1-4. The Query Editor window

At this point, a new query will have been created, called Query1, which has three steps already created for you that are listed in the Applied Steps section on the right-hand side of the screen in the Query Settings pane. The output of the third step, called ChangedType, will be visible in the Results Pane. If you click any of the other earlier steps, you will see the output of the query after that step has been executed there instead. (This makes it easy to debug a Power Query query because it allows you to see how each step changes the data.)

Now click the Apply & Close button in the top left-hand corner of the editor and the window will close. Since the Load to Worksheet check box (found under Load Settings in the bottom right-hand corner of the screen) was checked, a new worksheet will be created and the output of this query will be shown in a new Excel table located at cell A1 of the new worksheet, as shown in Figure 1-5.

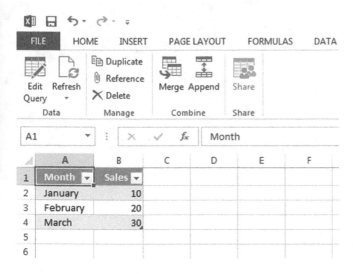

Figure 1-5. *Query output*

Congratulations! You have created your first Power Query query.

Editing an Existing Query

Queries can be edited after they have been created. Before you can do this, though, you need to go back to the Power Query tab on the ribbon and click the Workbook button in the Manage Queries section, so you can see a list of all the queries present in this workbook. When you do this, the Workbook Queries pane will appear on the right-hand side of the screen, as shown in Figure 1-6. The query you have just created, Query1, will be visible in this pane.

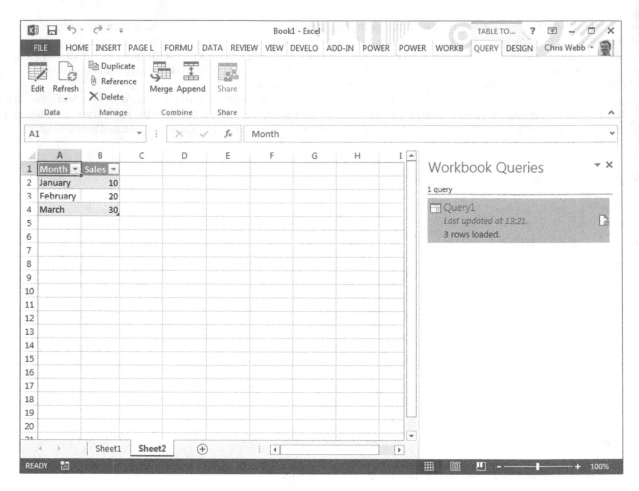

Figure 1-6. *The Workbook Queries pane*

Now, move your mouse cursor over the Workbook Queries pane and Query1. When you do this, a fly-out box will appear showing a preview of the data, when the query was last refreshed, and where the query is to be loaded . Also on the fly-out box is a series of clickable menu options plus ellipses that, when clicked, reveal even more menu options. (See Figure 1-7.) The menu options in this fly-out box are also available in a drop-down menu if you right-click the query in the Workbook Queries pane.

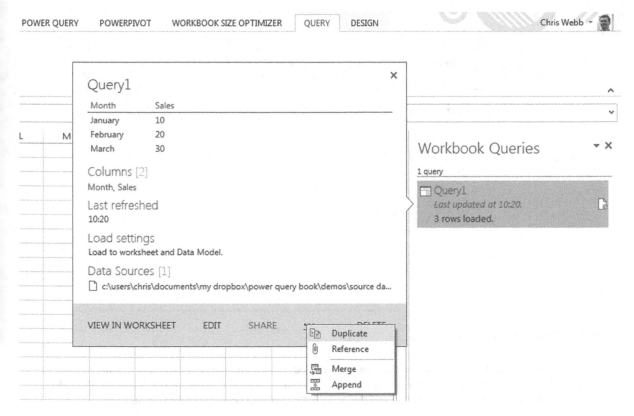

Figure 1-7. *The Workbook Queries fly-out menu*

Click the Edit option on the fly-out box and the Query Editor window will reopen, looking just as it does in Figure 1-4. Next, click the Remove Rows drop-down menu, which can be found in the center left of the Home tab of the Query Editor toolbar in the Reduce section, and click Keep Top Rows. This will add a new step onto the end of your query that filters out all but a given number of rows at the top of your query. Before it can do this, though, you will need to tell Power Query how many rows you want to keep. When you click the button, Power Query will open a dialog box, as shown in Figure 1-8, asking you for the number of rows to keep. Enter the value *2* to keep only the top two rows and click OK.

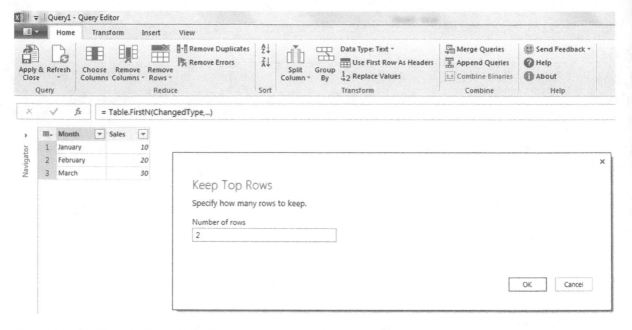

Figure 1-8. *The Keep Top Rows dialog box*

Once you have clicked OK, you will see the data has changed. Before, there were three months listed—January, February and March. Now, there are only two—January and February, as shown in Figure 1-9. A new step has also been added to the query called KeptFirstRows and the M code for this step is visible in the formula bar.

Figure 1-9. *The output of the KeptFirstRows step*

Finally, click the Apply & Close button, and you will see the new output of the query appear in the Excel table in the worksheet, as shown in Figure 1-10.

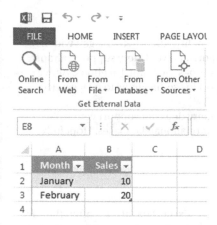

Figure 1-10. *The output of the edited query*

Why Use Power Query?

If you are an experienced Excel user, you may be thinking that you can already do everything that Power Query does by using the functionality present on the Data tab in combination with Excel formulas and maybe some VBA, without having to learn a completely new tool. That may be true up to a point, but there are some very strong arguments in favor of using Power Query over these well-known and trusted techniques. This section will make these arguments in some detail.

Faster Release Cycles

Microsoft Excel is one of the most widely used applications. As a result, every change that Microsoft makes to Excel has to be tested thoroughly; a bug could affect millions of users worldwide and cause untold disruption in their organizations. This means that Microsoft only releases a new version of Excel, on average, every three years—a very slow release cycle by modern standards and one that makes it difficult to get new functionality to users quickly. The new, streamed installation option for all Office products, which is available to Office 365 subscribers, will solve this problem eventually and allow Microsoft to push changes in Excel out to users as soon as they are available; however, it will be several years before most organizations change over to use this type of installation.

In the meantime, making the Power BI Excel functionality available through Excel add-ins rather than integrating it directly in Excel gives Microsoft a lot of flexibility it would not otherwise have. New releases of Power Query appeared on an almost monthly basis in the second half of 2013. Although the tempo has slowed since then, releases are still appearing regularly. This allows the Power Query team to release new features, fix bugs, and respond to user feedback much faster than if they were tied to the Office release cycle.

Based on the way Power Pivot started life as a completely separate add-in for Excel 2010 and then had its engine integrated natively into Excel 2013, it's a reasonable assumption to make that in the future Power Query functionality will be integrated into Excel in the same way. At the moment, there is a lot of overlap between what you can achieve on the Data tab in Excel and with Power Query; in the future, Power Query might be the replacement for the Data tab.

Therefore, if you are the kind of person who likes to get your hands on new functionality as soon as possible or if you have already run into the limitations of existing Excel functionality, Power Query is for you. Microsoft is making a huge investment in Power BI as a whole and Power Query in particular. Even if you find that Power Query can't do something that you need today, it could well be the case that it will be able to do it in a very short while.

Connectivity to New Data Sources

The most obvious example of where Power Query scores over native Excel functionality, and where the gap widens with each release of Power Query, is with the number of data sources that it supports. Power Query supports almost all of the data sources that can be accessed via the Data tab and it adds many new ones including Facebook, Active Directory, Exchange, SharePoint, OData feeds, and HDInsight. It also adds support for connections to web services. All of these data sources will be examined at length in Chapter 2.

Admittedly, at the time of writing, there are some data sources that Power Query does not support yet: SQL Server Analysis Services, ODBC, and some OLEDB data sources beyond the major relational databases. Hopefully, these gaps will be addressed in a future release.

Improved Connectivity to Existing Data Sources

Where Power Query supports a data source that is already supported natively by the Excel Data tab, it is often the case that it improves on the native functionality. One example is the ability to scrape data from a web page; Power Query is able to extract data from far more web pages than the native functionality is able to. Another example is the way that Power Query can merge data from a folder containing multiple csv files into a single result set with minimal effort.

Automate Data Loads

Power Query allows you to replace manual processes for loading data into Excel with a series of automated, repeatable steps that can be run with the click of a button. This not only saves time, but it is also much less prone to errors. Compared with VBA, Power Query is likely to offer better performance and also much easier maintenance for automating data loads, given that so many tasks require no code whatsoever.

Create Transformations and Calculations Easily

Building on from the previous point, as you saw in the walkthrough, Power Query makes it very easy to filter, aggregate, sort, pivot and unpivot, as well as to add calculations, just by clicking a button. Of course, not everything can be done through the user interface, but the Power Query development team has done an excellent job of identifying and implementing all of the common scenarios that need to be dealt with when loading data into Excel. Some more complex scenarios will require you to write M code; some scenarios will still be better handled using Excel formulas or by using DAX once the data has been loaded into the Excel Data Model. However, you will be pleasantly surprised at how easy Power Query is to use and how much it increases your productivity even if you are already a whiz at Excel formulas or VBA.

Do the Work in the Data Source, Not on the Desktop

One aspect of the way Power Query works that is not obvious but extremely important is the way that it will always try to push processing back to the data source. For example, if you are using a SQL Server data source and your query contains several steps, Power Query will translate all of the steps in your query into a single SQL SELECT statement, where possible. If the source table is very large, it will be much faster for any aggregation or filtering to take place in the SQL Server than for the whole of the table to be downloaded to Excel and the work to be done there. Note that this is not going to be possible with some types of data source (such as text files) or all of the transformations that Power Query is capable of. A full discussion of this behavior, called "query folding," is given in Chapter 3.

Share Queries between Workbooks and Users

Finally, Power BI's integration with Power BI Sites means that you can reuse queries in multiple workbooks and even share them with other users. Excel workbooks have a bad reputation for being silos of forgotten code and stale data. Power Query goes some way to try to address this problem, at least as far as data loading goes. If you think of all of the Excel reports and dashboards that exist in an organization, it's likely that a large number of them will use data from the same data sources and need to do the same things to that data before it can be of any use. If a single, shared query can be used to do this rather than multiple duplicated queries (with all the risk of errors or different implementations of business logic that go with that), then Excel reports will be faster to develop and more consistent between themselves.

Summary

By now, you should understand what Power Query does and what role it plays in the Power BI suite. You should also be familiar with the Power Query user interface and some basic concepts such as queries and steps. These topics have only been dealt with at a high level so, from now on, this book will concentrate on the details. In the next chapter, you will learn about all of the data sources supported by Power Query and how they can be accessed as well as related topics such as authentication and user locale.

■ ■ ■

CHAPTER 2

Power Query Data Sources

One of the best things about Power Query is the wide range of data sources that it supports. In addition to the obvious types of data source, such as relational databases and text files, it supports more exotic sources including Facebook, Active Directory, and OData, which are becoming more and more important in self-service BI scenarios. This chapter will deal with that all-important first step when creating a Power Query query—making a connection to a data source and extracting the raw data you want to work with. It will provide a guided tour of all of the data sources supported by Power Query, and it will also discuss related topics such as authentication.

Querying Relational Databases

Relational databases are the most commonly used type of data source for Power Query. The following relational database types are supported by Power Query: SQL Server, Windows Azure SQL Database, Access, Oracle, DB2, MySQL, PostgreSQL, Sybase, and Teradata. Unfortunately, there is no way of connecting directly to a relational database that is not on this list and, at the time of writing, there is no support for connections to other OLEDB or ODBC data sources. Luckily (at least for the purposes of this book), the user interface for connecting to each of these data sources is almost identical, so SQL Server will be used as the main example and then any differences for other databases will be listed afterwards.

Connecting to SQL Server

In order to create a new Power Query query that connects to and extracts data from SQL Server, you must first go to the Power Query tab in the Excel ribbon, click the From Database button, and then select From SQL Server Database (as shown in Figure 2-1).

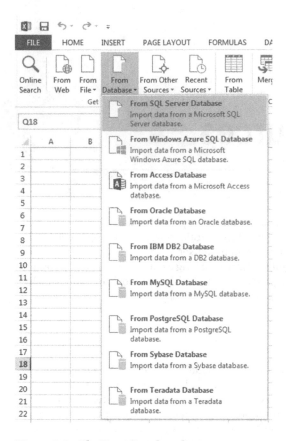

Figure 2-1. *The From Database button*

Once you have done this task, a dialog will appear that allows you to enter the name of the server and instance that you want to connect to and (optionally) the name of the database. You can also enter your own SQL query at this point if you have already written one. The dialog is shown in Figure 2-2.

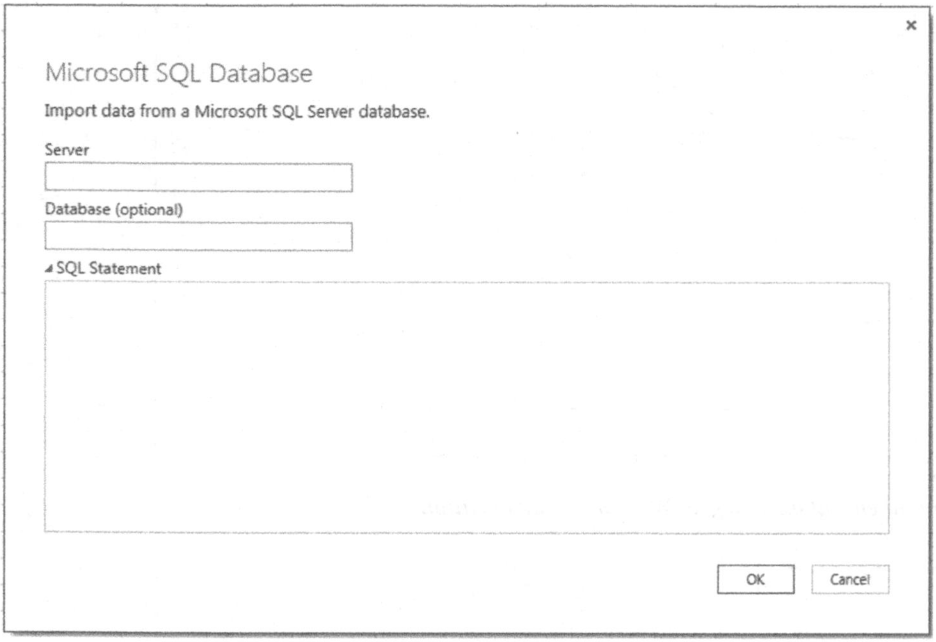

Figure 2-2. *The Microsoft SQL Database connection dialog*

The SQL Statement text box can take either a SQL Select Statement or a call to a stored procedure. In the latter case, the syntax you use is exactly the same as you'd use in SQL Server Management Studio, for example:

```
EXEC [sys].[sp_who];
```

If this is the first time you are connecting to the specified instance of SQL Server, Power Query will open a new dialog asking how the connection should be authenticated. Connections to SQL Server can use either Windows authentication, which means that your own Windows credentials will be used to authenticate your connection and nothing else needs to be entered or, if your database is in Mixed Mode, you can use SQL Server authentication and enter a username and password. When the dialog opens, you will see the Windows tab, shown in Figure 2-3; you will need to click the Database tab if you are using SQL Server authentication, as shown in Figure 2-4. In both cases, there is a check box to use an encrypted connection that is checked by default. If you are connecting to an instance of SQL Server that has not been configured to accept encrypted connections, you will need to uncheck this box. Your credentials will be saved after you have entered them and used automatically for all future connections to the same database.

Figure 2-3. *The SQL Server authentication dialog for Windows authentication*

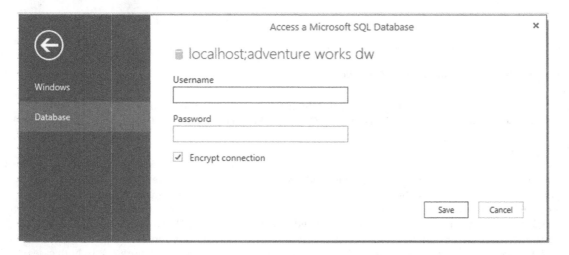

Figure 2-4. *The SQL Server authentication dialog for SQL Server authentication*

If you do enter your own query or call a stored procedure, once you click OK in the original Microsoft SQL Database connection dialog, the query or stored procedure will be run and the Query Editor window will open to show the results.

___

■ **Note** If your query returns a large number of rows and you intend to apply further transformations (such as filters or group bys) in subsequent steps inside your query, you may be better off not using your own query at all. You may get better performance connecting directly to the underlying tables in your database and using Power Query alone to implement the logic in your query. The reason for this advice will be explained in detail in Chapter 3 in the section on Query Folding.

___

If, on the other hand, you do not enter a database name or leave the SQL Statement text box blank, some extra functionality for navigating through a relational database is enabled. The first thing that will happen is a new pane called the Navigator pane appears on the right-hand side of the screen allowing you to select one or more tables, views, scalar functions, or table-valued functions in your database, as shown in Figure 2-5.

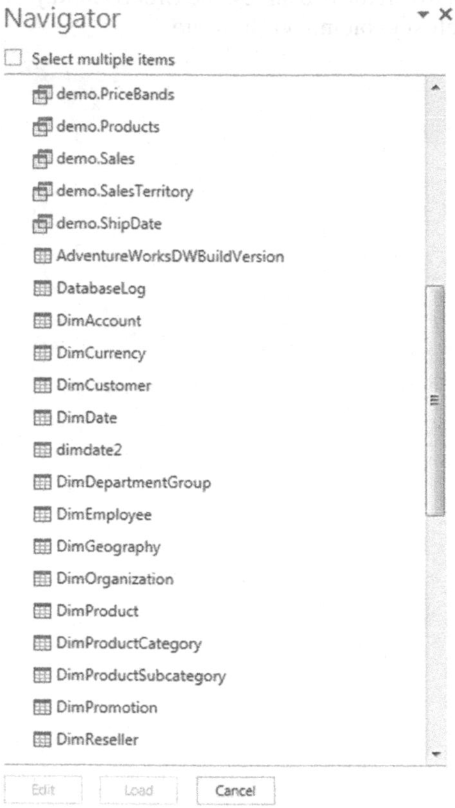

Figure 2-5. *The Navigator pane*

Initially, the Navigator pane will only allow you to select one object, but, if you check the Select Multiple Items box, you will be allowed to select multiple objects. Selecting multiple objects will result in multiple Power Query queries being created, one for each object that has been selected; the Edit button will disappear and new check boxes will appear asking whether you want to load the data to the Excel Data Model and/or direct to a worksheet when you click Load. If you do not check the Select Multiple Items box, you can open the Query Editor by clicking the Edit button or load data directly to the worksheet by clicking the Load button after you have made your selection.

■ **Note**   If you select a function in the Navigator pane, it will be imported as a Power Query function (a topic that will be dealt with in Chapter 5).

Navigating through a Database in the Query Editor

If you have imported a table into Power Query using the Navigator pane, then some extra functionality is enabled in the Query Editor for navigating along the relationships of your database. To illustrate this, I'm going to use the following tables from Microsoft's Adventure Works DW sample database: DimDate and FactInternetSales. These tables are shown in Figure 2-6. There are three foreign key relationships defined between the two tables: the OrderDateKey, DueDateKey, and ShipDateKey columns on FactInternetSales join to the DateKey column on DimDate.

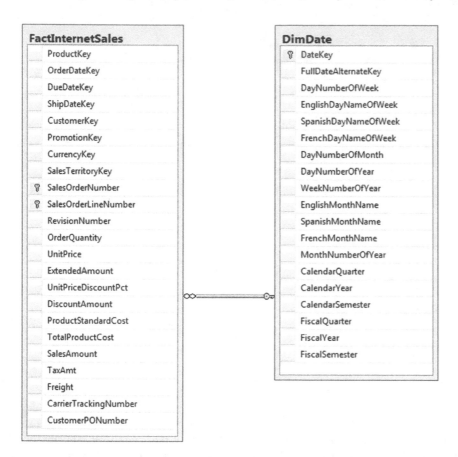

Figure 2-6. *Adventure Works DW table relationships*

Having imported just the DimDate table into Power Query using the Navigator pane, you will see a number of columns that contain the word "Table" if you scroll to the right-hand side of the table once you are in the Query Editor pane, as shown in Figure 2-7. These columns represent data from all tables that have a foreign key relationship with the DimDate table in the database.

	CalendarQuarter		CalendarYear		CalendarSemester		FiscalQuarter		FiscalYear		FiscalSemester		FactCallCenter		FactCurrencyRate		FactFinance		FactInternetSales(DateKey)	
7	3		2001		2		1		2002		1	Table		Table		Table		Table		
7	3		2001		2		1		2002		1	Table		Table		Table		Table		
7	3		2001		2		1		2002		1	Table		Table		Table		Table		
7	3		2001		2		1		2002		1	Table		Table		Table		Table		
7	3		2001		2		1		2002		1	Table		Table		Table		Table		
7	3		2001		2		1		2002		1	Table		Table		Table		Table		
7	3		2001		2		1		2002		1	Table		Table		Table		Table		
7	3		2001		2		1		2002		1	Table		Table		Table		Table		
7	3		2001		2		1		2002		1	Table		Table		Table		Table		
7	3		2001		2		1		2002		1	Table		Table		Table		Table		
7	3		2001		2		1		2002		1	Table		Table		Table		Table		
7	3		2001		2		1		2002		1	Table		Table		Table		Table		
7	3		2001		2		1		2002		1	Table		Table		Table		Table		
7	3		2001		2		1		2002		1	Table		Table		Table		Table		
7	3		2001		2		1		2002		1	Table		Table		Table		Table		

Figure 2-7. *Relationship columns on the DimDate table*

There are two ways to navigate from the DimDate table to the FactInternetSales table. The first is to click the word "Table" in any of the rows in the FactInternetSales(DateKey) column. This will return a table containing the rows from the FactInternetSales column that are related to the row you clicked by following the relationship from DateKey on DimDate to DueDateKey on FactInternetSales. So, for example, if you clicked the row for the date July 21st 2001 in the DimDate table, Power Query would return all of the rows in FactInternetSales that have a DueDateKey value for that particular date. In addition, once you have done this, a new pane will appear on the left-hand side of the Query Editor. This pane (shown in Figure 2-8) is also called the Navigator pane, but it's not the same as the Navigator pane we saw earlier. (I will refer to this pane as the Query Editor Navigator pane from now on to avoid confusion.) It shows you the table you started at and the table you have navigated to. To go back to where you came from, you just need to click the relevant table in the Query Editor Navigator pane.

Figure 2-8. *The Query Editor Navigation pane*

The second way to navigate from DimDate to FactInternetSales is to click the icon in the column header that looks like two arrows pointing left and right, as shown in Figure 2-9.

FactInternetSales(DateKey)	⇆
Table	
Table	

Figure 2-9. *The Expand icon*

When you click this icon, you will see two options, shown in Figure 2-10: Expand, which will perform an inner join between the two tables, and Aggregate, which will add new columns to your table containing values aggregated from the destination table.

Figure 2-10. *The Expand/Aggregate dialog with the Expand option selected*

By default, the Expand option is selected. If all of the columns in the destination table (FactInternetSales, in this case) are checked, you will get a table that contains all of the columns from both DimDate and FactInternetSales when you click OK. Because Power Query is performing an inner join, the resulting table will have as many rows as there are in the destination table that have an equivalent row in the source table. The same thing can also be achieved by selecting the column in the Results Pane and clicking the Expand button on the Transform tab of the Query Editor toolbar.

If you select the Aggregate option (as shown in Figure 2-11), you will only see the numeric columns from the destination table, but you will see each numeric column listed multiple times, once for each possible aggregate function that can be applied to it. Each box that you check will result in a new column added to the source table containing a value aggregated from the destination table.

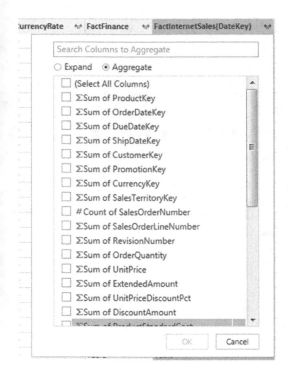

Figure 2-11. *The Expand/Aggregate dialog with the Aggregate option selected*

It is also possible to navigate "up" a relationship as well as "down" a relationship. When an appropriate relationship exists—for example, if you started in the FactInternetSales table and wanted to look up a value from the DimDate table—you will see a column in your table containing the value "Value" as shown in Figure 2-12.

SalesAmount ▼	TaxAmt ▼	Freight ▼	CarrierTrackingNumber ▼	CustomerPONum... ▼	DimCurrency ⁴⁺	DimCustomer ⁴⁺
3578.27	286.2616	89.4568	null	null	Value	Value
3578.27	286.2616	89.4568	null	null	Value	Value
3578.27	286.2616	89.4568	null	null	Value	Value
3578.27	286.2616	89.4568	null	null	Value	Value
699.0982	55.9279	17.4775	null	null	Value	Value

Figure 2-12. *Relationship columns on the FactInternetSales table*

Clicking "Value" in a cell will return a record object—basically the single row from the lookup table that joins to the row in the table you just clicked, but unpivoted. An example of a record is shown in Figure 2-13; it can easily be converted to a table by clicking the Into Table button on the toolbar above.

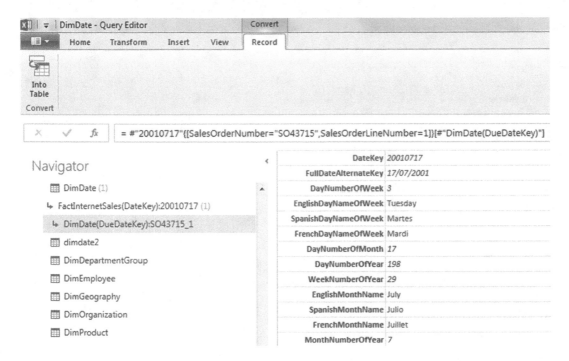

Figure 2-13. *A record object*

Alternatively, you may click the Expand icon at the top of the column. This will perform a join between the two tables in the same way that it did when navigating down a relationship. The only difference here is that there is no option to aggregate values, so you can only expand and add new columns containing lookup values from the destination table.

Connecting to Other Databases

As mentioned earlier, the experience of connecting to other types of relational database with Power Query is mostly the same as it is with SQL Server, although some of these other databases do not support all of the functionality previously described. For example, while most databases allow you to connect to tables or views, most do not support connecting to functions. One other consideration is that before you can connect to these databases, you need to ensure that you have the correct client components installed on your PC. Full details of what is supported for each relational database, the minimum version numbers of the client components required, and download links for those components can be found here:

http://tinyurl.com/PQRelDataSource

Extracting Data from Files

After relational databases, data file formats such as CSV are likely to be the most frequently used type of data source for Power Query. This section covers all of the many, diverse file formats supported by Power Query such as CSV, TXT, Excel, XML, and JSON.

Working with CSV Files

The comma-separated value (CSV) family of text file format is widely used to exchange data because of its simplicity. There is a lot of diversity in how the format is implemented but in general any plain text file that contains data arranged into records (usually where each line represents a single record), where each record is divided up into fields by a single character delimiter, and where each record has the same fields, can be referred to as a CSV file. Most CSV files use the file extension ".CSV" but that is not always the case, and some may use the file extension ".TXT".

The file 01 January Sales.CSV in the demo folder for this chapter is a simple example of a CSV file. Its contents can be seen in Figure 2-14.

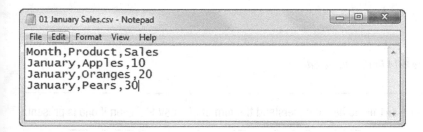

Figure 2-14. *A typical CSV file*

To import this data using Power Query, you need to click the From File button on the Power Query tab in the ribbon and then select From CSV as shown in Figure 2-15.

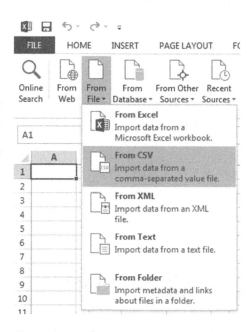

Figure 2-15. *The From CSV and From Text buttons*

Once you have done this, you will see a dialog asking for the location of the CSV file. When you have entered the location and clicked OK, the contents of the file will be imported. Power Query has a lot of built-in intelligence that will detect which delimiter you are using, whether the first line of the file contains column headers, and so on, which generally works very well. In fact, every time you try to open a text file that looks as though it could be a CSV file, even when you use the From Text button in the ribbon, Power Query will use this intelligence to convert the data in it into a table. The CSV file in Figure 2-14 will appear in the Query Editor as shown in Figure 2-16.

⊞▾	Month ▾	Product ▾	Sales ▾
1	January	Apples	10
2	January	Oranges	20
3	January	Pears	30

Figure 2-16. *The CSV file shown in Figure 2-14 in the Query Editor*

▪ **Note** Power Query will not use a schema.ini file to help it understand the format of a CSV file, even if one is present.

Working with Text Files

If you want to import data from a text file that is not formatted as a CSV file and that actually does contain text (such as the one shown in Figure 2-17), you can use the From Text button, visible in Figure 2-15.

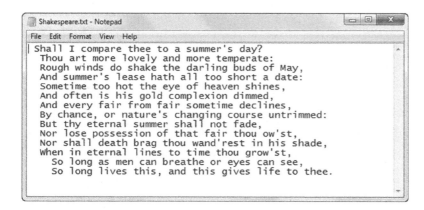

Figure 2-17. *A typical text file*

Text files like this become tables with one column and one row for each line once they have been imported into Power Query. Figure 2-18 shows what the text file in Figure 2-17 looks like in the Query Editor.

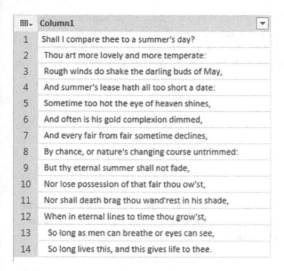

⊞▾	Column1	▼
1	Shall I compare thee to a summer's day?	
2	Thou art more lovely and more temperate:	
3	Rough winds do shake the darling buds of May,	
4	And summer's lease hath all too short a date:	
5	Sometime too hot the eye of heaven shines,	
6	And often is his gold complexion dimmed,	
7	And every fair from fair sometime declines,	
8	By chance, or nature's changing course untrimmed:	
9	But thy eternal summer shall not fade,	
10	Nor lose possession of that fair thou ow'st,	
11	Nor shall death brag thou wand'rest in his shade,	
12	When in eternal lines to time thou grow'st,	
13	So long as men can breathe or eyes can see,	
14	So long lives this, and this gives life to thee.	

Figure 2-18. *The text file shown in Figure 2-17 in the Query Editor*

Working with XML Files

Importing an XML file is a little bit more complex than importing data from a CSV file because, unlike CSV files, the data in an XML file is not usually tabular in structure. Luckily, once you are in the Query Editor window, Power Query allows you to navigate through the structure of an XML file to find the data that you need in the same way that you can navigate through the structure of a SQL Server database.

To import an XML file you first need to click the From File button and then click From XML. Once again a file open dialog will appear and you can select the location of your XML file. Figure 2-19 shows the contents of a simple XML file.

```
<?xml version="1.0" encoding="UTF-8"?>
- <company>
      <companyname>Crossjoin Consulting Ltd</companyname>
      <country>UK</country>
    - <employees>
       - <employee>
            <firstname>Chris</firstname>
            <lastname>Webb</lastname>
        </employee>
       - <employee>
            <firstname>Helen</firstname>
            <lastname>Lau</lastname>
        </employee>
      </employees>
  </company>
```

Figure 2-19. *A typical XML file*

Once this file has been imported into Power Query, Figure 2-20 shows what the Query Editor will look like.

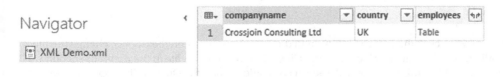

Navigator   ‹ | ⊞▾ | companyname | ▼ | country | ▼ | employees | ⇤⇥ |

XML Demo.xml

	companyname	country	employees
1	Crossjoin Consulting Ltd	UK	Table

Figure 2-20. *The contents of an XML file in the Query Editor*

There are two ways to reach the employee level data, depending on whether you want to see just the employee data or whether you want to see the company data, too. The first way is by clicking the value "Table" in the "employees" column; that will return another table with one column and one row, which again contains the value "Table." Clicking that will give you the table shown in Figure 2-21, which contains just the employee data.

Figure 2-21. *Drilled-down employee data from an XML file*

Alternatively, you can click the Expand icon in the "employees" column of the table shown in Figure 2-20, choose the default "Expand" option, and click OK. If you do this again, the end result will be as shown in Figure 2-22, where you can see the company level data is included along with the employee data.

▦▾	companyname	▾	country	▾	employees.employee.firstname	▾	employees.employee.lastname	▾
1	Crossjoin Consulting Ltd		UK		Chris		Webb	
2	Crossjoin Consulting Ltd		UK		Helen		Lau	

Figure 2-22. *Expanded employee data from an XML file*

Working with JSON Files

Although there is no option in the user interface for importing data from JSON files, Power Query has full support for them. You will often encounter JSON files if you are using web services as data sources. Figure 2-23 shows the contents of a simple JSON file.

```
JSON Demo.json - Notepad
File  Edit  Format  View  Help
{
        "Company": "Crossjoin Consulting Ltd",
        "Country": "UK",
        "Employees" : [
                {
                        "FirstName": "Chris",
                        "LastName": "Webb"
                } ,
                {
                        "FirstName": "Helen",
                        "LastName": "Lau"
                } ]
}
```

Figure 2-23. *A simple JSON file*

To import data from a JSON file, click the From Text button in the Power Query tab on the ribbon, change the file extension drop-down to "All Files," select the file's location, and click OK. While the XML file in the previous section was treated as a table when it was loaded, in this case, you will see a record object when the Query Editor opens, as shown in Figure 2-24.

Company	Crossjoin Consulting Ltd
Country	UK
Employees	List

Figure 2-24. *The contents of a JSON file in the Query Editor*

In this case, the only option to reach the employee level data is to click the "List" value in the "Employees" row, which reveals two "Record" links; clicking one of these "Record" links will return the data for one employee, as shown in Figure 2-25. Notice how, in this case, the Query Editor Navigator pane keeps track of where you have drilled to in the file.

Figure 2-25. *Employee data from a JSON file*

Working with Excel Files

Power Query can extract data from Excel files other than the one you are currently working with. When it does this, it treats each worksheet in the external Excel file as a table; it can also extract data from tables and named ranges, but not specific cells. Figure 2-26 shows one worksheet of a simple Excel workbook containing some sales data (there is a second worksheet in the same workbook with an identically structured table containing data for another month).

	A	B	C
1	Month	Product	Sales
2	January	Apples	10
3	January	Oranges	20
4	January	Pears	30
5			

Figure 2-26. *Sales data in an Excel worksheet*

To import data from this workbook using Power Query, you need to click the From File button and then the From Excel button in the Power Query tab in the ribbon, select the location of the Excel file, and click OK. When you do this, the Navigator pane will appear on the right-hand side of the current worksheet and you can select which worksheets, tables, or named ranges you want to load data from in the target workbook, as shown in Figure 2-27.

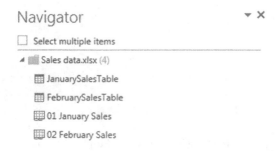

Figure 2-27. The Navigator pane showing worksheets in the target workbook

Just as when you are importing data from SQL Server, selecting a single item will light up the Edit and Load buttons. Clicking the Edit button will open the Query Editor, and clicking the Load button will load the data to a new worksheet in the current workbook. If you check the "Select multiple items" box and select more than one item, the Edit button disappears but new check boxes appear giving you the option of importing data to a worksheet or to the Excel Data Model when you click Load.

Working with Folders and Multiple Files

Power Query can treat the Windows file system itself as a data source, and while this is in itself useful, it also exposes one of Power Query's most practical features: the ability to combine data from multiple, identically structured text files.

Working with Data from the Windows File System

To load data from the Windows file system, click the From File button in the Power Query tab on the ribbon and then click From Folder. Doing this will open a dialog asking for a folder path, as shown in Figure 2-28.

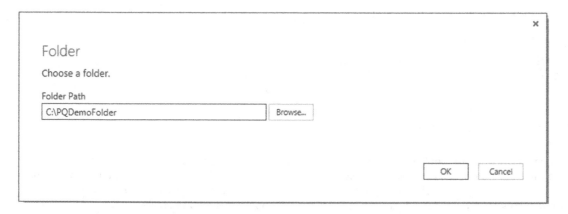

Figure 2-28. Choosing a folder for the From Folder option

Clicking OK will open the Query Editor, and you will see a table containing one row for each file in the folder you have specified and in all subfolders inside that folder (although the subfolders themselves are not shown), similar to you see in Figure 2-29.

⊞▾	Content	±±	Name	▾	Extension	▾	Date accessed	▾	Date modified	▾	Date created	▾	Attributes	▾↿	Folder Path	▾
1	Binary		01 JanuarySales.txt		.txt		21/10/2013 10:24:08		10/07/2013 12:22:56		21/10/2013 10:24:08	Record		C:\PQDemoFolder\	
2	Binary		02 FebruarySales.txt		.txt		21/10/2013 10:24:08		10/07/2013 12:22:50		21/10/2013 10:24:08	Record		C:\PQDemoFolder\	
3	Binary		03 MarchSales.txt		.txt		21/10/2013 10:24:08		10/07/2013 12:22:43		21/10/2013 10:24:08	Record		C:\PQDemoFolder\	

Figure 2-29. *The contents of a folder shown in the Query Editor*

Clicking the Expand icon—which works in exactly the same way as the Expand icon in other data sources—in the Attributes column of this table will allow you to add extra columns containing file attributes to the table.

Combining Data from Multiple Text Files

In Figure 2-29, you can see that each row in the "Content" column contains the value "Binary." Clicking "Binary" for one row will import the file that that row represents. In addition, there is an icon next to the column name in the "Content" column that looks like two arrows pointing down toward a horizontal line. This is the Combine icon, shown in Figure 2-30. When you click this icon, Power Query will attempt to combine all of the binary files listed in the table into a single binary file containing all of the data in all of the files. So, for example, if you have a table listing a number of identically structured CSV files, clicking the Combine icon will import all of the data from all of the CSV files shown. This technique does not work for all file formats, however, (Excel files cannot be combined in this manner, for example) and it will only work well if each of the files shares the same format. That means that if you are attempting to combine multiple CSV files, they should all contain the same fields in the same order; if they don't, the combine will succeed but the data returned will be very difficult to work with.

Figure 2-30. *The Combine icon*

The files shown in Figure 2-29 are CSV files similar to the one shown in Figure 2-16. Clicking the Combine icon in this case means that Power Query will combine the files, treat the result as a single CSV file, and output the table shown in Figure 2-31, which contains all of the rows from all of the files shown.

⊞▾	Column1	▾	Column2	▾	Column3	▾
1	January		Apples		1	
2	January		Oranges		2	
3	January		Pears		3	
4	February		Apples		4	
5	February		Oranges		5	
6	February		Pears		6	
7	March		Apples		1	
8	March		Oranges		2	
9	March		Pears		3	

Figure 2-31. *The output of the Combine operation*

Working with Data from the Current Excel Workbook

Power Query is able to use data from tables in the current Excel workbook as a data source for a query. The data has to be formatted as a table, however—Power Query cannot read data from individual cells or named ranges.

Figure 2-32 shows an Excel worksheet with a table of data in it. The table has the name "SalesTable." (You can find and change the name of a table by clicking inside the table and going to the Design tab in the Excel ribbon.)

Figure 2-32. *An Excel table*

If a cell inside the table is selected and you click the From Table button on the Power Query tab in the ribbon, the Query Editor will open and all of the data from the table will be imported, as shown in Figure 2-33. The name of the query will be the same as the table that you have imported.

▦	Month ▼	Sales ▼
1	January	2
2	February	3
3	March	5
4	April	3
5	May	6
6	June	8
7	July	7
8	August	6
9	September	6
10	October	9
11	November	8
12	December	5

Figure 2-33. *The contents of an Excel table in the Query Editor*

■ **Note**   If you click a cell in the current worksheet that is not part of a table and then click the From Table button, Power Query will ask you if you want the current selection to be formatted as a table in Excel; if you click OK, a new table will be created and the data from it will be imported. In Excel itself there are several ways of formatting a range of cells as a table—for example, by selecting the cells and then clicking the Table button on the Insert tab of the ribbon. It is better to use these options and create your table manually rather than let Power Query create the table for you because doing so gives you the chance to give it a meaningful name before you create your query. One way of working with data sources that Power Query does not explicitly support is to import the data into an Excel table (either using the functionality in the Data tab on the Excel ribbon or by copying and pasting) and then to use that as the source for your Power Query query.

Working with Data from the Web

There are a number of different ways to access data from the web using Power Query: You can scrape data from web pages, you can call web services, and you can even use Power Query's own built-in web data search functionality.

Scraping Data from Web Pages

For a long time, Excel has allowed you to scrape data from HTML tables in web sites. Power Query extends this functionality by allowing you to treat the HTML returned by a web page as a data source. This means that Power Query is able to scrape data from a much larger number of web pages than the native Excel feature although, at the time of writing, Power Query has a much less user-friendly interface for this.

Figure 2-34 shows part of a web page, `http://sqlbits.com/information/Pricing.aspx`, which contains data formatted as a table.

Register early to take advantage of our discounts.

All prices are exclusive of VAT. Prices are in UK Pounds Sterling (GBP).

	Cut-Off Date	Pre-Conference	Deep Dive	Full Conference	Community Day
	midnight on the	Thursday	Friday	Thursday & Friday	Saturday
Early Bird	3 Feb 2013	£260.00	£135.00	£395.00	
Standard	7 Apr 2013	£310.00	£185.00	£495.00	FREE
Full		£360.00	£235.00	£595.00	

Discounts available from most local usergroups. Contact your usergroup organiser for details.

Extra Discount - 20% off when 6 or more people book for the whole conference. Please see our Terms & Conditions for full details.

Figure 2-34. *Part of a web page containing a table of data*

To import this data into Power Query, click the From Web button on the Power Query tab in the ribbon, enter the URL of the web page in the dialog box that appears, and click OK. Once you have done this, the Navigator pane will appear on the right-hand side of the screen, as shown in Figure 2-35.

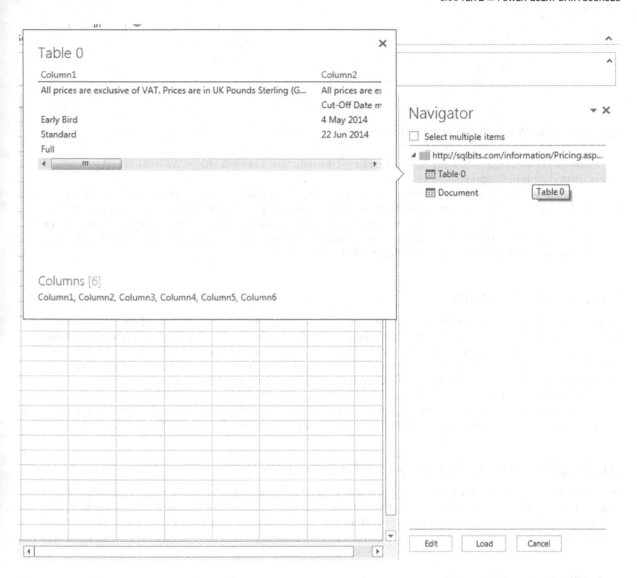

Figure 2-35. *The Navigator pane for a web page*

In this case, the Navigator pane will display any likely tables that you might want to import (in this instance, there is one, shown as "Table 0") as well as the entire HTML source for the page, which is listed as "Document." If you move your mouse over one of the tables shown, a fly-out box displaying a preview of the data in that table appears. Again, there is the option to select multiple items and either edit the query or load data direct to the worksheet or the Excel Data Model. Selecting "Table 0" and clicking Edit then opens the Query Editor to show the data from that table, as in Figure 2-36.

▦▾	Column1 ▾	Column2 ▾	Column3 ▾	Column4 ▾	Column5 ▾	Column6 ▾
1	All prices are exclusive of VAT.	All prices are exclusive of VAT.	All prices are exclusive of VAT.	All prices are exclusive of VAT. I	All prices are exclusive of VAT.	null
2		Cut-Off Date	Pre-Conference	Deep Dive	Full Conference	Community Day
3	Early Bird	4 May 2014	£275.00	£150.00	£425.00	FREE
4	Standard	22 Jun 2014	£325.00	£200.00	£525.00	FREE
5	Full		£375.00	£250.00	£625.00	FREE

Figure 2-36. *Data from a web page in the Query Editor*

Some extra cleaning and filtering is necessary to get the data into a useable shape. We will cover the techniques necessary to do this in Chapter 3.

If you instead click "Document" in the Navigator pane, the Query Editor will open and you will be able to navigate through the HTML in more or less the same way you can navigate through an XML file, as you saw earlier in this chapter. Finding the data you need in the HTML of all but the simplest web pages is extremely difficult. The best approach is to click the Expand button on any column that has one until you can see the data you need. Only then should you start filtering out the rows and columns that you don't need.

Calling a Web Service

Many web sites make data available through web services. Power Query can query RESTful web services (that is to say, web services that can be queried using only information passed through a URL) using the From Web button. Instead of entering the URL of a web page, you just need to enter the URL of the web service. Responses from RESTful web services usually return data in XML or JSON format, and Power Query will recognize the format used automatically. When querying web services using the From Web button through the user interface, Power Query is only able to issue GET requests; it is possible to issue POST requests as well using custom code.

In most cases, you will need to write your own M code to work with web services properly. More details on how to do this can be found in Chapter 5. There is also a worked example of how to call a web service in Chapter 8.

Finding Data Using Power Query Online Search

The Online Search button in the Power Query tab on the ribbon is actually the gateway to access two different data sources. First, it will allow you to query a number of public data sources curated by Microsoft, and secondly, if you have a Power BI for Office 365 subscription, it will allow you to search for data that you or other people have shared through the Power BI Data Catalog.

Searching for Public Data

Clicking the Online Search button will result in the Online Search pane appearing on the right-hand side of the screen inside Excel, as shown in Figure 2-37.

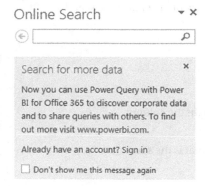

Figure 2-37. The Online Search pane

Entering a search term in the text box will return results from all of the public data sources that Power Query knows about, as shown in Figure 2-38. A brief list of some of the public data sources that can be queried can be found here: http://tinyurl.com/PQPublicData.

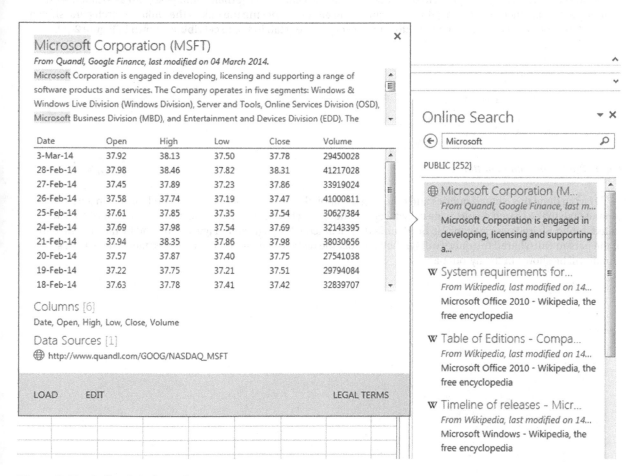

Figure 2-38. Online Search results

Hovering over one of the results will display a fly-out pane containing a preview of the data in the search result, which contains a number of clickable options:

- Load will create a query and load the data.

- Edit will open the Query Editor.

- Legal Terms will open a dialog showing the terms of use for this data.

- Clicking one of the column names in the Columns section will highlight the column in the preview of the table above.

- Clicking the link in the Data Sources section will open the web page that is the source of the data.

Searching for Shared Queries and Other Organizational Data

If you have a Power BI for Office 365 subscription, you can also search for queries and other organizational data sources that you or your colleagues have shared through the Power BI Data Catalog using the Online Search functionality. Details on how queries can be shared will be given in Chapter 7.

Before you can search, you need to be signed in using the Office 365 username and password associated with your Power BI for Office 365 subscription. You can sign in either by clicking the link in the Online Search pane shown in Figure 2-37 or by clicking the Sign In button on the Power Query tab in the Excel ribbon shown in Figure 2-39.

Figure 2-39. *The Sign In button*

Having done this, shared queries and other organizational data will appear in your search results in a new, separate tab in the search results pane called Organization; search results from public data sources appear in a tab called Public. Shared queries can also be identified by their icon, highlighted in Figure 2-40, and by the fact the name of the person who shared the query will be shown under the name of the query in the results pane (the person's e-mail will be shown in the fly-out pane).

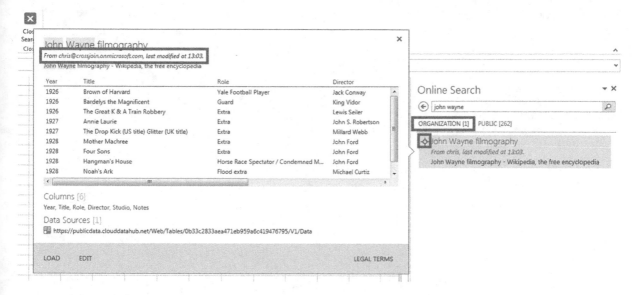

Figure 2-40. *A shared query in the Online Search results*

You can find a list of the queries you have shared with others in your organization by clicking the Shared button in the Power Query tab in the ribbon shown in Figure 2-41.

Figure 2-41. *The Shared button*

Clicking the Shared button will open the Shared Queries pane on the right-hand side of the screen, as shown in Figure 2-42. This pane behaves in exactly the same way as the Online Search results pane in terms of how you import data.

Figure 2-42. *The Shared Queries pane*

Using the Search Tab

When you perform a search using the Online Search button, a new tab will appear on the Excel ribbon: the Search tab, shown in Figure 2-43.

Figure 2-43. *The Search tab*

In the Refine section, the buttons allow you to search for terms in specific pieces of the metadata associated with a query. Clicking one of these buttons will add an advanced filter to your search term in the format `filtername:(searchterm)`. So, clicking the Name button will allow you to search for queries or datasets that have specific text in their names; for example, `name:(John Wayne)` will search for queries or datasets that have the text "John Wayne" in their name, as shown in Figure 2-44. Multiple advanced filters can be used in a query, and they can be combined with regular search terms. Advanced filters can also be typed manually without clicking the buttons and they can also be deleted like any other text.

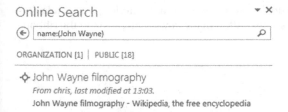

Figure 2-44. *Using an advanced filter on name*

Following is the full list of advanced filters:

- `name:()` filters on text in the name of the query or dataset.

- `description:()` filters on text in the description of the query or dataset.

- `from:()` filters on queries or datasets shared by specific people or web sites. For people, you can supply some or all of an e-mail address; for web-sites, it will filter on the name of the site. For example, `from:(cwebb)` will search for queries shared by users with the text "cwebb" in their e-mail address and `from:(data.gov)` will search for datasets from `www.data.gov/`.

- `datasource:()` filters on queries or datasets from a specific underlying data source. For example, `datasource:(wikipedia)` will search for data from Wikipedia and `datasource:(salesdatawarehouse)` will search for data from a database called "salesdatawarehouse."

- `lastmodifieddate:` allows you to search for queries modified in a specific date range. Clicking the This Week button shown in Figure 2-43 opens a drop-down box with a number of built-in date ranges; for example, `lastmodifieddate:this year` will return queries modified in the current calendar year.

- `columnname:()` filters on text that appears in column names.

- `iscertified:` filters shared queries depending on whether they have been certified by a data steward or not. For example, `iscertified:yes` only returns shared queries that have been certified. Certified queries will be described in more detail in Chapter 7; briefly, a certified query should return more trustworthy data than a noncertified query.

Finally, clicking the Recent Searches button will display a list of recent search terms.

Using Other Queries as Data Sources

There are a number of different ways in which Power Query queries can be used to feed data to other queries in the same workbook: by using another query as a data source, by duplicating an existing query, and by referencing an individual value from another query.

Referencing Entire Queries

A Power Query query can use another query defined elsewhere in the same workbook as a data source; this is known as "referencing" a query. It might seem strange to want to do this, but in certain circumstances splitting up a large query into multiple smaller parts can make it easier to develop and maintain. Also, if you have many queries that share the same logic, separating that logic into a separate query can prevent you from repeating the same code in many places.

There are two ways to reference another query. First, you can do this from the Workbook Queries pane. If it isn't currently displayed, you can make it visible by clicking on the Workbook button in the Power Query tab on the ribbon, as shown in Figure 2-45.

Figure 2-45. *The Workbook button*

The Workbook Queries pane displays a list of all the queries in the current workbook. Right-clicking a query as shown in Figure 2-46 and then selecting Reference will result in a new query being created that uses the query you have clicked on as a data source.

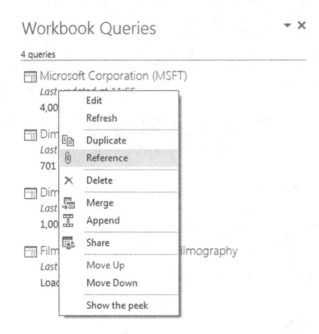

Figure 2-46. *Referencing a query through the Workbook Queries pane*

The second way to reference a query is from the Query tab in the Excel ribbon. This is visible after a query has been loaded into a table in the worksheet. As you can see in Figure 2-47, it contains the same options as the right-click menu shown in Figure 2-46, and clicking the Reference button has exactly the same effect as the Reference right-click menu item does in the Workbook Queries pane.

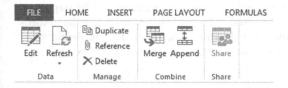

Figure 2-47. *The Query tab*

When you reference a query in another query, you must be very careful because changing your source query could break any other queries that reference it.

Duplicating Queries

It is also possible to create a copy of an existing query by using either the Duplicate right-click menu item in the Workbook Queries pane or by clicking on the Duplicate button in the Query tab. When you duplicate a query, there is no dependency between the new query and the original query in the way that there is when you reference a query—you can edit the original query and the new query will be unaffected.

Using Individual Values from Queries

Finally, it is also possible to take individual values from cells in existing queries and use these values as the starting point for a new query. This is only possible inside the Query Editor, and you can do this by right-clicking in a cell containing a value in the results pane and selecting Add as New Query, as shown in Figure 2-48.

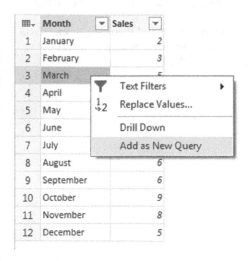

Figure 2-48. *The Add as New Query option*

Once you have done this, a dialog will appear telling you that a new query has been created successfully and what its name is. When you click OK, you can find this new query by closing the Query Editor and looking in the Workbook Queries pane.

When you reference a value in this way, Power Query will create a duplicate query containing all of the steps up to and including the step you had open in the Query Editor when you clicked in the cell, plus an extra step that returns just the value in the cell that you clicked. Therefore, this option is more like the Duplicate option than the Reference option—there is no dependency on the source query, and changes to the source query will not break the newly created query.

OData Data Sources

OData is an extremely important part of Microsoft's self-service BI strategy. A full description of what it is can be found at www.odata.org/, but it can be summed up as "ODBC for the web." OData is a standard for implementing RESTful web services that query or update data and, as such, it provides a uniform interface for a wide variety of different types of data source. Part of the appeal of OData is that it makes a web service look like a relational database: What it calls "entities" are basically tables of data, entities have relationships defined between them just like foreign key relationships, and an OData query is very similar to a SQL query but expressed in the form of a URL.

Microsoft is one of the main sponsors of OData, but SAP and IBM are also supporting it. In addition, Microsoft is enthusiastically implementing OData web services across a lot of its products such as SharePoint, Windows Azure, and Dynamics CRM Online. Microsoft has also made it very easy for developers to implement OData feeds in their own applications, for example, using Visual Studio Lightswitch. Power Query has support for generic OData data sources, and it also has more specialized interfaces for certain types of OData data sources such as the Windows Azure Marketplace.

Working with Generic OData Web Services

The test service available from www.odata.org/ is a good example that can be used to illustrate Power Query's support for OData. The first thing to find out about any OData web service that you are working with is its service root URL, which provides information on the resources available from this particular data source. The service root URL of the test service is http://services.odata.org/OData/OData.svc/.

In the Power Query tab in the ribbon, if you click the From Other Data Sources button and then click From OData Feed, a dialog will appear asking for the URL of the OData feed that you want to work with. Entering the URL above will open the Navigator pane on the right-hand side of the screen, as shown in Figure 2-49.

Navigator　　　　　▼ ✕

☐ Select multiple items

◢ ▦ http://services.odata.org/OData/OData.svc/ (8)

　　▦ Advertisements

　　▦ Categories

　　▦ PersonDetails

　　▦ Persons

　　▦ ProductDetails

　　▦ Products

　　▦ Suppliers

　　fx GetProductsByRating

Figure 2-49. *The Navigator pane for an OData web service*

By now, you should be familiar with the way the Navigator pane works. What you can see here for this OData feed is very similar to what you saw when connecting to a relational database. Underneath the service root URL is a list of entities and service operations, which are treated as tables of data and functions, respectively. Selecting the entity

"Products" and then clicking the Edit button to open the Query Editor will show a table containing all of the data for that entity, as shown in Figure 2-50.

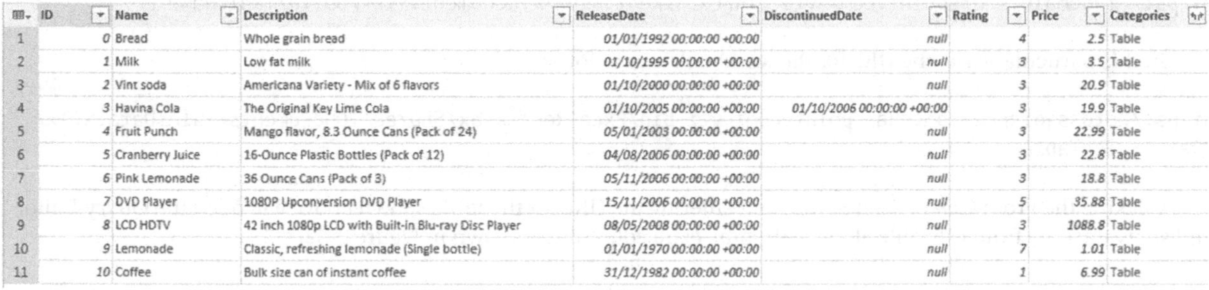

	ID	Name	Description	ReleaseDate	DiscontinuedDate	Rating	Price	Categories
1	0	Bread	Whole grain bread	01/01/1992 00:00:00 +00:00	null	4	2.5	Table
2	1	Milk	Low fat milk	01/10/1995 00:00:00 +00:00	null	3	3.5	Table
3	2	Vint soda	Americana Variety - Mix of 6 flavors	01/10/2000 00:00:00 +00:00	null	3	20.9	Table
4	3	Havina Cola	The Original Key Lime Cola	01/10/2005 00:00:00 +00:00	01/10/2006 00:00:00 +00:00	3	19.9	Table
5	4	Fruit Punch	Mango flavor, 8.3 Ounce Cans (Pack of 24)	05/01/2003 00:00:00 +00:00	null	3	22.99	Table
6	5	Cranberry Juice	16-Ounce Plastic Bottles (Pack of 12)	04/08/2006 00:00:00 +00:00	null	3	22.8	Table
7	6	Pink Lemonade	36 Ounce Cans (Pack of 3)	05/11/2006 00:00:00 +00:00	null	3	18.8	Table
8	7	DVD Player	1080P Upconversion DVD Player	15/11/2006 00:00:00 +00:00	null	5	35.88	Table
9	8	LCD HDTV	42 inch 1080p LCD with Built-in Blu-ray Disc Player	08/05/2008 00:00:00 +00:00	null	3	1088.8	Table
10	9	Lemonade	Classic, refreshing lemonade (Single bottle)	01/01/1970 00:00:00 +00:00	null	7	1.01	Table
11	10	Coffee	Bulk size can of instant coffee	31/12/1982 00:00:00 +00:00	null	1	6.99	Table

Figure 2-50. *Data from an OData entity in the Query Editor*

Clicking the Table and Record links that are visible in some columns will allow you to navigate from entity to entity in the same way that you can navigate between tables in a relational database.

Working with Data from Excel Workbooks Stored in SharePoint

When you upload an Excel workbook to SharePoint (either on-premises or SharePoint Online), every table in that workbook is exposed as an OData feed that can be used in Power Query—a great example of OData's usefulness in the real world. Figure 2-51 shows an Excel workbook containing a table displayed in the Excel Web App.

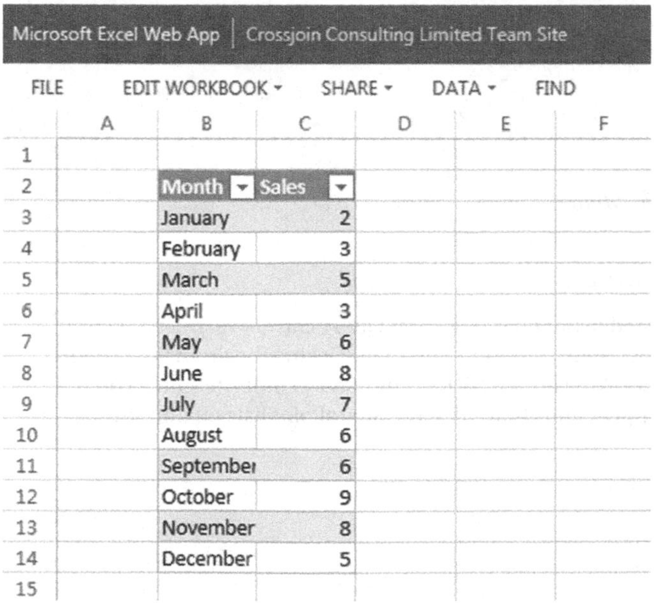

	A	B	C	D	E	F
1						
2		Month	Sales			
3		January	2			
4		February	3			
5		March	5			
6		April	3			
7		May	6			
8		June	8			
9		July	7			
10		August	6			
11		Septembei	6			
12		October	9			
13		November	8			
14		December	5			
15						

Figure 2-51. *An Excel workbook containing a table viewed in the Excel Web App*

The URL for a table in an Excel workbook stored in SharePoint is in the following format (the three parts of the URL that you need to replace, the domain, the Excel workbook's path and name, and the table name, are in bold):

```
https://mydomain.sharepoint.com/_vti_bin/ExcelRest.aspx/mydocument.xlsx/OData/TableName
```

In this particular case, the URL for the workbook is as follows:

```
https://crossjoinpowerbi.sharepoint.com/_vti_bin/ExcelRest.aspx/Shared%20Documents/SalesData.xlsx/
OData/SalesTable
```

Clicking the From OData Feed button and entering the URL for the table shown above will open the Query Editor and show the data from the table along with some extra columns, as shown in Figure 2-52.

▦.	Month	Sales	excelRowID	excelUpdated
1	January	2	0	10/02/2014 22:18:47
2	February	3	1	10/02/2014 22:18:47
3	March	5	2	10/02/2014 22:18:47
4	April	3	3	10/02/2014 22:18:47
5	May	6	4	10/02/2014 22:18:47
6	June	8	5	10/02/2014 22:18:47
7	July	7	6	10/02/2014 22:18:47
8	August	6	7	10/02/2014 22:18:47
9	September	6	8	10/02/2014 22:18:47
10	October	9	9	10/02/2014 22:18:47
11	November	8	10	10/02/2014 22:18:47
12	December	5	11	10/02/2014 22:18:47

Figure 2-52. Data from an Excel OData feed in the Query Editor

Working with Data from SharePoint Lists

As well as being able to extract data from Excel tables stored in SharePoint, Power Query can also extract data from SharePoint lists. This is possible by clicking the From Other Sources button and then clicking the From SharePoint List button. Once you have done this, a dialog will appear asking for the URL of your SharePoint site. Once you have entered a URL and clicked OK, the Navigator pane will appear and show all of the SharePoint lists on that site, as shown in Figure 2-53.

Navigator ▼ ✕

☐ Select multiple items

▲ ■ https://crossjoinpowerbi.sharepoint.com (9)

⊞ AccessRequests

⊞ Appdata

⊞ ComposedLooks

⊞ ContentTypePublishingErrorLog

⊞ ConvertedForms

⊞ Employees

⊞ ProjectPolicyItemList

⊞ TaxonomyHiddenList

⊞ UserInformationList

Figure 2-53. *SharePoint lists shown in the Navigator pane*

As you would expect, selecting a list in the Navigator pane and clicking the Edit button will open the Query Editor and show the contents of that list in a table, along with a lot of extra (not very useful) columns, as shown in Figure 2-54.

⊞▾	Id	ContentTypeID	ContentType	Title	Modified	Created
1	2	0x010050DD96AE6BB3BF42AB7A9F81CB04CF	Item	Power Pivot	28/11/2013 13:48:50	28/11/2013 13:48:50
2	3	0x010050DD96AE6BB3BF42AB7A9F81CB04CF	Item	Power Query	28/11/2013 13:48:58	28/11/2013 13:48:58
3	4	0x010050DD96AE6BB3BF42AB7A9F81CB04CF	Item	Power Map	28/11/2013 13:49:06	28/11/2013 13:49:06
4	5	0x010050DD96AE6BB3BF42AB7A9F81CB04CF	Item	Power BI Sites	28/11/2013 13:49:15	28/11/2013 13:49:15
5	6	0x010050DD96AE6BB3BF42AB7A9F81CB04CF	Item	Q&A	28/11/2013 13:49:20	28/11/2013 13:49:20

Figure 2-54. *The contents of a SharePoint list shown in the Query Editor*

Working with Data from the Windows Azure Marketplace

The Windows Azure Marketplace (`https://datamarket.azure.com/`) is a Microsoft web site where you can download third-party data to use for analysis purposes. One example of where this could be useful is if you were a retailer studying the effect of the weather on sales in your stores. You could download historical weather data and combine it with your own sales data to see whether there was any correlation between the two. Some of the data available in the Marketplace must be purchased, but there is a lot of free data available there as well. To be honest, a lot of the datasets (especially the free ones) are not very useful at all; that said, there are a few very useful services hidden in there such as the Bing Search API and new data is being added regularly.

To use data from the Windows Azure Marketplace in Power Query, you first need to subscribe to some datasets. To do this you need to go to the Windows Azure Marketplace web site and click the Data tab. This will display a list of available datasets, as shown in Figure 2-55.

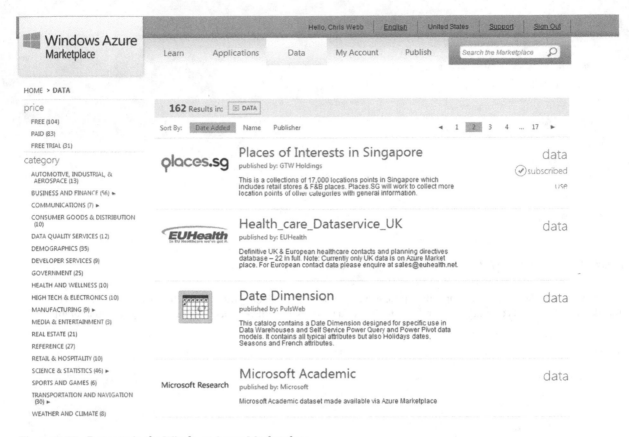

Figure 2-55. Datasets in the Windows Azure Marketplace

To subscribe to a dataset, click its name and then click the Sign-up button on the top right-hand side of the screen, as shown in Figure 2-56.

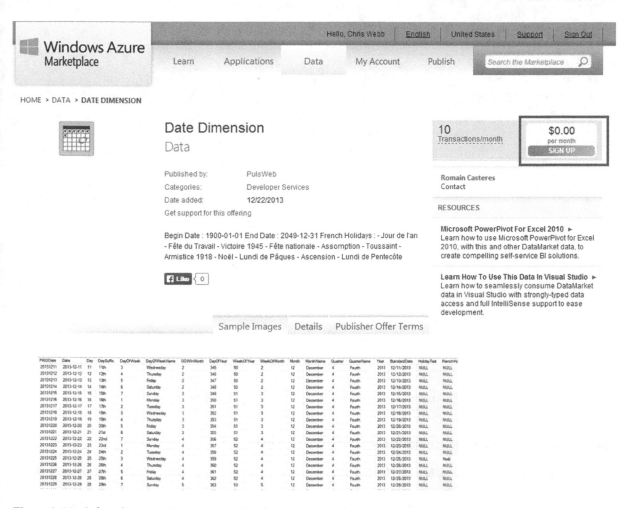

Figure 2-56. *Subscribing to a dataset in the Windows Azure Marketplace*

Having done this, you can now go back to Power Query. To use a dataset that you have subscribed to, click the From Other Sources button and then From Windows Azure Marketplace. If this is the first time you are using this option, you may be prompted to sign in. There are two options for doing this in the authentication dialog:

- Using a Microsoft account (the email address that you use to sign into Microsoft products and services, which used to be known as a Windows Live ID).

- Using a Windows Azure Marketplace account key. This can be found by going to the Windows Azure Marketplace web site, signing in there, and going to the My Account tab.

Once you have signed in, the Navigator pane will appear and display a list of all of the datasets you have subscribed to, as shown in Figure 2-57. Expanding a dataset will show a list of tables and functions that can be used in Power Query. Clicking the Add Data Feeds link at the bottom of the Navigator pane will take you to the Windows Azure Marketplace web site so you can subscribe to new feeds.

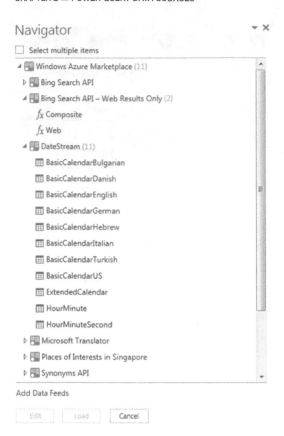

Figure 2-57. *Windows Azure Marketplace datasets in the Navigator pane*

As usual, selecting a table and then clicking Edit will create a query in the Query Editor which uses the table as a data source.

Working with Data from Windows Azure Blob Storage and Table Storage

Extracting data stored in either Windows Azure Blob Storage or Windows Azure Table Storage to Power Query is straightforward. The first step to doing so in both cases is to click the From Other Sources button and then either the From Windows Azure Blob Storage button or the Windows Azure Table Storage button. When you do this, a dialog will appear asking for the name of your Azure Storage account. Then, if this is the first time you are accessing this account, you will be asked to enter your account key (which can be found in the Windows Azure Management Portal, where it is called an Access Key). The Navigator pane will then open. For Windows Azure Blob Storage, each container becomes a table in the Navigator pane; for Windows Azure Table Storage, each table becomes a table in the Navigator pane. Selecting a table in the Navigator pane and clicking Edit will open the Query Editor as normal. Once there, you can expand Table and Record values in the way you have already seen with other data sources.

Working with Data from HDFS and HDInsight

While it would not be correct to call Power Query a "big data" tool, Power Query can come in very useful for importing files stored in the Hadoop Distributed File System (HDFS) for any Hadoop distribution that supports the WebHDFS protocol. It can also connect to files stored in Microsoft's cloud-based distribution of Hadoop, HDInsight. At the time of writing, Power Query is unable to generate HIVE queries.

To connect to Hadoop, click the From Other Data Sources button and then click the From Hadoop File (HDFS) button. A dialog will open asking you to enter the name or the IP address of your Hadoop server. Once you have done this, the Query Editor will open and the experience will be exactly the same as if you were using the From Folder option described earlier in this chapter: The contents of individual files can be returned, or multiple files can be combined into a single table of data.

To connect to HDInsight, the process is slightly different. Click the From Other Data Sources button and then click From Windows Azure HDInsight. A dialog will appear asking you to enter your account name and then your account key (just as if you were connecting to Windows Azure Blob Storage). Once you have done that, a list of all of the Windows Azure Blob Storage containers associated with your account will appear in the Navigator pane. By default, there will be a container with the same name as your HDInsight cluster. Selecting a container and clicking Edit will open the Query Editor to show all of the files stored in that container. Again, from this point, the experience will be exactly the same as if you were using the From Folder option described earlier.

Working with Active Directory Data

Power Query can connect to Active Directory and extract data from there. To do this, click the From Other Sources button and then From Active Directory. A dialog box will appear asking for the name of the domain to connect to, which may have the name of the domain you are currently logged in to already filled in. Once you click OK, if this is the first time you are connecting to this domain, the authentication dialog will appear and you can use either your Windows credentials or supply a username and password to connect. Next, the Navigator pane will appear on the right-hand side of the screen displaying all of the domains and sub-domains that you have access to; you can expand a domain and see all of the objects associated with that domain such as users, groups, and computers. Selecting a domain or an object and then clicking the Edit button will open the Query Editor window with a table of data and you will be able to navigate through the data using Record links in the usual way.

Working with Data from Microsoft Exchange

If you use Microsoft Exchange, you can use Power Query to extract data from there on e-mails you have received, your calendar, contacts, tasks, and meeting requests. To connect to Exchange, click the From Other Sources button and then From Microsoft Exchange. If this is the first time you are connecting to Exchange, you may need to enter your e-mail address and password in the authentication dialog box at this point. Only one Exchange account can be set up in Power Query at any time. When you have done this, the Navigator pane will appear on the right-hand side of the screen showing the various types of information you can extract, as shown in Figure 2-58.

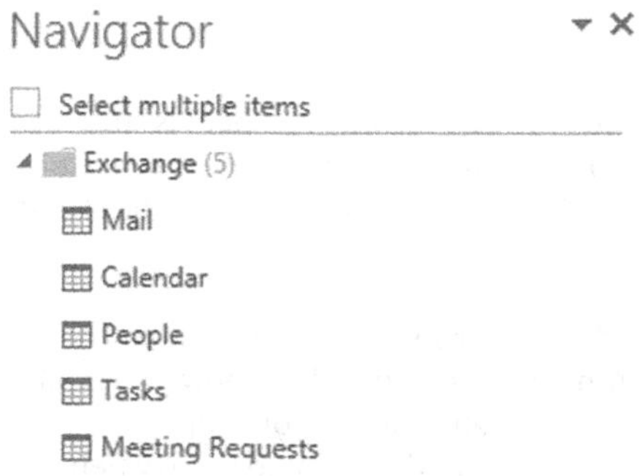

Navigator ▾ ✕

☐ Select multiple items

◢ ▦ Exchange (5)

▦ Mail

▦ Calendar

▦ People

▦ Tasks

▦ Meeting Requests

Figure 2-58. Resources from Microsoft Exchange in the Navigator pane

Selecting an item and clicking the Edit button will open the Query Editor window. If you select Mail, you will see a table containing all of the e-mails you have stored in your Exchange account, as shown in Figure 2-59; Calendar will show a table containing all of the items in your calendar; People will show a table containing all of your contacts; Tasks will show a table containing all of your tasks; and Meeting Requests will show a table containing all of your meeting requests.

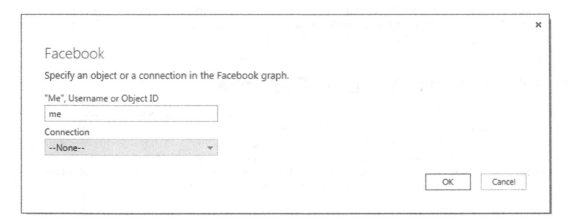

⊞▾	Folder Path ▾	Subject ▾	Sender ♠▾	DisplayTo ▾	DisplayCc ▾	ToRecipients ♠▾	CcRecipients ♠▾	BccRecipients ♠▾	DateTimeSent ▾
1	\Inbox\	Scheduled Refresh: SQLBitsRegonline.xlsx has just failed to refresh	Record	Chris Webb; chris@crossjoin.co.uk	null	Table	Table	Table	03/05/2014 23:48:15
2	\Inbox\	Scheduled Refresh: SQLBitsRegonline.xlsx has just failed to refresh	Record	Chris Webb; chris@crossjoin.co.uk	null	Table	Table	Table	02/05/2014 23:48:20
3	\Inbox\	Scheduled Refresh: SQLBitsRegonline.xlsx has just failed to refresh	Record	Chris Webb; chris@crossjoin.co.uk	null	Table	Table	Table	01/05/2014 23:47:57
4	\Inbox\	Scheduled Refresh: SQLBitsRegonline.xlsx has just failed to refresh	Record	Chris Webb; chris@crossjoin.co.uk	null	Table	Table	Table	01/05/2014 22:46:47
5	\Inbox\	Chris Webb wants to share 'Weather2013V2'	Record	Chris Webb	null	Table	Table	Table	23/07/2012 22:09:05
6	\Inbox\	RE: Chris Webb (chris@Crossjoin.onmicrosoft.com) has invited you to coll	Record	'Jamie Thomson'; Chris Webb	null	Table	Table	Table	17/07/2012 14:13:48
7	\Inbox\	RE: Chris Webb (chris@Crossjoin.onmicrosoft.com) has invited you to coll	Record	'Jamie Thomson'; Chris Webb	null	Table	Table	Table	17/07/2012 13:53:07
8	\Inbox\	Getting the most out of SharePoint	Record	Chris Webb	null	Table	Table	Table	17/07/2012 11:17:40
9	\Inbox\	FW: Chris Webb (chris@Crossjoin.onmicrosoft.com) has invited you to col	Record	Chris Webb; chris@crossjoin.co.uk	null	Table	Table	Table	17/07/2012 13:46:16

Figure 2-59. *E-mails from Exchange shown in the Query Editor*

Working with Data from Facebook

Power Query is able to connect to and extract data from the Facebook Graph both for personal accounts and any company pages you manage. To do this, click the From Other Sources button and then click the From Facebook button. When you do this, the dialog shown in Figure 2-60 will appear, asking you for some initial information about what data you want to extract.

```
                                                                    ✕

    Facebook

    Specify an object or a connection in the Facebook graph.

    "Me", Username or Object ID

    me

    Connection

    --None--                              ▾


                                           OK          Cancel
```

Figure 2-60. *The Facebook connection dialog*

The upper text box shown in Figure 2-60 asks you who you want to connect as. The default value here is "me," which will connect using your personal account. However, if you are an administrator of another Facebook page, for example for a company, you can enter a different username or use a Facebook Object ID (both of which can be found on the Page Info tab of your page on the Facebook web site).

The lower text box allows you to choose a particular part of the graph to return. The default option is "—None—", which means that the Query Editor will open and display a root record from which you can navigate to all of the data associated with the user you have chosen in the upper text box. Choosing another option in this drop-down box will go directly to a specific part of the graph, such as the friend list or the news feed, and return a table of data.

If you haven't already signed in to Facebook, the authentication dialog will appear and ask you to do so when you click OK. Clicking the Sign In button will open another window where you will need to enter your Facebook password. Once you have done this, click the Save button to close the authentication dialog.

Once you are in the Query Editor, you can navigate through the Facebook graph by clicking Table and Record links in the usual way.

Working with Data from SAP BusinessObjects

Data from SAP BusinessObjects UNX (but not UNV) universes can be accessed from Power Query by clicking the From Other Data Sources button and selecting From SAP BusinessObjects BI Universe. For this to work, you will need to have the following SAP BusinessObjects components installed:

- SAP BusinessObjects Platform version 4.1 with SP2

- SAP BI 4.1.2 REST Web Service

Having clicked the button, you will be prompted to enter the URL of your SAP BusinessObjects BI4 Server universe, as shown in Figure 2-61. This will be in the format `http://<hostname>:<portnumber>/biprws`. By default, the REST Web Service uses port number 6405.

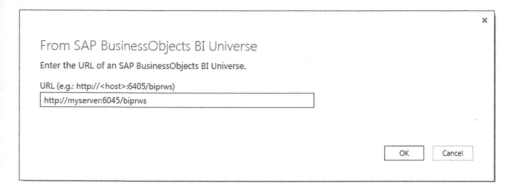

Figure 2-61. *Connecting to a SAP BusinessObjects universe*

You will then need to choose the credential type you want to use to connect to the SAP BI4 Server universe and then enter your credentials. Once you have done this, you will see a list of universes in the Navigator pane. Under each universe, you can see a list of the dimensions, attributes, and measures in that universe, and you can select the attributes and measures you want to import data for, as shown in Figure 2-62.

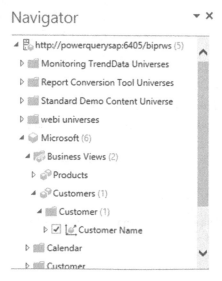

Figure 2-62. *The Navigator Pane showing the contents of a universe*

Once in the Query Editor, you can modify your selection by clicking the Add Items and Collapse Columns buttons, as shown in Figure 2-63.

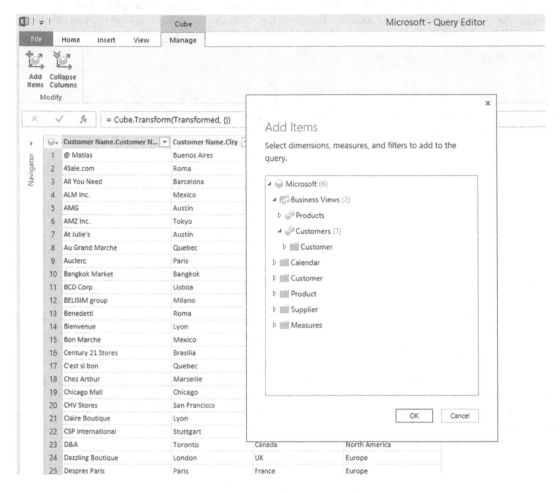

Figure 2-63. *Modifying a selection in the Query Editor*

■ **Note**　At the time of writing, the SAP BusinessObjects-related functionality in Power Query was still in Preview and, therefore, is likely to change in future releases. Also, any future support for SQL Server Analysis Services data sources will probably be very similar to what is shown here.

Reusing Recent Data Sources

Once you have used a data source in Power Query, it will appear on the list of data sources shown when you click the Recent Sources button on the Power Query tab in the Excel ribbon (see Figure 2-64).

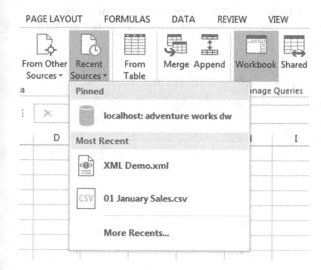

Figure 2-64. *The Recent Sources drop-down box*

Clicking one of the data sources in this list will automatically create a new query that uses that data source and open the Query Editor. Clicking the More Recents option at the bottom of the drop-down list opens the Manage Recent Sources dialog, as shown in Figure 2–65, where you can pin data sources to the list, delete data sources from the list, and copy the path to text file data sources to the clipboard.

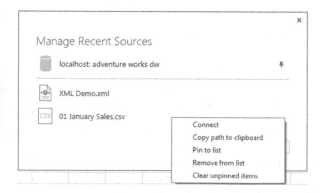

Figure 2-65. *The Manage Recent Sources dialog*

Managing Credentials

You have already seen several times how Power Query handles authentication when connecting to different types of data source. You may also have noticed how Power Query saves the information on authentication for future connections to the same data source. What happens when your workbook is sent to someone else though? Power Query saves all authentication data to an encrypted file on your local hard drive, so any usernames or passwords you type in are held securely. This file is separate from any workbook. If you send your workbook to another user or open it on another machine, Power Query will search the encrypted file on the new machine to see if credentials are saved for all data sources used in that workbook. If the credentials are present on the new machine, they are used. If they are not, the user is prompted to enter new credentials.

You can edit the credentials stored on your local machine by clicking the Data Source settings button on the Power Query tab in the Excel ribbon. This opens the Data Source settings dialog, as shown in Figure 2-66. Clicking a data source will light up the Edit Credential and Delete buttons.

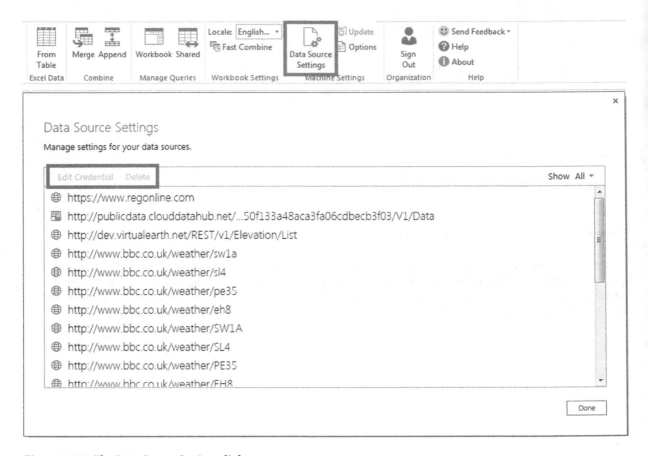

Figure 2-66. *The Data Source Settings dialog*

If you are using a shared query and do not have access to a data source used by it, you may see a "Request Access" link in the top right-hand corner when the authentication dialog box for the data source appears. This link will either be a web page or an e-mail address to allow you to contact someone who will be able to grant you access to the data source. More details on how data sources can be managed by data stewards, including how this type of "Request Access" link can be created, will be given in Chapter 7.

The Importance of Locale

If you are working with data from many different countries, you must take into account international variations in the way data is formatted. For example, in the United States, the data 07/01/2015 is July 1st 2015, but in Europe the same date would be read as January 7th 2015. Similarly, in English-speaking countries, a period (also known as a full stop or decimal point) is used as a decimal separator, and a comma is used as a thousands separator. In many European countries, the opposite is true and a comma is used as a decimal separator and a period is used as a thousands separator. This section shows how you can deal with these issues in Power Query when importing data. In Chapter 3, you will learn how you can set the locale used for specific transformations.

Setting a Default Locale

To see what the impact is of changing locale in Power Query, Figure 2-67 shows the contents of a semicolon separated file containing date, product, and sales data.

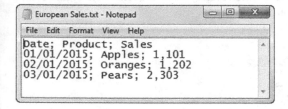

Figure 2-67. *Data for testing the effect of different locales*

When you create a new Excel workbook, Power Query will use the current operating system locale as its default. You can see what this is and override it by going to the Power Query tab in the ribbon and looking at the Locale drop-down box, as shown in Figure 2-68.

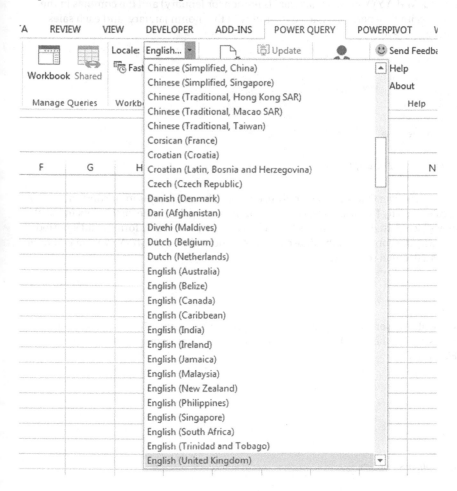

Figure 2-68. *The default locale drop-down box*

With the default locale set to English (United States), the dates will be interpreted as being in MM/DD/YYYY format and the commas in the Sales column will be interpreted as thousands separators if the file in Figure 2-68 is imported into Power Query. Two custom columns have been added to the query to make the results easier to interpret: one to return the name of the month used in the Date column and a second to return True if the value in the Sales column is less than 3. The output of the query using the English (United States) locale is as shown in Figure 2-69; each date is in a different month, and each sales value is greater than 3.

	A	B	C	D	E
1	Date	Product	Sales	Month Name	Value Of Sales Less Than 3?
2	01/01/2015	Apples	1101	January	FALSE
3	01/02/2015	Oranges	1202	February	FALSE
4	01/03/2015	Pears	2303	March	FALSE

Figure 2-69. *Data imported with the English (United States) locale*

If you change the default locale to be French (France) instead, however, and refresh the query, you will see that the dates are interpreted as being in DD/MM/YYYY format ("janvier" is French for January) and the commas in the sales column are interpreted as being decimals separators. Each date is now in the month January, and each sales value is now less than 3, as shown in Figure 2-70.

	A	B	C	D	E
1	Date	Product	Sales	Month Name	Value Of Sales Less Than 3?
2	01/01/2015	Apples	1.101	janvier	TRUE
3	02/01/2015	Oranges	1.202	janvier	TRUE
4	03/01/2015	Pears	2.303	janvier	TRUE

Figure 2-70. *Data imported with the French (France) locale*

It is very important to realize that the Power Query locale is only used when Power Query is importing and transforming data; the Windows locale, used by Excel, is always used when displaying the results of the data in Excel. In Figures 2-69 and 2-70, the Windows locale used is English (UK), which uses a DD/MM/YYYY format and a period as a decimal separator. This explains why the contents of the date column are shown in DD/MM/YYYY format and the sales values shown are use a period as a decimal separator.

CSV Files and Code Pages

When importing CSV files, it is also possible to set the code page used to interpret its contents. To do this, open the Query Editor and, in the Applied Steps box on the right-hand side, double-click the Gears icon next to the step that imports the CSV file, as shown in Figure 2-71.

Figure 2-71. *The Gears icon in the Applied Steps box*

Once you have done this, a dialog will open (shown in Figure 2-72) and you can use the File Origin drop-down box to set the code page used to interpret this CSV file.

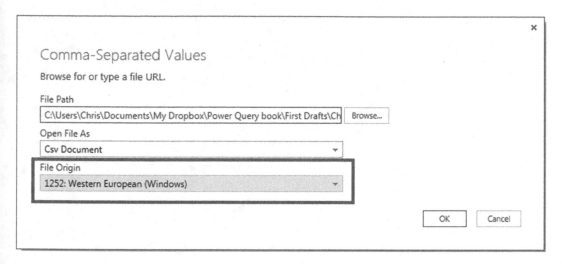

Figure 2-72. The File Origin drop-down box

Summary

In this chapter, you have seen the wide variety of data sources that you can connect to using Power Query. Hopefully, you have also seen the similarities in the way that Power Query treats all of these data sources so that once you have learned how to work with one data source, it is very easy to learn how to work with all of them. In the next chapter, you will learn about how you can filter, sort, aggregate, and otherwise manipulate the data now that you have loaded it into Power Query.

CHAPTER 3

■ ■ ■

Transforming Data with Power Query

Now that you have extracted the data that your need from your source, it is very likely that you are going to want to change it or clean it before you load it into the worksheet or the Excel Data Model. It's rarely the case that your source data is in exactly the right format and, of course, this is where Power Query shows its worth. In this chapter, you'll learn about all of the functionality in the Power Query query editor for filtering, sorting, aggregating, and unpivoting your data, and you will take a first look at how you can use the M language to define calculations in custom columns.

Most of the examples in this chapter use the same CSV file, Chapter3SourceData.csv, which can be found in the samples for this book. This file contains sales information with a number of problems and inconsistencies that are typical of real-world data.

Queries and Steps

In Chapter 1, you learned that Power Query queries are composed of one or more steps, each of which either loads data from a data source or applies some kind of change to the output of another step. You also learned how the final step in the query gives the output of the query. If you load Chapter3SourceData.csv into Power Query using the From CSV button, the Query Editor shows the data found in Figure 3-1.

▦▾	InvoiceNumber ▾	SalesDate ▾	ProductName ▾	UnitsSold ▾	SalesValue ▾	ShippingCost ▾	SalesPeople ▾	ShipToCity ▾	ShipToCountry ▾
1	123	01/01/2014	Apples	1	0.45	10	Chris	London	UK
2	124	01/01/2014	Oranges	2	0.6	20	Chris,Helen	Washington DC	USA
3	125	02/02/2014	Apples	2	0.9	20	HELEN	Dublin	Ireland
4	126	02/02/2014	Oranges	1	0.3	10	Helen	Paris	France
5	Invoice127	03/03/2014	Pears	5	1	40	Chris	Berlin	Germany
6	128	03/03/2014	Apples	3	1.2	30	CHRIS,Natasha	Zurich	Switzerland
7	129	03/03/2014	Oranges	3	0.9	30	Chris,Mimi	Oslo	Norway
8	129	03/03/2014	Oranges	3	0.9	30	chris,mimi	Oslo	Norway
9	130	03/04/2014	Grapes	1	2	100	Helen,Natasha	Oslo	
10	131	04/04/2014	Apples	1	0.45	10	Chris	London	

Figure 3-1. *Data from Chapter3SourceData.csv in the Query Editor*

If you look in the Applied Steps pane, you will see that three steps have been added to your query automatically, as shown in Figure 3-2.

◢ APPLIED STEPS

Figure 3-2. *Steps created automatically when a CSV file is imported*

The last step, called ChangedType, is highlighted and it is the output of that step that is shown in Figure 3-1. Because it is the last step in this query, this will be the output of the query. Clicking on a different step will show the output of that step. The three steps that have been created do the following:

- Source loads the data from the CSV file.

- FirstRowAsHeader takes the first row of the CSV file and uses the values as the column names.

- ChangedType automatically applies a data type to each of the columns. For example, Power Query thinks that the Date column only contains data of type date, so it sets the type of that column to be date. That column can now only contain date values.

The Source step has a Gears icon next to it. As you saw in the section on locales in Chapter 2, clicking this icon allows you to edit the settings for how the CSV file is imported. Any step in a query where a dialog was used to configure some settings will have the same icon next to it. You can click the Gears icon if you want the same dialog to reappear so you can change something.

You can also see from Figure 3-2 that with the ChangedType step highlighted, a Cross icon is visible next to it; clicking this icon will delete the step. Any step can be deleted after it has been selected, not just the last one in the query. If you right-click a step, the Delete Until End menu option will delete the current step and any subsequent steps.

The order of steps can also be changed by right-clicking a step and selecting either Move Up or Move Down. Steps can also be renamed from the right-click menu by selecting Rename.

■ **Note** Moving or deleting steps could result in errors elsewhere in your query. For example, if you delete a step that creates a new column in your table and that column is referenced in a later step, that later step will throw an error. If this is likely to happen, Power Query will show a warning dialog when you try to delete a step. In general, though, Power Query is quite tolerant of change and, if you rename a step, it will update any other steps with the new name.

One last thing to mention here is that when you click a step and see the results that it returns in the Query Editor, Power Query doesn't always reload your source data and recalculate the values. To make the user interface responsive, it caches intermediate results on disk. Therefore, if your source data has changed, you may need to click the Refresh button on the Home tab of the Query Editor toolbar to see the latest results.

■ **Note**   If you work with very large datasets, Power Query can use a lot of disk space to hold the cached, intermediate results you see in the Query Editor. The location of this cache is `C:\Users\username\AppData\Local\Microsoft\Power Query`. The documentation mentions that there is a soft limit of 4GB for the size of this cache—"soft" because this limit can be exceeded for short periods of time.

Working with Columns

One of the first things you will want to do with your data as soon as you have loaded it is to make sure your columns are in the right place, are named appropriately, and are using the correct data types. This section will show you all of the functionality available in Power Query to do this.

Naming Columns

Deleting the second and third steps (called FirstRowAsHeader and ChangedType), which were created automatically when the sample CSV file was loaded into Power Query, will mean the Query Editor will show the output of just the first step, Source, as in Figure 3-3.

▦▾	Column1 ▾	Column2 ▾	Column3 ▾	Column4 ▾	Column5 ▾	Column6 ▾	Column7 ▾	Column8 ▾	Column9 ▾
1	InvoiceNumber	SalesDate	ProductName	UnitsSold	SalesValue	ShippingCost	SalesPeople	ShipToCity	ShipToCountry
2	123	1/1/2014	Apples	1	0.45	10	Chris	London	UK
3	124	1/1/2014	Oranges	2	0.60	20	Chris,Helen	Washington DC	USA
4	125	2/2/2014	Apples	2	0.90	20	HELEN	Dublin	Ireland
5	126	2/2/2014	Oranges	1	0.30	10	Helen	Paris	France
6	Invoice127	3/3/2014	Pears	5	1.00	40	Chris	Berlin	Germany
7	128	3/3/2014	Apples	3	1.20	30	CHRIS,Natasha	Zurich	Switzerland
8	129	3/3/2014	Oranges	3	.90	30	Chris,Mimi	Oslo	Norway
9	129	3/3/2014	Oranges	3	.90	30	chris,mimi	Oslo	Norway
10	130	3/4/2014	Grapes	1	2.00	100	Helen,Natasha	Oslo	
11	131	4/4/2014	Apples	1	0.45	10	Chris	London	

Figure 3-3. *The output of the Source step*

At this point, the column names from the CSV file are shown in the first row of the table. To recreate what Power Query did automatically earlier and make these values the column names in the table, click the Use First Row As Headers button on the Home tab in the Query Editor toolbar (shown in Figure 3-4). Once you have done this, a new step will be created called FirstRowAsHeader, and the Query Editor will display its output.

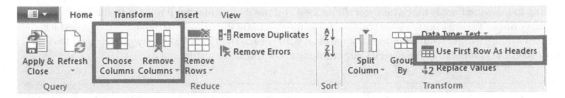

Figure 3-4. *The Use First Row as Headers, Remove Columns, and Choose Columns buttons*

Column names can also be edited manually either by double-clicking the name or by right-clicking the column and selecting Rename. Even if you rename multiple columns, Power Query will do its best to include those changes in a single new step rather than multiple steps; this step will be called RenamedColumns by default.

Moving Columns

Columns can be moved left or right in the table by dragging and dropping them in the appropriate place, or by right-clicking the column and then selecting Move and either Left, Right, To Beginning or To End. Again, where possible, Power Query will include all of those changes in a single step, called ReorderedColumns by default.

Removing Columns

It is often the case that when you import data, you do not need all of the columns from your source. It is also important that you do not import columns that you do not need if you are loading data into the Excel Data Model because these columns will increase the amount of memory needed to store the data.

You can remove columns from a table in a number of ways. If you select one or more columns in the Results pane and right-click, you can choose the Remove Columns option to remove the selected columns or the Remove Other Columns option to remove all but the selected columns. The Remove Columns drop-down box on the Home tab of the Query Editor toolbar has the same options. You can also click the Choose Columns button on the Home tab of the Query Editor toolbar (shown in Figure 3-4) to open the Choose Columns dialog, where you can select all the columns you want to keep or remove from your table.

Splitting Columns

Having renamed and reordered some columns, the example query will look something like what is shown in Figure 3-5.

▦▾	Invoice Number ▾	Product Name ▾	Sales Date ▾	Sales Value ▾	Units Sold ▾	Shipping Cost ▾	Sales People ▾	Ship To City ▾	Ship To Country ▾
1	123	Apples	1/1/2014	0.45	1	10	Chris	London	UK
2	124	Oranges	1/1/2014	0.60	2	20	Chris,Helen	Washington DC	USA
3	125	Apples	2/2/2014	0.90	2	20	HELEN	Dublin	Ireland
4	126	Oranges	2/2/2014	0.30	1	10	Helen	Paris	France
5	Invoice127	Pears	3/3/2014	1.00	5	40	Chris	Berlin	Germany
6	128	Apples	3/3/2014	1.20	3	30	CHRIS,Natasha	Zurich	Switzerland
7	129	Oranges	3/3/2014	.90	3	30	Chris,Mimi	Oslo	Norway
8	129	Oranges	3/3/2014	.90	3	30	chris,mimi	Oslo	Norway
9	130	Grapes	3/4/2014	2.00	1	100	Helen,Natasha	Oslo	
10	131	Apples	4/4/2014	0.45	1	10	Chris	London	

Figure 3-5. *Query Editor showing columns to be split and merged*

Notice how in the Sales People column, some rows contain two names in a comma-delimited list. If you want each of these names shown in a separate column, click the column to select it, then click the Split Column button on the Transform tab of the Query Editor toolbar, and then select By Delimiter, as shown in Figure 3-6, or make the same selection from the right-click menu.

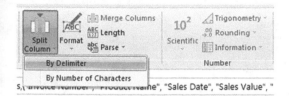

Figure 3-6. *The Split Column by Delimiter button*

When you do this, the "Split a column by delimiter" dialog will appear, as shown in Figure 3-7.

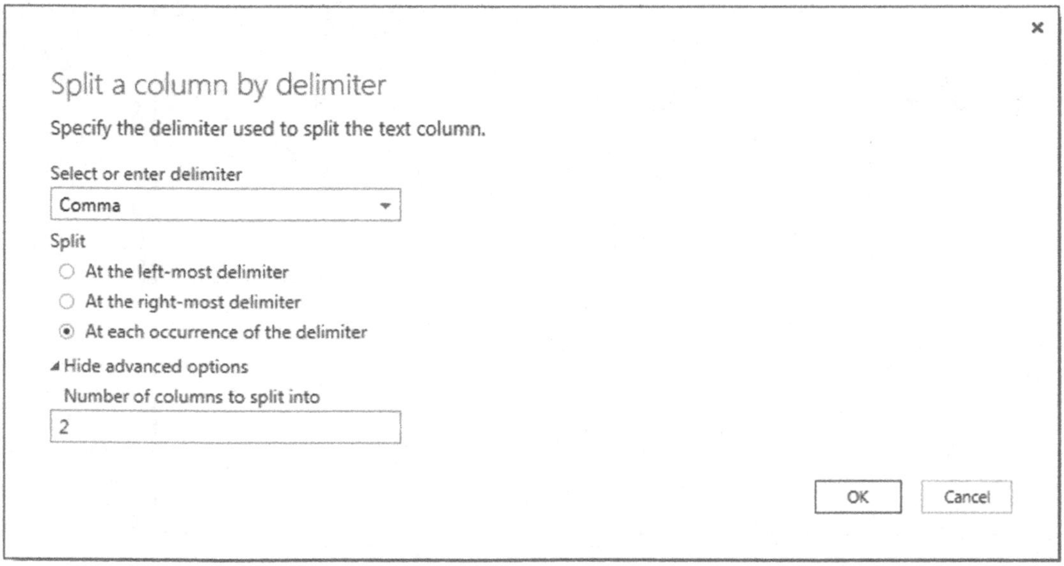

Figure 3-7. *The "Split a column by delimiter" dialog*

In this particular case, the default options are the ones you want to use: You want to split the column at each occurrence of a comma and end up with two columns. Clicking OK will result in the existing Sales People column being removed from your table and being replaced with two columns called Sales People.1 and Sales People.2, which can then be renamed to something more meaningful like Sales Person 1 and Sales Person 2, as shown in Figure 3-8.

⠿▾	Invoice Number ▾	Product Name ▾	Sales Date ▾	Sales Value ▾	Units Sold ▾	Shipping Cost ▾	Sales Person 1 ▾	Sales Person 2 ▾	Ship To City ▾	Ship To Country ▾
1	123	Apples	01/01/2014	0.45	1	10	Chris		null London	UK
2	124	Oranges	01/01/2014	0.6	2	20	Chris	Helen	Washington DC	USA
3	125	Apples	02/02/2014	0.9	2	20	HELEN		null Dublin	Ireland
4	126	Oranges	02/02/2014	0.3	1	10	Helen		null Paris	France
5	Invoice127	Pears	03/03/2014	1	5	40	Chris		null Berlin	Germany
6	128	Apples	03/03/2014	1.2	3	30	CHRIS	Natasha	Zurich	Switzerland
7	129	Oranges	03/03/2014	0.9	3	30	Chris	Mimi	Oslo	Norway
8	129	Oranges	03/03/2014	0.9	3	30	chris	mimi	Oslo	Norway
9	130	Grapes	03/04/2014	2	1	100	Helen	Natasha	Oslo	
10	131	Apples	04/04/2014	0.45	1	10	Chris		null London	

Figure 3-8. Query Editor results showing split columns

As you will already have noticed, it is also possible to split a column into multiple columns of a certain number of characters by clicking the By Number Of Characters option shown in Figure 3-6. The dialog for this is shown in Figure 3-9.

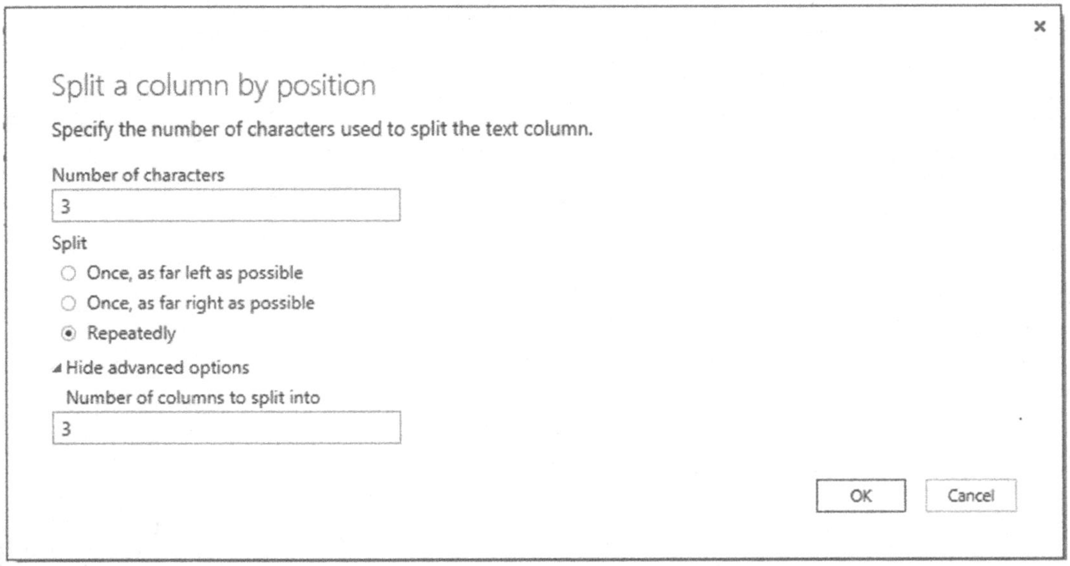

Figure 3-9. The "Split a column by position" dialog

Even though it makes no sense to do this, the result of splitting the Product Name into columns of three characters is shown in Figure 3-10. All subsequent examples in this chapter will assume this step has been deleted!

Product Name.1 ▾	Product Name.2 ▾	Product Name.3 ▾
App	les	*null*
Ora	nge	s
App	les	*null*
Ora	nge	s
Pea	rs	*null*
App	les	*null*
Ora	nge	s
Ora	nge	s
Gra	pes	*null*
App	les	*null*

Figure 3-10. *The Product Name column split into columns of three characters*

Merging Columns

It is also possible to merge two columns containing text data into a single column. In Figure 3-8, you can see two columns called Ship to City and Ship to Country. To merge these columns into a single text column, click one of them and then click the other while holding down either the Shift key or the Ctrl key on the keyboard, so that both columns are selected. Then select the Merge Columns option from the right-click menu as shown in Figure 3-11. Alternatively, you can click the Merge Columns button on the Transform tab in the Query Editor toolbar. Note that the Merge Queries button on the Home tab of the toolbar is not for merging columns, but for merging two queries.

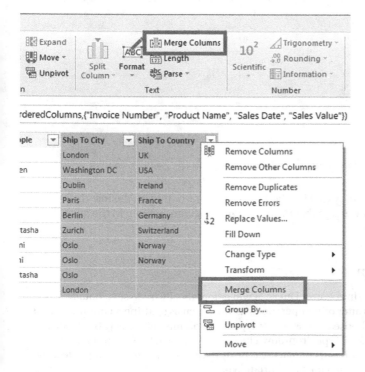

Figure 3-11. *The Merge Columns option and button*

When you have done this, the Merge Columns dialog will appear, as shown in Figure 3-12, and you will be able to choose a character to separate the values from the two columns in the new, merged column.

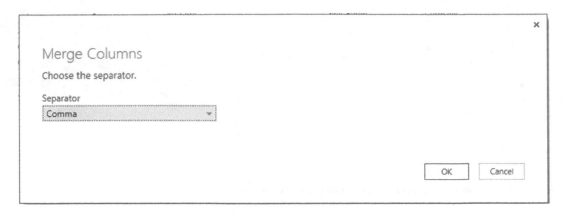

Figure 3-12. *The Merge Columns dialog*

Choosing a comma and clicking OK will result in the Ship to City and Ship to Country columns being replaced by a single column containing the values from both of those columns, separated by a comma. The new column will be called Merged. (Again, it's a good idea to rename the column immediately afterward to something more meaningful like Ship to Address.) The end result is shown in Figure 3-13.

▦▾	Invoice Number ▾	Product Name ▾	Sales Date ▾	Sales Value ▾	Units Sold ▾	Shipping Cost ▾	Sales Person 1 ▾	Sales Person 2 ▾	Ship To Address ▾
1	123	Apples	01/01/2014	0.45	1	10	Chris	*null*	London,UK
2	124	Oranges	01/01/2014	0.6	2	20	Chris	Helen	Washington DC,USA
3	125	Apples	02/02/2014	0.9	2	20	HELEN	*null*	Dublin,Ireland
4	126	Oranges	02/02/2014	0.3	1	10	Helen	*null*	Paris,France
5	Invoice127	Pears	03/03/2014	1	5	40	Chris	*null*	Berlin,Germany
6	128	Apples	03/03/2014	1.2	3	30	CHRIS	Natasha	Zurich,Switzerland
7	129	Oranges	03/03/2014	0.9	3	30	Chris	Mimi	Oslo,Norway
8	129	Oranges	03/03/2014	0.9	3	30	chris	mimi	Oslo,Norway
9	130	Grapes	03/04/2014	2	1	100	Helen	Natasha	Oslo,
10	131	Apples	04/04/2014	0.45	1	10	Chris	*null*	London,

Figure 3-13. *The Query Editor showing the Ship to Address merged column*

Merging columns is also possible from the toolbar by clicking the Merge Columns button on the Insert tab of the Query Editor toolbar; it works in almost the same way except that the two original columns remain in the query and a new column containing the merged values is added.

Setting the Data Type of a Column

As you have already seen, when you import a CSV file into Power Query, it will automatically try to set a data type for each column. In fact, Power Query will try to do this after other operations as well, such as splitting a column. In most cases, Power Query will do a good job but you can choose your own data type for a column quite easily by clicking it and then selecting the appropriate type from the Data Type drop-down box on the Home tab of the toolbar in the Query Editor, as shown in Figure 3-14. Alternatively, you can change the type by right-clicking the column, selecting Change Type from the right-click menu, and then selecting the appropriate type.

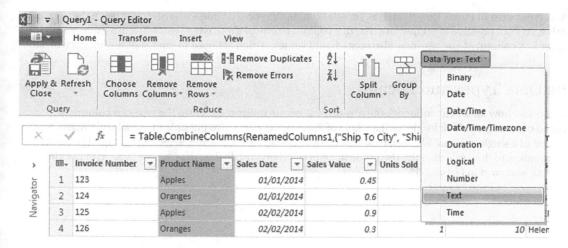

Figure 3-14. *The Data Type drop-down box*

The following data types can be used for columns in Power Query:

- *Binary*, which is for storing sequences of bytes. This data type can be used to store images and the contents of files from disk.

- *Date*, which is for storing date values. Power Query can store any date between January 1st 0001 CE and December 31st 9999 CE in the Gregorian calendar.

- *Date/Time*, which is for storing values that represent both a date and a time.

- *Date/Time/Timezone*, which is for storing values that contain a date, a time, and a time zone. A time zone value is a stored as the difference in the number of minutes between a local time and Universal Coordinated Time (UTC).

- *Duration*, which is for storing values that represent the difference between two times, date/times, or date/time/timezones. The minimum granularity of a duration value is 100 nanoseconds.

- *Logical*, which can only store true or false values.

- *Number*, which is for storing any numeric value. This includes integers and fractional numbers; the number will be stored with at least the precision of a Double.

- *Text*, which is for storing Unicode text. Power Query is case sensitive, meaning that it distinguishes between uppercase and lowercase text. For example, the text "HELLO WORLD" is treated as a different value from the text "hello world." This has important implications when it comes to doing things such as filtering and transforming text values.

- *Time*, which is for storing time-of-day values.

- *Any*, which can be used to store any type of value. The Any data type is not displayed in the Data Type drop-down box because you cannot explicitly set a column to be of type Any. However, when you import data from some data sources, such as an Excel table, you will see that no selection is made in the Data Type drop-down box. This means that the column is of type Any. When this happens, it is a good idea to select another, more appropriate type for the column such as Text or Number so you can use Power Query's special functionality for these types.

Other data types exist in Power Query, such as *Tables*, *Lists*, and *Records*. While we have already seen these values in cells in a table, it is not possible to set the data type of a column to one of these types; you will learn more about them in Chapter 5. A column of any type may also contain null values, which are used to represent the absence of data.

Changing Data Types and Locales

In Chapter 2, you saw how locale can influence the way text values are interpreted when the type of a column is changed. Instead of setting a default locale for the whole of Power Query, it is also possible to use a locale when changing the type of a single column. This can be achieved by right-clicking a column, selecting Change Type from the right-click menu, and then selecting the Using Locale option. When you do this, the Change Type with Locale dialog will appear, as shown in Figure 3-15.

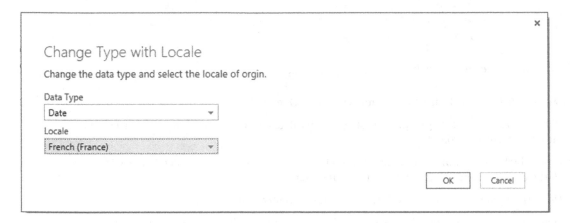

Figure 3-15. *The Change Type with Locale dialog*

This dialog allows you to change the type of a column while specifying the locale used for the data source. For example, the sample CSV file contains the text "3/4/2014" in one of the rows of the SalesDate column. If this value is cast to a date type using the locale French (France), this will be interpreted as a date in the format DD/MM/YYYY, and it will become the date 3rd April 2014. If, on the other hand, this value is cast to a date type using the locale English (US), it will be interpreted as a date in the format MM/DD/YYYY and become the date 4th March 2014.

Filtering Rows

It's very likely that you will not need all of the data you have imported and that you will have to filter out some rows. There are a number of ways to do this in Power Query, which you will learn about in this section.

Filtering Rows Using Auto-Filter

Probably the easiest way to filter rows in a table is to use the Auto-Filter box. You can find this by clicking the down-arrow icon next to a column name in the Query Editor, as shown in Figure 3-16.

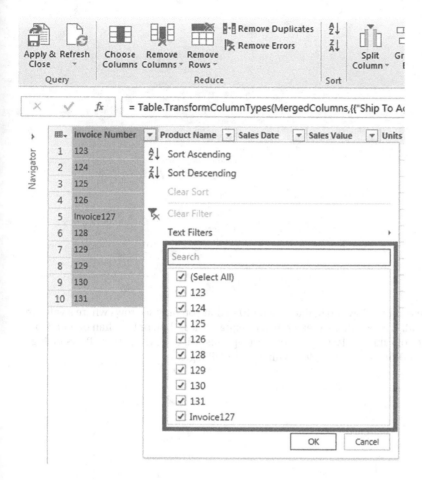

Figure 3-16. *The Auto-Filter box*

The Auto-Filter box displays the first 1,000 distinct values that it finds in a column. If there are more than 1,000 distinct values in a column, a Load More button appears which, if you click it, will load 1,000 more distinct values. Unchecking a value in the Auto-Filter box will mean that any row that contains that value for the selected column will be removed from the table. By default, all values are selected. Unchecking the (Select All) box at the top of the list of values will uncheck all of the values underneath it, so you can check just the values that you want. You can also search for values in the Search box. As soon as you start to type in the Search box, the values in the Auto-Filter box will be filtered down to those that match your search term. To clear the Search box, click the X icon on the far right-hand side of it.

Filtering Rows Using Number, Text, and Date Filters

Depending on the data type of the column, just above the Auto-Filter box specialized number, text and date filter options will be available.

Number Filters

Figure 3-17 shows the Number Filters menu that is available just about the Auto-Filter box for columns of type *number*.

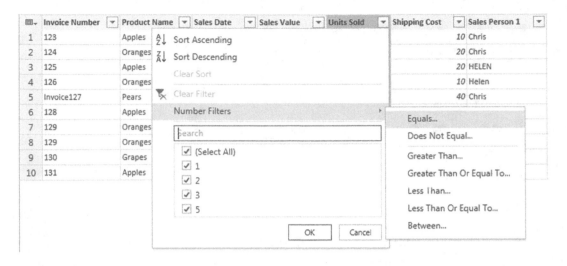

Figure 3-17. *The Number Filters menu*

The options here are self-explanatory: They allow you to filter the table so that you only see rows where a value in the selected column equals, does not equal, is greater than, greater than or equal to, less than or less than or equal to a given value. You can also filter by ranges of values. Selecting one of these options will display the Filter Rows dialog as shown in Figure 3-18. Multiple filter conditions can be applied with AND or OR logic.

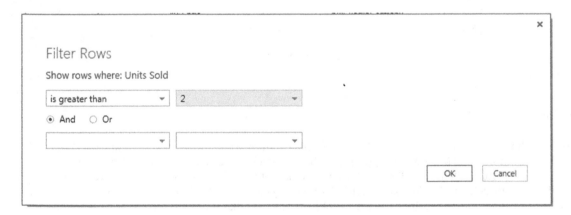

Figure 3-18. *The Filter Rows dialog*

Once a filter has been applied, the Clear Filter menu option (shown in Figure 3-17) will be enabled; selecting this menu option will remove the filter.

Text Filters

Columns of type *text* have a different set of specialized filters that can be applied to them, as shown in Figure 3-19.

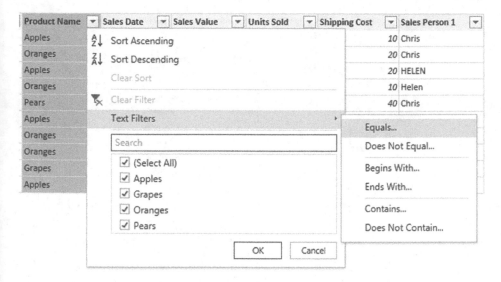

Figure 3-19. *The Text Filters menu*

Again, the options here are self-explanatory: You can filter rows in a table according to whether values in a text column equal or do not equal a text value you supply, or according to whether they begin with, end with, contain, or do not contain any given piece of text. Clicking one of these options will open a Filter Rows dialog that is essentially the same as the one shown in Figure 3-18.

Date Filters

Columns of type *date* have a large number of options for filtering, as shown in Figure 3-20.

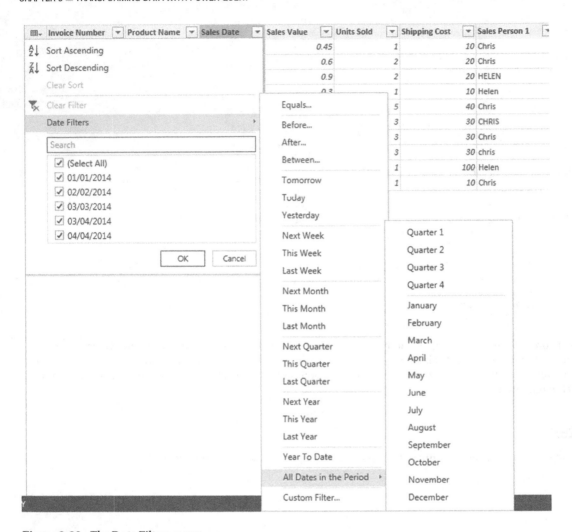

Figure 3-20. *The Date Filters menu*

Rows in a table can be filtered according to whether the date in that row is equal to, before, or after a given date. They can also be filtered according to whether the date is in one of many predefined date ranges such as the current week or the current month. All of these date ranges are based on a standard calendar that cannot be customized. Clicking the Custom Filter menu option will open the Filter Rows dialog and allow you to create more complex date filters.

Filtering Rows by Range

There are a number of options available for filtering rows by their position in the table. These options can be accessed from buttons in the Reduce section of the Home tab of the Query Editor toolbar, as shown in Figure 3-21.

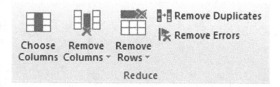

Figure 3-21. *The Reduce section of the Query Editor toolbar*

The same options can also be accessed by clicking on the Table icon in the top left-hand corner of the table in the Query Editor, as shown in Figure 3-22.

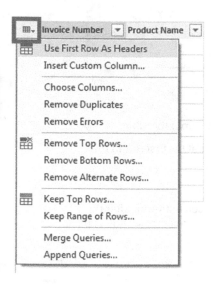

Figure 3-22. *The Table icon menu*

The Remove Rows drop-down box on the toolbar allows you to remove rows from a table in different ways. Remove Top Rows and Remove Bottom Rows remove a given number of rows from either the top or the bottom of the table; Keep Top Rows removes all but a given number of rows from the top of the table. Clicking either of these buttons opens a dialog where you specify the number of rows you want to keep or remove. The Keep Range button allows you to filter all but a given number of rows, starting from a given row number; clicking this button will open a dialog allowing you to enter the number of the first row and the number of rows to keep from that point.

Remove Alternate Rows removes an alternating number of rows from your table. Clicking this button opens the Remove Alternate Rows dialog, as shown in Figure 3-23.

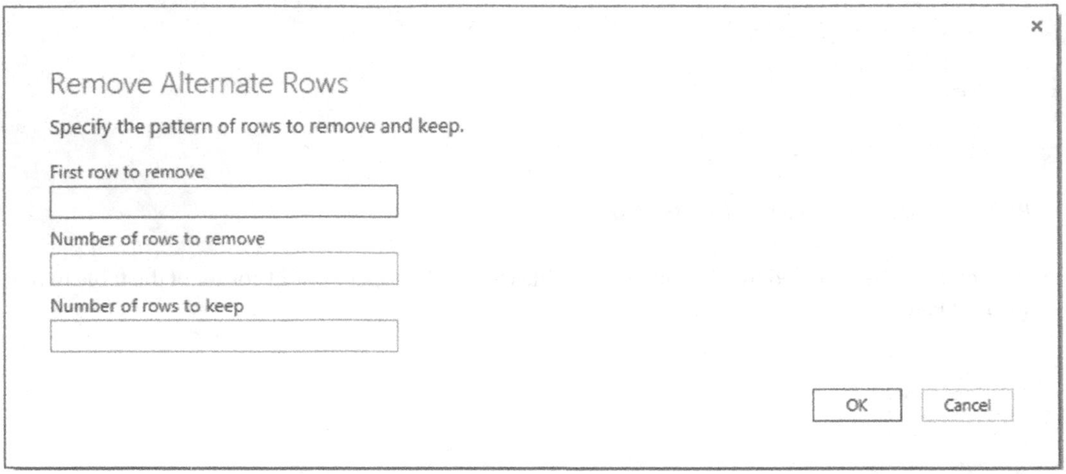

Figure 3-23. *The Remove Alternate Rows dialog*

In the Remove Alternate Rows dialog, you specify a pattern for removing rows from the table:

- The number of the first row to remove. Entering *1* here would mean that the first row in the table would be the first to be removed.

- The number of rows that will be removed from the table.

- The number of rows from the table that will be kept after rows have been removed. After the rows that have been kept, another section of rows will be removed, then another section kept, and so on, until the end of the table has been reached.

Removing Duplicate Values

It is also possible to filter rows from a table that have duplicate values in a certain column and also to remove duplicate rows. In Figure 3-24, you can see that Rows 7 and 8 in the table both have the value 129 in the Invoice Number column.

▦.	Invoice Number	Sales Date	Product Name	Units Sold	Sales Value	Shipping Cost	Sales Person 1	Sales Person 2
1	123	01/01/2014	Apples	1	0.45	10	Chris	null
2	124	01/01/2014	Oranges	2	0.6	20	Chris	Helen
3	125	02/02/2014	Apples	2	0.9	20	HELEN	null
4	126	02/02/2014	Oranges	1	0.3	10	Helen	null
5	Invoice127	03/03/2014	Pears	5	1	40	Chris	null
6	128	03/03/2014	Apples	3	1.2	30	CHRIS	Natasha
7	129	03/03/2014	Oranges	3	0.9	30	Chris	Mimi
8	129	03/03/2014	Oranges	3	0.9	30	chris	mimi
9	130	03/04/2014	Grapes	1	2	100	Helen	Natasha
10	131	04/04/2014	Apples	1	0.45	10	Chris	null

Figure 3-24. *Table rows with duplicated invoice numbers*

Selecting the Invoice Number column and then clicking the Remove Duplicates button in the Reduce section of the Home tab on the Query Editor toolbar will result in Row 8, the second row with the invoice number 129, being removed from the table. If you select multiple columns, Power Query will only remove a row if every value in the selected columns is duplicated.

To remove rows where every value in every column is duplicated, you either have to manually select every column and click the Remove Duplicates button in the toolbar or click the Table icon in the top left-hand corner of the table and select Remove Duplicates from the menu. Power Query is case sensitive when checking for duplicates so with the example data shown in Figure 3-24, no rows would be removed if you selected every column and clicked Remove Duplicates. This is because Row 7 contains the value "Chris" in the Sales Person 1 column, but Row 8 contains the value "chris."

Filtering Out Rows with Errors

Error values can appear in columns for a number of reasons: A calculated value could contain a syntax error, for example, or an error value could be the result of a failed type conversion. In the sample data shown in Figure 3-24, you can see that in Row 5 the Invoice Number column contains a non-numeric value; if you try to convert the Invoice Number column to type *Number*, you will see an error value appear in this row, as shown in Figure 3-25.

▦▾	Invoice Number ▼	Product Name ▼	Sales Date ▼
1	123	Apples	01/01/2014
2	124	Oranges	01/01/2014
3	125	Apples	02/02/2014
4	126	Oranges	02/02/2014
5	Error	Pears	03/03/2014
6	128	Apples	03/03/2014
7	129	Oranges	03/03/2014
8	129	Oranges	03/03/2014
9	130	Grapes	03/04/2014
10	131	Apples	04/04/2014

Figure 3-25. An error value in a cell

Rows containing error values can be filtered from a table in two ways. First of all, you can select one or more columns and click the Remove Errors button on the Home tab in the Query Editor toolbar. This will remove all rows that contain errors in the selected columns. Alternatively, you can click on the Table icon and then select the Remove Errors menu option. This will remove all rows from the table that contain errors in any column.

Sorting a Table

Tables in Power Query can be sorted in either ascending or descending order by one or more columns. To sort a table by a single column, select that column in the Query Editor and then either click one of the two sort buttons on the toolbar (shown in Figure 3-26) or click the down arrow next to the column name and select Sort Ascending or Sort Descending from the menu. When a column is sorted, a small arrow pointing upward or downward will appear in the column header, indicating whether the table is sorted in ascending or descending order.

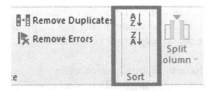

Figure 3-26. *The Sort buttons on the Query Editor toolbar*

If you select more than one column in the table, the sort buttons will be disabled. To sort by more than one column, you have to apply a sort to one column and then immediately afterward click another column and sort that. When you do this, both sort operations will be combined in a single step and a number will appear in the headers of both columns indicating which column will be sorted first and which will be sorted second. Figure 3-27 shows a table that has been sorted, first of all, by Sales Date in descending order, and then by Product Name in ascending order.

Sales Date	Sales Value
04/04/2014	0.45
03/04/2014	2
03/03/2014	0.9
03/03/2014	0.9
03/03/2014	1

Figure 3-27. *A table sorted by two columns*

If there are multiple steps in a query where sorting is applied to a table (they will have to be separated by other steps that do something else), the last sort step will override any previous sorting that has been applied.

You can also reverse the order of the rows in your table by clicking the Reverse Rows button on the Transform tab of the Query Editor toolbar.

Changing Values in a Table

Power Query also allows you to alter values within a table in a number of ways.

Replacing Values with Other Values

The Replace Values button, found in the Column section of the Transform tab on the Query Editor toolbar (see Figure 3-28), allows you to search for values in columns and replace them with other values. The same functionality can be accessed by right-clicking a column and selecting the Replace Values menu item.

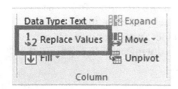

Figure 3-28. *The Replace Values button*

After you have clicked this button, the Replace Values dialog will appear, as shown in Figure 3-29.

☒	

Replace Values

Replace one value with another in the selected columns.

Value To Find

Oranges

Replace With

Lemons

☑ Match entire cell contents

OK   Cancel

Figure 3-29. *The Replace Values dialog*

The options here are straightforward: You must enter the value to find, the value to replace with, and whether the entire cell contents must be matched. Note that the matching is case sensitive so, for example, the text "Oranges" will not be matched to the text "oranges."

To delete occurrences of a value completely, you need to leave the Replace With box empty. In our sample data, one row in the Invoice Number column contains the value "Invoice127," and, as you have already seen, this results in an error when the Invoice Number column is cast to the data type Number. To prevent the error, before casting the column you could select the Invoice Number column, click Replace With, enter "Invoice" in the Value To Find text box, leave the Replace With text box blank, leave the Match entire cell check box unchecked and click OK. This would mean the value "Invoice127" would become just "127" and the cast to Number would succeed.

To replace blank text values with a null value, you need to leave the Value To Find text box empty and enter the value "null" in the Replace With text box. To replace any other text value with a null, you have to enter a value in the Value To Replace text box and then ensure that the Match entire cell check box is checked; if it is not checked, you will get an error in any matched cells.

Text Transforms

Selecting one or more text columns in the Query Editor will enable the Format drop-down box on the Transforms tab of the Query Editor toolbar, as shown in Figure 3-30. The same functionality can also be accessed from the right-click menu.

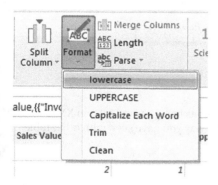

Figure 3-30. *The Format drop-down box*

Following are the five items on this menu:

- *Lowercase,* which sets all text in the selected columns to lower case.

- *UPPERCASE,* which sets all text in the selected columns to upper case.

- *Capitalize Each Word,* which makes all words in the selected column start with a capital letter and sets all subsequent letters in a word to lower case.

- *Trim,* which removes any leading or trailing whitespace characters from text.

- *Clean,* which removes any unprintable characters from text in the selected columns.

In the source data, the names in the Sales Person 1 and Sales Person 2 columns are in a mixture of upper and lower case; selecting these columns and then using the Capitalize Each Word transform will format all of these names consistently, as shown in Figure 3-31. This is important not just for aesthetic reasons: Remember that Power Query is case sensitive, so you usually have to use these text transforms for other functionality such as Replace With to work effectively.

Sales Person 1	Sales Person 2
Chris	null
Helen	Natasha
Chris	Mimi
Chris	Mimi
Chris	null
Chris	Natasha
Helen	null
Helen	null
Chris	null
Chris	Helen

Figure 3-31. *The result of using the Capitalize Each Word transform*

The two options on the Parse drop-down box, also on the Transform tab of the Query Editor toolbar, allow you to transform a piece of text in a cell into either an XML document or a JSON document. Figure 3-32 shows some sample data in the Query Editor where there is a table containing two rows and one text column and each cell contains XML.

▦▾	Column1
1	<?xml version="1.0" encoding="UTF-8"?><company><name>Crossjoin Consulting Ltd</name><country>UK</country></company>
2	<?xml version="1.0" encoding="UTF-8"?><company><name>Microsoft Corporation</name><country>USA</country></company>

Figure 3-32. *XML data stored in table cells*

Using the XML text transform on this column would result in each cell's contents being turned into an XML table (as shown in Figure 3-33), which can then be aggregated or expanded in the way you have seen with other table values.

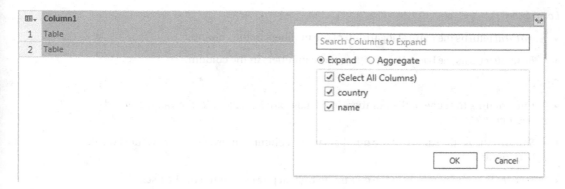

Figure 3-33. Table cells containing XML table values

Number Transforms

Selecting a column of data type *Number* will enable a number of items in the Number section of the Transform tab in the toolbar, as shown in Figure 3-34. Again, the same functionality can be accessed from the right-click menu.

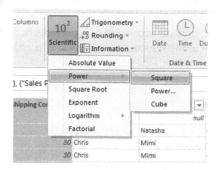

Figure 3-34. The Number section of the Transform tab

The functionality in this section allows you to apply various types of calculation to the values in the selected column.

The Rounding drop-down box has the following three options:

- *Round* allows you to round the numbers in the column up to a given number of decimal places, entered by the user.

- *Round Up* rounds the numbers in the column up to the nearest whole number.

- *Round Down* rounds the numbers in the column down to the nearest whole number.

The Scientific drop-down box has the following options:

- *Absolute Value* returns the absolute value of the numbers in the column; that is to say that positive numbers are not changed, and negative numbers become positive. For example, the number 3 would remain as 3, but -4 would become 4.

- *Factorial* returns the factorial of numbers in the column. For example, the value 4 would become 4*3*2*1=24.

- *Logarithm*
    - *Natural* returns the natural logarithm of the numbers in the column.
    - *Base-10* returns the base-10 logarithm of the numbers in the column.
- *Power*
    - *Cube* returns the cube of the numbers in the column. For example, the value 2 would become 2*2*2=8.
    - *Square* returns the square of the numbers in the column. For example, the value 3 would become 3*3=9.
    - *Power* raises the numbers in the column to a given power, entered by the user.
- *Square Root* returns the square root of the numbers in the column.
- *Exponent* returns the exponent of the numbers in the column.

The Information drop-down box has the following options:

- *Is Even* returns TRUE if the values in the column are even, and FALSE otherwise.
- *Is Odd* returns TRUE if the values in the column are odd, and FALSE otherwise.
- *Sign* returns 1 if the values in the column are positive, -1 if they are negative, and 0 otherwise.

The Trigonometry drop-down box allows you to find the sine, cosine, tangent, arcsine, arccosine, and arctangent of the values in the selected columns. Note that these transforms expect the values in the selected columns to be in radians and not degrees.

Date/Time/Duration Transforms

Selecting a column of data type *Date*, *Time*, or *Duration* (or any hybrid type) will enable either the Date, Time, or Duration drop-down boxes in the Date & Time section of the Transform tab in the toolbar, as shown in Figure 3-35. Again, the same functionality can be accessed from the right-click menu.

Figure 3-35. *The Date/Time/Timezone Transforms menu*

The options on the Date drop-down box:

- *Date Only* returns just the Date part of a DateTime value
- Year
  - *Year* returns just the year part of the dates in the column.
  - *Start of Year* returns the first date in the year for each date in the column.
  - *End of Year* returns the last date in the year for each date in the column.
- Month
  - *Month* returns the month number of the date.
  - *Start of Month* returns the first date in the month.
  - *End of Month* returns the last date in the month.
  - *Days in Month* returns the number of days in the month.
- Day
  - *Day* returns the day number of the date.
  - *Day of Week* returns the number representing the day of the week.
  - *Day of Year* returns the day number of the year.
  - *Start of Day* returns a DateTime value for the start of the day.
  - *End of Day* returns a DateTime value for the end of the day.
- Quarter
  - *Quarter of Year* returns the quarter number of the date.
  - *Start of Quarter* returns the first date in the quarter.
  - *End of Quarter* returns the last date in the quarter.
- Week
  - Week of Year returns the week number of the year.
  - *Week of Month* returns the week number of the month.
  - *Start of Week* returns the first date in the week.
  - *End of Week* returns the last date in the week.

The options on the Time drop-down box:

- *Time Only* returns just the Time part of each DateTime value in the column.
- *Hour* returns the hour number of the time.
- *Minute* returns the minute number of the time.
- *Second* returns the second number of the time.

The options on the Duration drop-down box:

- *Days* returns a number representing the days component of a duration value.
- *Hours* returns a number representing the hours component of a duration value.

- *Minutes* returns a number representing the minutes component of a duration value.

- *Seconds* returns a number representing the seconds component of a duration value.

- *Total Days* returns the total number of days in the duration.

- *Total Hours* returns the total number of hours in the duration.

- *Total Minutes* returns the total number of minutes in the duration.

- *Total Seconds* returns the total number of seconds in the duration.

For these Duration transforms, it's worth pointing out the difference between the first and second groups of options. For example, given a duration value of 1 day and 2 hours, the Hours option would return 2 whereas the Total Hours option would return 26.

Filling Up and Down to Replace Missing Values

The Fill drop-down box on the Transform tab of the Query Editor toolbar (shown in Figure 3-36) contains two options: Fill Down allows you to replace null values in a column with the last non-null value in a column, and Fill Up does the same but uses the next non-null value in the column.

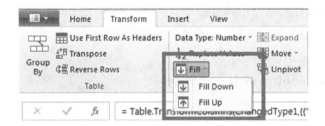

Figure 3-36. *The Fill Down button on the Query Editor toolbar*

This functionality is extremely useful for cleaning data that contains missing values. For example, Figure 3-37 shows the contents of the Ship To Country and the Ship To City columns in our sample data before they were merged. As you can see, in two cases the name of the country is missing.

Ship To City	Ship To Country
London	UK
Washington DC	USA
Dublin	Ireland
Paris	France
Berlin	Germany
Zurich	Switzerland
Oslo	Norway
Oslo	Norway
Oslo	
London	

Figure 3-37. *Sample data showing missing country values*

If you make the assumption that each city name should always be associated with the same country name (so that Oslo should be associated with the country Norway, and London should be associated with the country UK), and that there is always going to be one row where the country is given for each city, then you can use the Fill Down button along with some of the other functionality we have already seen to fill in the missing values.

The first step is to use the Replace Values button to replace the empty text in the Ship To Country column with null values; how to do this was described above in the section "Replacing Values with Other Values." Once you have done this, the data will be as shown in Figure 3-38. This is important because the Fill Down button will only replace null values and not blank text.

Ship To City	Ship To Country
London	UK
Washington DC	USA
Dublin	Ireland
Paris	France
Berlin	Germany
Zurich	Switzerland
Oslo	Norway
Oslo	Norway
Oslo	null
London	null

Figure 3-38. Sample data with empty text values replaced by nulls

Next, you need to order your table first of all by the Ship To City column (either in ascending or descending order) and then by the Ship To Country column in descending order, as shown in Figure 3-39.

Ship To City	Ship To Coun...
Berlin	Germany
Dublin	Ireland
London	UK
London	null
Oslo	Norway
Oslo	Norway
Oslo	null
Paris	France
Washington DC	USA
Zurich	Switzerland

Figure 3-39. Sample data sorted by Ship To City and Ship To Country

Finally, you are ready to click the Fill Down button: The null values are now directly underneath the values you want to replace them with. Clicking Fill Down will result in the null values being replaced with the correct country name, as shown in Figure 3-40. Remember that the table can be reordered in subsequent steps without affecting this change.

Ship To City	Ship To Country
Berlin	Germany
Dublin	Ireland
London	UK
London	UK
Oslo	Norway
Oslo	Norway
Oslo	Norway
Paris	France
Washington DC	USA
Zurich	Switzerland

Figure 3-40. *Sample data with filled down values*

Aggregating Values

Numeric values in a table can be aggregated (that is to say, summed, counted, averaged, or otherwise summarized) by clicking the Group By button on the Home tab of the toolbar of the Query Editor, as shown in Figure 3-41. This functionality is named after its equivalent in the SQL database query language, the Group By clause, and it works in almost the same way.

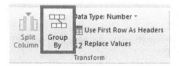

Figure 3-41. *The Group By button in the Query Editor toolbar*

Clicking this button opens the Group By dialog, as shown in Figure 3-42.

Group By...

Specify the columns to group by.

Group by   +

| Product Name | ▼ | − |

New column name   Operation   Column   +

| Count of Sales | Count Rows ▼ | ▼ | − |

OK   Cancel

Figure 3-42. *The Group By dialog*

There are two main sections in the Group By dialog. First of all, the upper, Group by section allows you to specify which columns you want to group by when aggregating. By default, any columns that were selected in the Query Editor will be included in this section; you can add or remove columns using the + and – buttons. The output of the group by operation will include all of the distinct combinations of values from the selected columns.

Secondly, the lower section allows you to specify the aggregation operations that you want to perform on any of the remaining columns. Again, multiple aggregation operations can be specified here by clicking on the + and – buttons. Each aggregation operation will result in a new column being added to the output and the name of that column is specified in the New column name text box.

The following aggregation operations are available in the Operation drop-down box:

- Sum, which returns the sum of values in the column selected in the Column drop-down box.

- Average, which returns the average of values in the column selected in the Column drop-down box.

- Min, which returns the minimum of the values in the column selected in the Column drop-down box.

- Max, which returns the maximum of the values in the column selected in the Column drop-down box.

- Count Rows, which returns a count of the number of rows (the Column drop-down box is disabled in this case).

- Count Distinct Rows, which returns the number of rows containing distinct combinations of values in each column of the table (again the Column drop-down box is disabled in this case).

- All Rows, which returns a value of type Table in a single cell. This option has little practical use unless you are planning to use these Table values in your own custom M code.

With all of the changes made so far to the sample data in this chapter, the Query Editor will show what is displayed in Figure 3-43.

🁢▾	Invoice Number ▾	Product Name ▾	Sales Date ▾	Sales Value ▾	Units Sold ▾	Shipping Cost ▾	Sales Person 1 ▾	Sales Person 2 ▾	Ship To Address ▾
1	123	Apples	01/01/2014	0.45	1	10	Chris	null	London,UK
2	124	Oranges	01/01/2014	0.6	2	20	Chris	Helen	Washington DC,USA
3	125	Apples	02/02/2014	0.9	2	20	Helen	null	Dublin,Ireland
4	126	Oranges	02/02/2014	0.3	1	10	Helen	null	Paris,France
5	127	Pears	03/03/2014	1	5	40	Chris	null	Berlin,Germany
6	128	Apples	03/03/2014	1.2	3	30	Chris	Natasha	Zurich,Switzerland
7	129	Oranges	03/03/2014	0.9	3	30	Chris	Mimi	Oslo,Norway
8	129	Oranges	03/03/2014	0.9	3	30	Chris	Mimi	Oslo,Norway
9	130	Grapes	03/04/2014	2	1	100	Helen	Natasha	Oslo,Norway
10	131	Apples	04/04/2014	0.45	1	10	Chris	null	London,UK

Figure 3-43. Sample data for aggregation

Using this sample data, the settings shown in figure 3-42 will return a table with two columns, as shown in Figure 3-44: a column called Product Name that contains all of the distinct values from the Product Name column and a column called Count of Sales, containing the number of rows from the original table that are associated with each value in Product Name.

⊞▾	Product Name ▾	Count of Rows ▾
1	Pears	1
2	Apples	4
3	Oranges	4
4	Grapes	1

Figure 3-44. *Count of Sales grouped by Product Name*

A slightly more complex example would involve selecting both the Product Name and Sales Person 1 columns and aggregating the Sales Value both by Sum and Average, as shown in Figure 3-45.

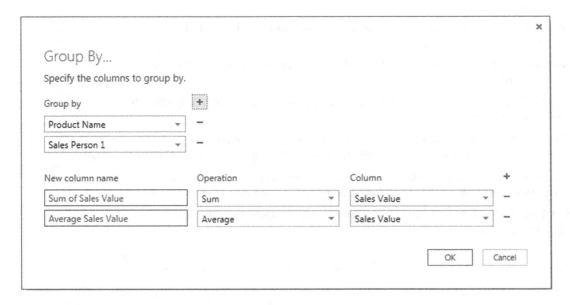

Figure 3-45. *Grouping by Product Name and Sales Person 1*

The output of this is shown in Figure 3-46: a table with four columns, containing all of the distinct combinations of values from Product Name and Sales Person 1 that existed in the original table, and Sales Value summed and averaged.

⊞▾	Product Name ▾	Sales Person 1 ▾	Sum of Sales Value ▾	Average Sales Value ▾
1	Pears	Chris	1	1
2	Apples	Helen	0.9	0.9
3	Apples	Chris	2.1	0.7
4	Oranges	Chris	2.4	0.8
5	Grapes	Helen	2	2
6	Oranges	Helen	0.3	0.3

Figure 3-46. *Sales Value grouped by Product Name and Sales Person 1*

Finally, the All Rows aggregation option can be used with the Product Name column, as shown in Figure 3-47.

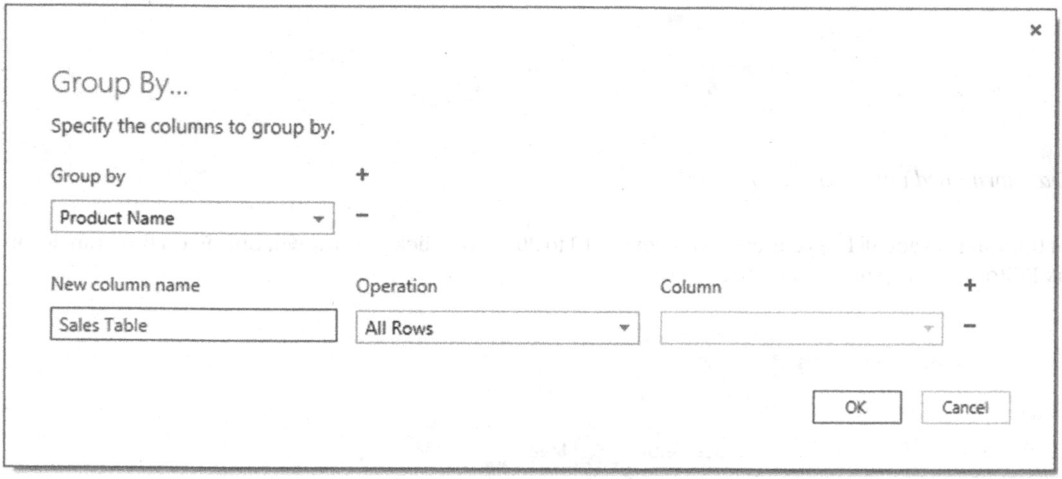

***Figure 3-47.** The All Rows aggregation option*

The output of this is shown in Figure 3-48. Clicking the Expand icon next to the Sales Table column header will allow you to add extra columns or aggregated values to the table in exactly the same way as you saw in Chapter 2 when navigating through a SQL Server database. This option is useful for scenarios where you need to write M code for aggregating data in ways that are not available through the Group By dialog.

	Product Name	Sum of Sales Value
1	Apples	Table
2	Oranges	Table
3	Pears	Table
4	Grapes	Table

***Figure 3-48.** The output of the All Rows aggregation option*

Unpivoting Columns to Rows

One very common problem that you will encounter in your source data is pivoted data. For example, your source data might contain one column for each year's sales. While this might be how the data is usually displayed in a report, for many purposes (such as aggregating data) it's much more convenient to have a single column for your sales values and one row for each year. Figure 3-49 shows a simple example of sales data formatted in this way.

⊞▾	Product ▾	2010 ▾	2011 ▾	2012 ▾	2013 ▾	2014 ▾
1	Apples	5	6	7	2	3
2	Pears	1	1	4	7	8
3	Grapes	9	6	4	5	6

Figure 3-49. *Data formatted with years as columns*

To unpivot this data, select all five year columns from 2010 to 2014 and click the Unpivot button on the Transform tab of the Query Editor toolbar (shown in Figure 3-50).

Figure 3-50. *The Unpivot button*

The unpivoted version of this data is shown in Figure 3-51. What were the column names are now stored in a new column called Attribute; the values are now stored in a new column called Value.

⊞▾	Product ▾	Attribute ▾	Value ▾
1	Apples	2010	5
2	Apples	2011	6
3	Apples	2012	7
4	Apples	2013	2
5	Apples	2014	3
6	Pears	2010	1
7	Pears	2011	1
8	Pears	2012	4
9	Pears	2013	7
10	Pears	2014	8
11	Grapes	2010	9
12	Grapes	2011	6
13	Grapes	2012	4
14	Grapes	2013	5
15	Grapes	2014	6

Figure 3-51. *Unpivoted data with one row for each product and year*

Unpivoting data can also be useful for handling many-to-many relationships in data. In the sample data in Figure 3-43, you can see that each sale has either one or two sales people associated with it in the Sales Person 1 and Sales Person 2 columns. If you wanted to find out the total value of sales for each sales person, taking into account the fact that one sale may be linked to two sales people, you could select the Sales Person 1 and Sales Person 2 columns and click the Unpivot button. The output from this is shown in Figure 3-52. Notice how there are no rows where Sales Person 2 contained a null value.

	Invoice Number	Product Name	Sales Date	Sales Value	Units Sold	Shipping Cost	Ship To Address	Attribute	Value
1	123	Apples	01/01/2014	0.45	1	10	London,UK	Sales Person 1	Chris
2	124	Oranges	01/01/2014	0.6	2	20	Washington DC,USA	Sales Person 1	Chris
3	124	Oranges	01/01/2014	0.6	2	20	Washington DC,USA	Sales Person 2	Helen
4	125	Apples	02/02/2014	0.9	2	20	Dublin,Ireland	Sales Person 1	Helen
5	126	Oranges	02/02/2014	0.3	1	10	Paris,France	Sales Person 1	Helen
6	127	Pears	03/03/2014	1	5	40	Berlin,Germany	Sales Person 1	Chris
7	128	Apples	03/03/2014	1.2	3	30	Zurich,Switzerland	Sales Person 1	Chris
8	128	Apples	03/03/2014	1.2	3	30	Zurich,Switzerland	Sales Person 2	Natasha
9	129	Oranges	03/03/2014	0.9	3	30	Oslo,Norway	Sales Person 1	Chris
10	129	Oranges	03/03/2014	0.9	3	30	Oslo,Norway	Sales Person 2	Mimi
11	129	Oranges	03/03/2014	0.9	3	30	Oslo,Norway	Sales Person 1	Chris
12	129	Oranges	03/03/2014	0.9	3	30	Oslo,Norway	Sales Person 2	Mimi
13	130	Grapes	03/04/2014	2	1	100	Oslo,Norway	Sales Person 1	Helen
14	130	Grapes	03/04/2014	2	1	100	Oslo,Norway	Sales Person 2	Natasha
15	131	Apples	04/04/2014	0.45	1	10	London,UK	Sales Person 1	Chris

Figure 3-52. *Sample data with Sales Person 1 and Sales Person 2 unpivoted*

You can now rename the Value column to something more meaningful, such as Sales Person, and use the Group By functionality to find the sum of the Sales Value column for each sales person, as shown in Figure 3-53.

	Sales Person	Sum of Sales Value
1	Chris	5.5
2	Helen	3.8
3	Natasha	3.2
4	Mimi	1.8

Figure 3-53. *Sales aggregated by Sales Person*

There is no way to do the opposite of an unpivot—in other words, to pivot rows into columns—in the Query Editor toolbar. However, it is possible if you write your own M code. (An example is given in Chapter 5.)

Transposing a Table

Transposing a table involves turning the rows of a table into columns and the columns into rows, and it can be achieved by clicking the Transpose button in the Transform tab of the Query Editor toolbar (as shown in Figure 3-54).

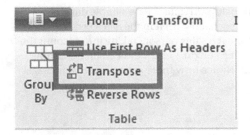

Figure 3-54. *The Transpose button on the Query Editor toolbar*

Transposing the table shown in Figure 3-49 gives the table shown in Figure 3-55.

▦▾	Column1 ▾	Column2 ▾	Column3 ▾
1	Apples	Pears	Grapes
2	5	1	9
3	6	1	6
4	7	4	4
5	2	7	5
6	3	8	6

Figure 3-55. *The result of transposing the table shown in Figure 3-49*

As you can see, the column names have been completely lost, and the values from the first column in the original table are now held in the first row. (You would be able to use them as column names by clicking the Use First Rows As Headers button, of course.)

Creating Custom Columns

New columns containing calculated values can be added to your table in the Query Editor. These columns, called custom columns, can be created with a number of built-in calculations, or you can write your own calculation using Power Query's M language.

Built-in Custom Columns

All of the built-in custom column types can be found on the Insert tab of the Query Editor toolbar, as shown in Figure 3-56. The same functionality can also be found on the right-click menu and by clicking the Table icon.

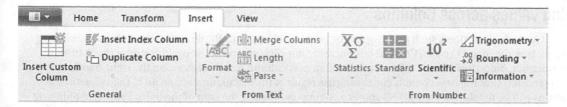

Figure 3-56. The Insert tab of the Query Editor toolbar

Index Columns

The Insert Index Column button adds a new column to your table containing values from zero to one less than the number of rows in your table, with the first row in the table containing the zero value. An example of an index column is shown in Figure 3-57.

⊞▾	Product Name ▾	Count of Sales ▾	Index ▾
1	Apples	5	0
2	Oranges	7	1
3	Pears	1	2
4	Grapes	2	3

Figure 3-57. An example of an index column

Index columns are typically not very useful on their own, but they are extremely useful as an intermediate step when creating other, more complex calculations, as you will see in Chapter 5.

Duplicating Columns

As with index columns, the ability to duplicate a column in a table isn't very useful on its own, but it is important when creating other calculations—for example, when you are using one of the built-in transformations described earlier in this chapter and you want to preserve the original contents of a column.

To duplicate a column, simply select the column you want to duplicate in the Query Editor and then click the Duplicate Column button in the toolbar. When you do this, a new column called "Copy of x," where "x" is the name of the original column, will be added onto the right-hand side of the table, as shown in Figure 3-58. This column will contain the same values as the original column and will be unaffected by any subsequent changes to the original column.

⊞▾	Product Name ▾	Count of Sales ▾	Index ▾	Copy of Product Name ▾
1	Apples	5		Apples
2	Oranges	7		Oranges
3	Pears	1		Pears
4	Grapes	2		Grapes

Figure 3-58. An example of a duplicated column

Calculating Values across Columns

Many different types of calculations, such as sums, can be performed across multiple numeric columns by selecting the columns, clicking the Insert Custom Column button, and then clicking one of the options under the Statistics, Standard, or Scientific drop-down boxes. When you do this, a new column will be created on the right-hand side of the table, and each row of the new column containing the result of the calculation across all of the values in the selected columns will be displayed. Figure 3-59 shows a column containing the sum of the Sales Value and Shipping Cost columns, created by selecting those two columns and selecting the Sum option on the Statistics drop-down box.

▦▾	Invoice Number ▼	Product Name ▼	Sales Date ▼	Sales Value ▼	Units Sold ▼	Shipping Cost ▼	Sum ▼
1	123	Apples	01/01/2014	0.45	1	10	10.45
2	124	Oranges	01/01/2014	0.6	2	20	20.6
3	125	Apples	02/02/2014	0.9	2	20	20.9
4	126	Oranges	02/02/2014	0.3	1	10	10.3
5	127	Pears	03/03/2014	1	5	40	41
6	128	Apples	03/03/2014	1.2	3	30	31.2
7	129	Oranges	03/03/2014	0.9	3	30	30.9
8	129	Oranges	03/03/2014	0.9	3	30	30.9
9	130	Grapes	03/04/2014	2	1	100	102
10	131	Apples	04/04/2014	0.45	1	10	10.45

Figure 3-59. *A calculated column showing the sum of Sales Value and Shipping Cost*

It is important to understand that these options allow you to calculate values vertically, over the values in different columns in the same row in a table. If you want to perform a calculation over all of the values in all rows in a single column, you will probably want to use the Group By functionality described earlier in this chapter.

The following options are available under the Statistics drop-down box:

- *Sum* adds all the values in the selected columns.

- *Min* finds the minimum of the values in the selected columns.

- *Max* finds the maximum of the values in the selected columns.

- *Average* finds the average of the values in the selected columns.

- *Standard Deviation* finds the standard deviation of the values in the selected columns.

- *Count Values* counts the number of values in the selected columns. Null values are ignored.

- *Count Distinct Values* counts the number of distinct values in the selected columns. Null values are ignored.

The following options are available under the Standard drop-down box:

- *Add* adds all the values in the selected columns. This does exactly the same thing as the Sum option above.

- *Multiply* multiplies all the values in the selected columns.

- *Subtract* subtracts the values in the column selected first from the values in the column selected second when two columns are selected.

- *Divide* divides the values in the column selected first by the values in the column selected second when two columns are selected.

- *Divide (Integer)* does the same as Divide but only returns the integer part of the result.

- *Modulo* does the same as Divide but only returns the remainder (or modulo).

The Power option is also enabled under the Scientific drop-down when only two columns are selected. This creates a new column that raises the values column you selected first to the power of the value in the same row in the second column you selected.

Custom Columns with M Calculations

The real power of custom columns becomes apparent once you define your own calculations using the M language. A full introduction to the M language will be given later on in this book in Chapter 5, but it is easy to write simple M expressions without needing to know much about the language itself.

To create a custom column that uses an M expression, click the Insert Custom Column button in the toolbar. When you do this, the Insert Custom Column dialog will appear, as shown in Figure 3-60.

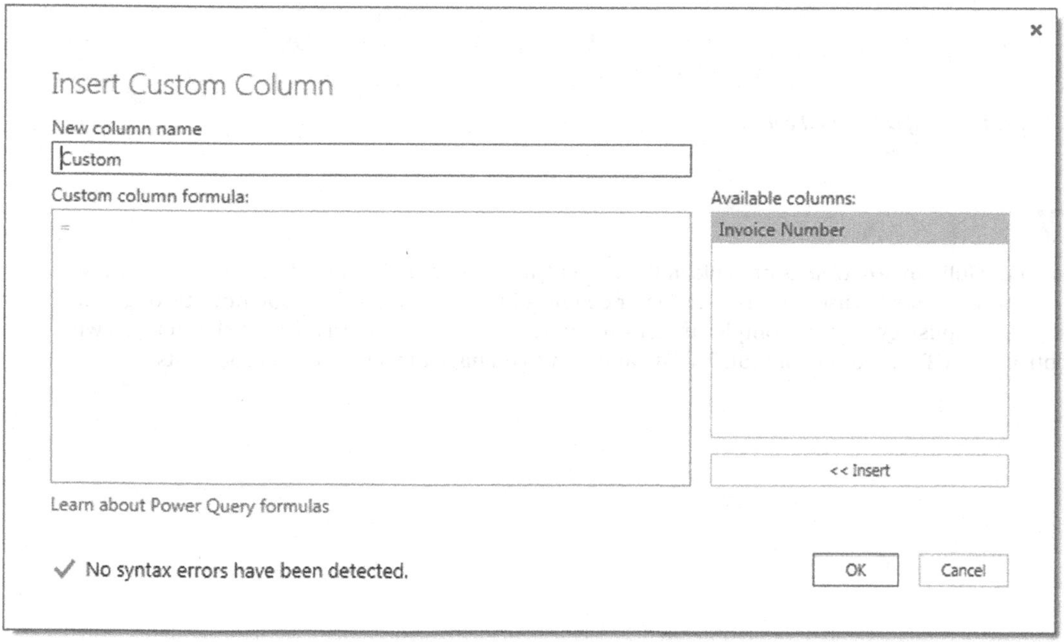

Figure 3-60. The Insert Custom Column dialog

Calculations based on values from other columns in the same row are easy to create in this dialog. To reference a value in another column, select the column name in the Available Columns box and then either double-click it or click the Insert button. When you do this, the name of the column, surrounded by square brackets to show it is a column reference, will appear in the Custom Column Formula text box and you can then add to the expression in that text box yourself. When you have finished writing your expression, click the OK button and a new column will be added to the right-hand side of the table containing the calculated values. You can enter the name of the new column in the New column name box.

Using the sample data for this chapter, the M expression [Sales Value] * 1.2 will return the value from the Sales Value column in the current row multiplied by 1.2, and the M expression [Sales Value] + [Shipping Cost] will return the value from the Sales Value column in the current row plus the value from the Shipping Cost column. The results of these two calculations are shown in Figure 3-61.

	Sales Value	Shipping Cost	Sales Times 1.2	Sales Plus Shipping
1	0.45	10	0.54	10.45
2	0.6	20	0.72	20.6
3	0.9	20	1.08	20.9
4	0.3	10	0.36	10.3
5	1	40	1.2	41
6	1.2	30	1.44	31.2
7	0.9	30	1.08	30.9
8	0.9	30	1.08	30.9
9	2	100	2.4	102
10	0.45	10	0.54	10.45

Figure 3-61. *Two examples of calculated columns*

Summary

You have now seen the full range of what is possible in the Power Query Query Editor and, for many users, this will be all they will ever want or need to use. Nevertheless, later chapters in this book will show you how, through the M language, you can accomplish even more complex transformations and calculations. In the next chapter, you will learn how to control where Power Query outputs its data and how to manage the data refresh process itself.

CHAPTER 4

■ ■ ■

Data Destinations

You've got hold of the data you need. You've filtered, sorted, aggregated, and otherwise transformed it. Now, the last thing you need to do is decide where the data should end up. Power Query gives you two choices for where the output of a query will be loaded: a table in a worksheet or the Excel Data Model. In this chapter, you will learn how to use both of these destinations and how to refresh a query so your data is up-to-date.

Choosing a Destination for Your Data

When you have finished working in the Query Editor, you can choose a destination for your data using the check boxes in the Load Settings section in the bottom right-hand side of the screen (as shown in Figure 4-1).

Figure 4-1. *The Load Settings options in the Query Editor*

The Load to worksheet option will result in the output of your query being loaded to a table in the worksheet; the Load to Data Model will result in the output of your query being loaded to a table in the Excel Data Model. Both boxes can be checked with the result that data will be loaded to both destinations. You can also leave both boxes unchecked, which will disable the query, meaning that the data will not be loaded anywhere by Power Query; however, the query can still be used as a source for other queries in your workbook. When you click on the Apply & Close button in the Query Editor toolbar to close the Query Editor, data will be loaded to the selected destinations.

■ **Note**   The Load to Data Model option is only available if you are using Power Query with Excel 2013. If you are using Excel 2010, this option is not available because the Excel Data Model does not exist as a feature in this version of Excel.

You can set your own default values for these settings for all new queries by clicking the Options button on the Power Query tab in the Excel ribbon, as shown in Figure 4-2.

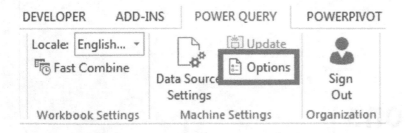

Figure 4-2. *The Options button on the Power Query tab in the Excel ribbon*

Clicking the Options button opens the Options dialog, as shown in Figure 4-3. Here you can either choose to use the standard Power Query load settings or have the Load to worksheet and/or the Load to Data Model options checked by default.

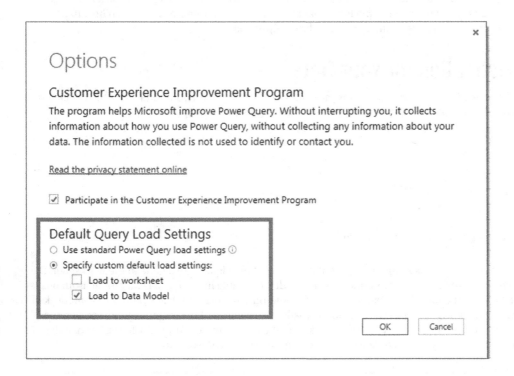

Figure 4-3. *Setting default query load settings*

Loading Data to the Worksheet

If you want to load data from Power Query directly to an Excel worksheet, you have two options: use the built-in Load to worksheet functionality or create your own tables in Excel and connect them to Power Query.

Using the Default Excel Table Output

When you use the Load to worksheet option on a new query, a new worksheet will be added to your workbook and the data from your query will be added to a new Excel table whose top left-hand cell will be in cell A1 of the new worksheet the first time the query is run. The Excel table will have the same name as your Power Query query. For example, take a query that returns the data shown in Figure 4-4 in the Query Editor.

Figure 4-4. *The output of a query in the Query Editor*

When loaded to a table in the worksheet using the Load to worksheet option, you will see the table shown in Figure 4-5.

Figure 4-5. *The data from the query shown in Figure 4-4 in the worksheet*

One drawback of the Load to worksheet option is that there is no way of controlling where the table is created—it will always be in cell A1 of the newly created worksheet. However, once the table has been created, you can change the format and add extra columns. These customizations will remain after the query has been refreshed.

Loading Data to Your Own Excel Tables

An alternative to using the Load to Worksheet option is to create your own Excel tables in the worksheet and connect them to Power Query. This is possible because every time you create a query using Power Query, an OLE DB connection is created inside Excel that points to the output of this query. This connection is useable even when the query itself is disabled.

To create a new query table in Excel, you need to go to the Data tab on the Excel ribbon and then click the Existing Connections button, shown in Figure 4-6.

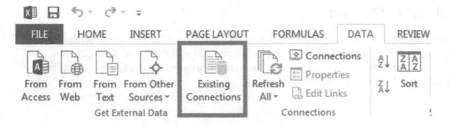

Figure 4-6. *The Existing Connections button on the Data tab*

When you do this, the Existing Connections dialog will open, as shown in Figure 4-7. All Power Query connections will be listed in the Connections In This Workbook section on the Connections tab, and they will have names in the format "Power Query-queryname".

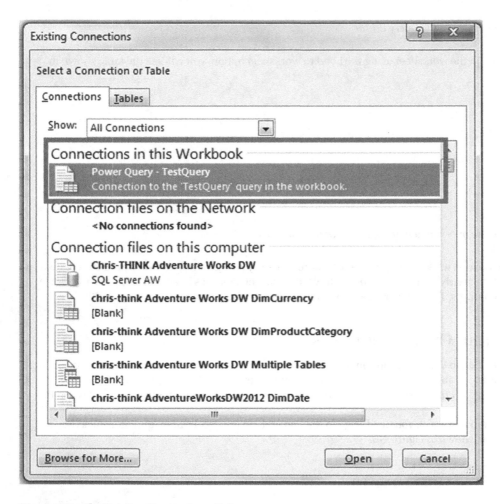

Figure 4-7. *The Existing Connections dialog*

Double-clicking the connection for your query will open the Import Data dialog, as shown in Figure 4-8.

Figure 4-8. *The Import Data dialog*

Selecting the Table option will create a new query table from the output from your query at the position specified in the Where do you want to put the data? section. The new query table will behave in the same way as an Excel table connected to any other type of data source, and you can create multiple Excel tables connected to the same Power Query query. You can give the table a new name, format the data in columns, and add new columns to the table. These changes will be preserved even when you refresh the data.

Loading Data to the Excel Data Model

As you learned in Chapter 1, the Excel Data Model is an in-memory database engine that is a new feature in Excel 2013—it is the database engine behind Power Pivot, natively integrated into Excel. If you are using Power Query with Excel 2013, there are a number of advantages to loading data into the Excel Data Model over loading it directly to the worksheet that you will learn about in this section. A full description of what you can do with the Excel Data Model and Power Pivot is outside the scope of this book. (If you are unfamiliar with this topic, it is good idea to learn more about it before you proceed.)

Viewing Tables in the Excel Data Model

Once you have loaded the output of a query to the Excel Data Model using the Load to Data Model option in the Query Editor, you can see that table either through the Existing Connections dialog that you saw above or by opening the Power Pivot window, if you have the Power Pivot add-in enabled.

Tables in the Excel Data Model and the Existing Connections Dialog

On the Data tab in the Excel ribbon, clicking the Existing Connections button (shown in Figure 4-5) will open the Existing Connections dialog. To see tables loaded to the Excel Data Model, you have to go to the Tables tab, as shown in Figure 4-9.

Figure 4-9. *The Tables tab of the Existing Connections dialog*

The contents of this tab are divided into three sections. In the top section, clicking This Workbook Data Model will create a connection to the whole Excel Data Model. When you click on this section, the Import Data dialog will open as in Figure 4-7, but the radio button for loading data to a table will be grayed out and the radio buttons to create a Power View report or just create a connection will be enabled. If you create a PivotTable in this way it will be connected to all of the tables in the Excel Data Model.

In the next section down, named WorkbookName (This Workbook), you will see listed all of the tables in the worksheets in your workbook. This can be very confusing if you are using Excel tables as data sources for your queries using the From Table functionality, but nothing here is related to the Excel Data Model or Power Query.

Finally, you will see a list of all of the tables loaded into the Excel Data Model grouped by the connections they are associated with. You will see all of the tables you have loaded into the Excel Data Model from Power Query here, along with tables you have loaded into the Excel Data Model by other means (for example, via the Data tab in Excel or the Power Pivot window). Clicking one of the tables listed here will also open the Import Data dialog, this time with all of the radio buttons enabled so you can create tables, PivotTables, PivotCharts, and Power View reports from the table you have selected.

When you create an Excel table linked to a table in the Excel Data Model using this method, it will look just like the Excel tables you have seen earlier in this chapter, but with one well-hidden difference. These tables display all of the data from the table they are bound to when they are created, but they can be modified so that they display the results of a DAX query against the tables in the Excel Data Model instead. To do this, right-click inside the table and select Table and Edit DAX. Then, in the Edit DAX dialog, select DAX in the Command Type drop-down box, and you will be able to enter a DAX query in the Expression text box.

Tables in the Excel Data Model and the Power Pivot Window

If you have the Power Pivot add-in enabled in Excel (it is installed by default but not enabled—see `http://tinyurl.com/EnablePP` for instructions how to do this), you can also open the Power Pivot window to see the tables that you have loaded into the Excel Data Model. If you are doing any kind of serious BI work in Excel, this is the recommended option for viewing tables in the Excel Data Model.

You can open the Power Pivot window by going to the PowerPivot tab on the Excel ribbon and clicking the Manage button, as shown in Figure 4-10.

Figure 4-10. *The Manage button on the PowerPivot tab*

After you have done this, the Power Pivot window will open in Data View, as shown in Figure 4-11. You can see the data in each table in the Excel Data Model by clicking its name in the tab strip at the bottom of the screen.

Invoice Number	Sales Date	Product Name	Units Sold	Sales Value	Shipping Cost	Sales Times 1.2	Sales Plus Shipping	Sales Person 1	Sales Person 2	Ship to Address	Add Column
127	03/03/2014 0...	Pears	5	1	40	1.2	41	Chris		Berlin,Germany	
129	03/03/2014 0...	Oranges	3	0.9	30	1.08	30.9	Chris	Mimi	Oslo,Norway	
129	03/03/2014 0...	Oranges	3	0.9	30	1.08	30.9	Chris	Mimi	Oslo,Norway	
126	02/02/2014 0...	Oranges	1	0.3	10	0.36	10.3	Helen		Paris,France	
124	01/01/2014 0...	Oranges	2	0.6	20	0.72	20.6	Chris	Helen	Washington DC,USA	
130	03/04/2014 0...	Grapes	1	2	100	2.4	102	Helen	Natasha	Oslo,	
131	04/04/2014 0...	Apples	1	0.45	10	0.54	10.45	Chris		London,	
128	03/03/2014 0...	Apples	3	1.2	30	1.44	31.2	Chris	Natasha	Zurich,Switzerland	
123	01/01/2014 0...	Apples	1	0.45	10	0.54	10.45	Chris		London,UK	
125	02/02/2014 0...	Apples	2	0.9	20	1.08	20.9	Helen		Dublin,Ireland	

Figure 4-11. *The Power Pivot window in Data View*

Clicking the Diagram View button in the toolbar will move you to a view where you can see each of your tables in a diagram, as shown in Figure 4-12. Here you can more easily see and specify relationships between the tables.

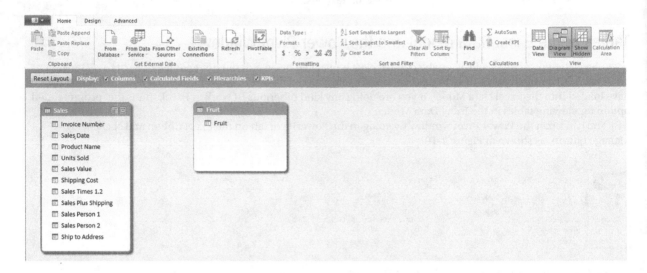

Figure 4-12. *The Power Pivot window in Diagram View*

Clicking the PivotTable button in the ribbon will create a new PivotTable on a worksheet connected to the data in the Excel Data Model.

Advantages of Using the Excel Data Model

If you are an experienced Excel user, you may feel more comfortable loading data from Power Query into a table on a hidden sheet rather than using the Excel Data Model. However, there are a number of compelling reasons to use the Excel Data Model as the destination for your data:

- An Excel 2013 worksheet can have a maximum of 1,048,576 rows. If you are working with large amounts of data, you may find you need to import more than this number of rows from a data source. The Excel Data Model can do this. There is no set limit on the amount of data that you can load into the Excel Data Model; it is dictated by a combination of a number of factors including the amount of memory on your PC, the number of distinct values in each column of your table, and the way your data is sorted. It is certainly the case that the Excel Data Model can handle tables with millions, even tens or hundreds of millions, of rows. Using the 64-bit version of Excel is a good idea if you are working with large data volumes because it can store much more data than the 32-bit version of Excel.

- The Excel Data Model is also capable of performing calculations such as aggregations across large tables much more quickly than the equivalent Excel spreadsheet formulas. The DAX language (which is really just an extension of the Excel formula language for the Excel Data Model) is capable of expressing complex calculations that would be very difficult to implement otherwise.

- Loading data into the Excel Data Model unlocks some very useful functionality when you are working with that data in a worksheet—for example, the ability to create a PivotTable linked to multiple tables of data and the ability to use Excel Cube Formulas such as the CubeMember() and CubeValue() functions. Power Map can only work with data stored in the Excel Data Model, and although Power View can work with data from the worksheet as well as the Excel Data Model, it works much more smoothly with the latter.

- Since the Excel Data Model compresses the data that it stores, workbooks that have data stored in the Excel Data Model are typically much smaller than workbooks that have the same data stored in tables in the worksheet. Workbook size is also significant if you are uploading a workbook to a Power BI site, where different limits are applied on the amount of data that is allowed in the Excel Data Model and in the worksheet. Although these limits are subject to change, when you upload a workbook to a Power BI site, you are allowed to have up to 250MB of data in the Excel Data Model while the rest of the workbook can be no more than 10MB in size, at the time of writing.

Learning about Power Pivot and the Excel Data Model may seem a daunting prospect, but the benefits of doing so are immense. For any moderately complex BI or reporting application, you are strongly advised to use the Excel Data Model to store your data.

If you have already used Power Pivot and the Excel Data Model, you are probably aware that you can also load data into the Excel Data Model from the Data tab in Excel 2013 and also from inside the Power Pivot window. While these options do not provide any of the rich functionality that Power Query has for cleaning and transforming data, they do support some data sources that Power Query (as yet) does not support such as generic OLE DB/ODBC connections. If you need to use one of these data sources then you have no choice but to use the Excel Data tab or the Power Pivot window to load your data. Also, if the data you are loading is already clean and in the format you need (for example, if you are loading data from a data warehouse), there may be no need to use Power Query.

Power Query and Table Relationships

In general, Power Query's role in a self-service BI solution is to extract, transform, and load data into the Excel Data Model; after that has happened, you use Power Pivot to model the data. One of the most important modeling tasks is to define relationships between tables. You can do this by dragging and dropping columns from one table to another in the Diagram View of the Power Pivot window. However, in some circumstances, Power Query is able to detect relationships between tables and create them for you automatically when it loads data into the Excel Data Model.

Table Relationships and Relational Databases

Where foreign key relationships exist between tables in a relational database such as SQL Server, Power Query will automatically create relationships in the Excel Data Model when you import these tables into the Excel Data Model. There is no indication that this is happening in the Power Query user interface, but you will see the relationships created when you look in Diagram View in the Power Pivot window.

Taking the Adventure Works DW sample database for SQL Server as an example, the DimDate, FactInternetSales, DimProduct, DimProductSubcategory, and DimProductCategory tables have foreign key relationships, as shown in Figure 4-13.

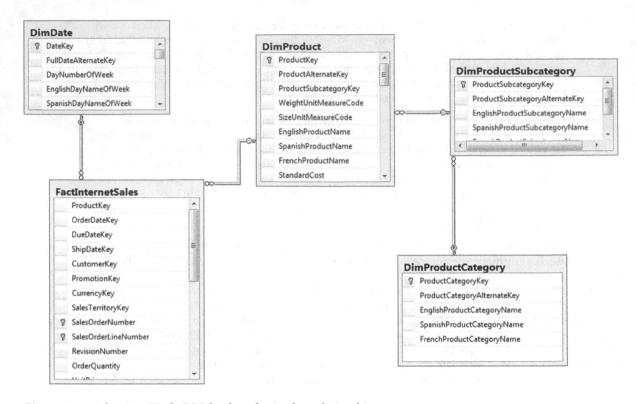

Figure 4-13. *Adventure Works DW database foreign key relationships*

If you connect to the Adventure Works DW database using the From SQL Server Database option (described in Chapter 2) and select these tables in the Navigator pane, as shown in Figure 4-14, the relationships between these tables will also be imported.

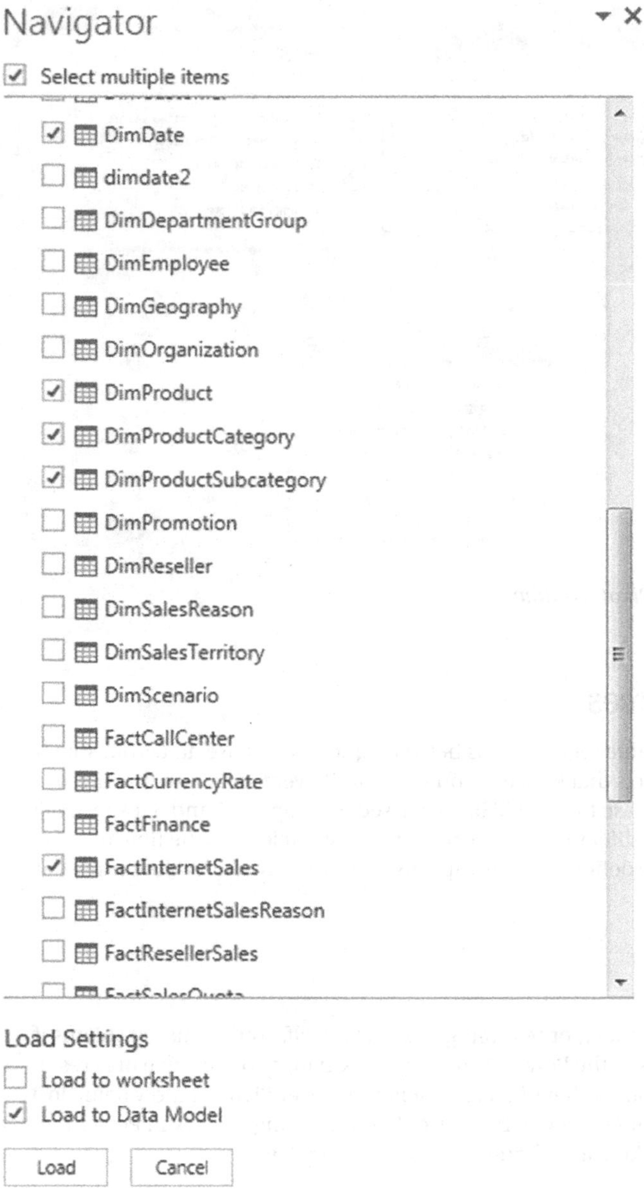

Navigator ▾ ✕

☑ Select multiple items

☑ ▦ DimDate
☐ ▦ dimdate2
☐ ▦ DimDepartmentGroup
☐ ▦ DimEmployee
☐ ▦ DimGeography
☐ ▦ DimOrganization
☑ ▦ DimProduct
☑ ▦ DimProductCategory
☑ ▦ DimProductSubcategory
☐ ▦ DimPromotion
☐ ▦ DimReseller
☐ ▦ DimSalesReason
☐ ▦ DimSalesTerritory
☐ ▦ DimScenario
☐ ▦ FactCallCenter
☐ ▦ FactCurrencyRate
☐ ▦ FactFinance
☑ ▦ FactInternetSales
☐ ▦ FactInternetSalesReason
☐ ▦ FactResellerSales
☐ ▦ FactSalesQuota

Load Settings

☐ Load to worksheet
☑ Load to Data Model

[Load] [Cancel]

Figure 4-14. *Importing multiple tables from SQL Server in the Navigator pane*

Opening the Power Pivot window in Diagram View will show that these relationships have been imported into the Excel Data Model, as seen in Figure 4-15.

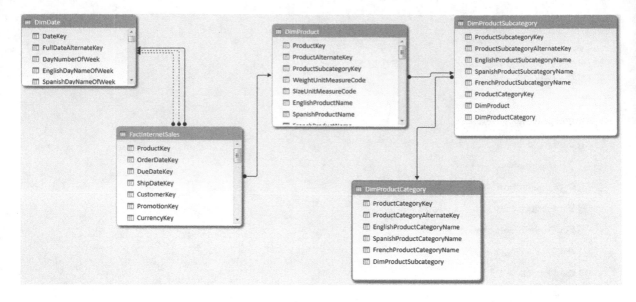

Figure 4-15. *Imported table relationships in the Power Pivot window*

Table Relationships and Other Data Sources

In certain circumstances, Power Query will also create table relationships between queries that use data from sources other than relational databases. It does this when it detects that keys exist on tables in Power Query and that these tables have been joined using the Merge functionality; these topics will be discussed in Chapters 5 and 6 respectively. However, the relationship detection functionality is very difficult to get working reliably—at least at the time of writing—so it is recommended that you always explicitly define relationships inside Power Pivot after the source data has been loaded.

Breaking Changes

Deleting or renaming the columns in your Power Query query, or renaming the query itself, could cause problems if you have created calculated columns or calculated fields in the Power Pivot window. Changes of this type may result in errors in Power Pivot or, at worst, lead to calculations and other objects built in the Power Pivot window being lost. Therefore, you are strongly advised to finish work on your Power Query queries before starting to work in Power Pivot, and to make sure you back up your workbook before making any changes in Power Query later on.

Refreshing Queries

After you have created a query, it is very likely that you will want to reload the data from your data source at some point, if it has changed. You can do this manually in various ways, or you can set each query to update automatically. Since neither Excel tables nor the Excel Data Model supports adding new data to what has already been loaded, Power Query does not allow you to do any kind of incremental refresh. When you refresh a query in Power Query, you always have to reload all of your data into your destination.

Refreshing Queries Manually

Queries can be refreshed manually from the Workbook Queries pane in one of two ways. First of all, when your mouse hovers over a query a Refresh button appears to the right of the name (as shown in Figure 4-16), and clicking this button will refresh the query. While a query is refreshing, you can cancel the refresh by clicking the same button. You can also refresh a querying by right-clicking it and selecting the Refresh option from the right-click menu.

Figure 4-16. *The Refresh button in the Workbook Queries pane*

The Workbook Queries pane displays the date and time that the query was last refreshed, as well as the number of rows that it returned.

Queries can also be refreshed from the Excel Data tab, either by clicking the Refresh All button, or by clicking the Connections button to open the Workbook Connections dialog, selecting the connection associated with the query, and then clicking the Refresh button, as shown in Figure 4-17.

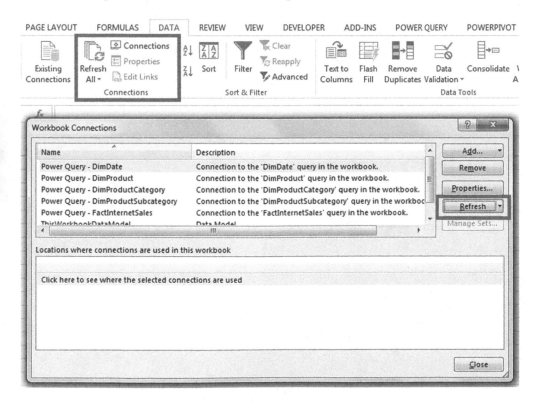

Figure 4-17. *The Excel Workbook Connections dialog*

Finally, queries can be refreshed by clicking the Refresh button on the Home tab of the Query Editor, as shown in Figure 4-18. You can cancel refresh in the Query Editor either by clicking the Cancel option on the drop-down box under the Refresh button, or by clicking the message in the bottom right-hand corner of the Query Editor window under the Load Settings area (if you are quick).

Figure 4-18. *The Refresh button in the Query Editor toolbar*

Automating Data Refresh

Because Excel sees Power Query queries as OLE DB connections, all of the methods you would usually use for automating data refresh will work with Power Query. Clicking the Properties button in the Workbook Connections dialog (shown in Figure 4-17) will open the Connection Properties dialog, as shown in Figure 4-19.

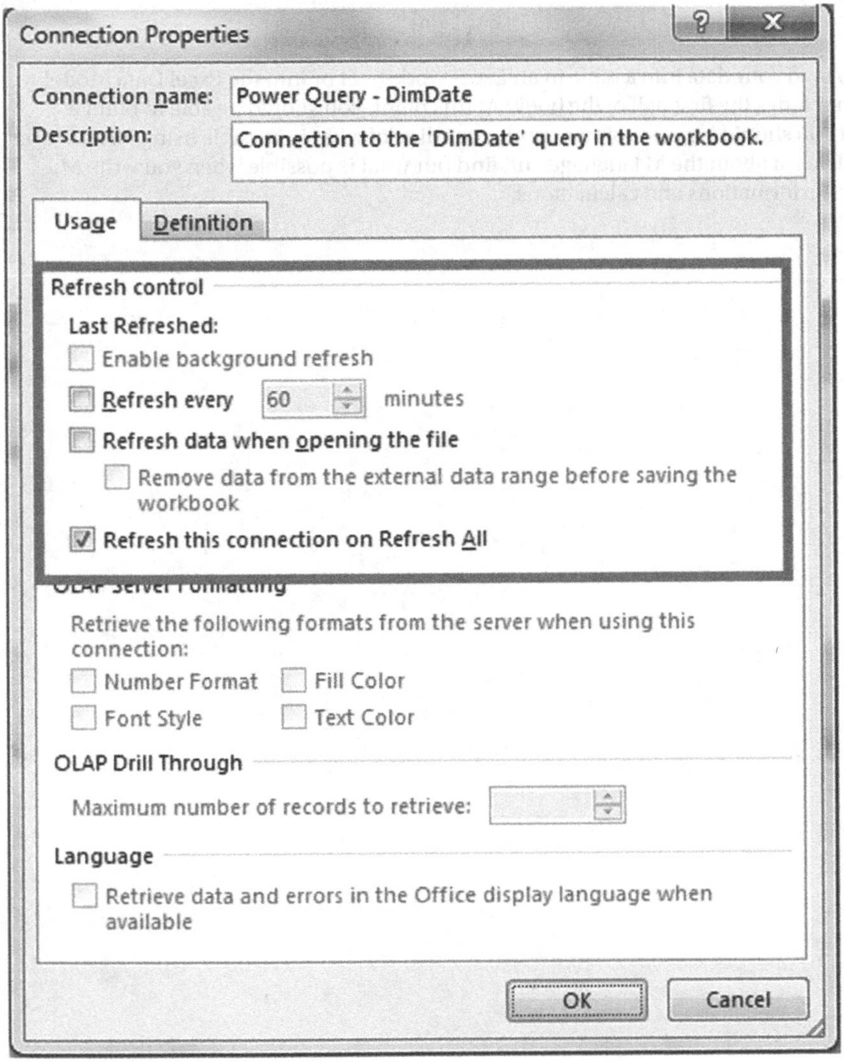

Figure 4-19. *The Connection Properties dialog*

In the Connection Properties dialog, you can configure a Power Query query to refresh after a given number of minutes and also for it to automatically refresh when you open the Excel workbook. This last option is very useful for ensuring that your workbook always displays up-to-date data.

Although there is no direct integration between Power Query and VBA, Power Query connections can be refreshed using VBA in the same way as any other Excel connection. Using ActiveWorkbook.Connections ("Power Query - QueryName"). Refresh in an Excel macro will refresh an individual query and ActiveWorkbook. RefreshAll will refresh all connections in a workbook, whether they were made by Power Query or not.

Summary

In this chapter, you have seen how to load your data into a table in an Excel worksheet or into the Excel Data Model, and how to refresh your data. This concludes the first half of the book: At this point, you should be able to build a complete Power Query solution, and you should have a thorough understanding of what is possible using just the user interface. In the next chapter, you will learn about the M language and find out what is possible when you write M code to implement more advanced transformations and calculations.

CHAPTER 5

Introduction to M

If you want to unlock the full potential of Power Query, you have to learn M. M is the unofficial name for Power Query's formula language, and Power Query generates M code for each step in your query. The Power Query user interface also allows you to write your own M expressions in situations where you need more flexibility and control over what your query does.

The biggest problem with the M language, from an Excel developer's point of view, is that it bears little resemblance to Excel formulas or VBA: it is a functional language like F#. You will have to learn new syntax, new functions, and new ways of doing familiar things, and there will be a learning curve. However, if you already have some programming experience you will find M quite easy to get going with, and once you have mastered it you will appreciate its elegance. Even if you aren't a confident programmer, you should be able to write simple expressions—for example, when you want to create custom columns. It's unlikely that you will ever need to write a lot of M code, though. In almost all cases you can use the user interface to generate the steps for your query, and only in the most complex cases will you need to edit the code that is generated for you or write the M code for a step yourself.

In this chapter you will learn about how to write your own M expressions; the M language and its syntax; commonly used objects such as Tables, Lists, and Records; and how to create your own M functions so you can share business logic between steps and even between queries.

Writing M in the Query Editor

Before learning *how* to write M, you need to know *where* in the Power Query user interface you can write it. There are two places you can create and edit the M expressions used by a query in the Query Editor: in the Formula Bar and in the Advanced Editor window. Also, for those situations where you want to write the code for your query from scratch, you can click the From Other Sources button on the Power Query tab in the Excel ribbon and then select the Blank Query option to create queries with no code in them at all.

The Formula Bar

The Formula Bar in the Query Editor (shown in Figure 5-1) allows you to view and edit the M code for an existing step and also to create new steps in your query using handwritten M expressions.

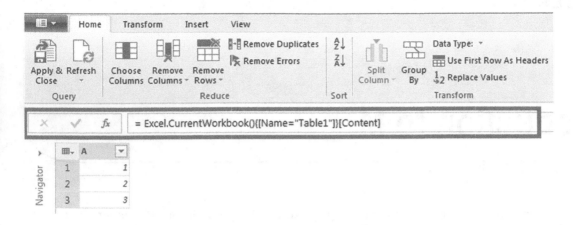

Figure 5-1. *The Formula Bar in the Query Editor window*

The Formula Bar always displays the M expression for the step in your query that is currently selected in the Applied Steps pane on the right-hand side of the Query Editor. Once you have selected a step you can click inside the Formula Bar to edit the M code generated for the step; when you have finished you can either press the Enter key on your keyboard or click the check button on the left of the Formula Bar to save your changes. When you do this you will see the new output of the step displayed. If you make a change and then want to discard it, you must click the cross button on the far left-hand side of the Formula Bar.

As you saw in Chapters 2 and 3, some steps visible in the Applied Steps pane have a Gears icon next to them, and clicking this icon allows you to edit the setting for this step using the same dialog that you used to create it. If you edit the M code for a step in the Formula Bar and make a change that is syntactically correct but is not supported in the user interface, the Gears icon will disappear, and you will have no choice after that but to edit the step using the Formula Bar.

You can also create a new step in your query by clicking the *f*x button on the left-hand side of the Formula Bar. When you do this a new step will be added to your query whose expression is simply the name of the step that was selected in the Applied Steps pane when you clicked the button. This means that the step will return exactly the same output as the previous step in the query. Once you have done this you can edit the M code in the Formula Bar as normal, altering the step to do whatever you want to do.

The Advanced Editor Window

The M code for an entire query can be viewed and edited in the Advanced Editor window. To open the Advanced Editor, go to the View tab on the ribbon inside the Query Editor and click the Advanced Editor button, as shown in Figure 5-2.

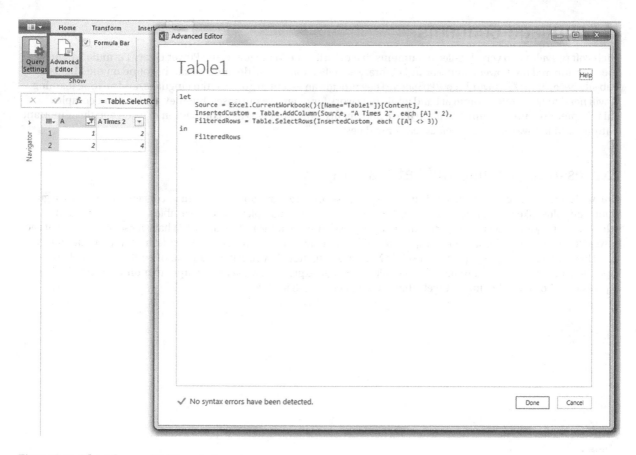

Figure 5-2. *The Advanced Editor window*

The Advanced Editor is nothing more than a basic text editor—there are no features like IntelliSense or syntax highlighting to help you write code, only a message at the bottom left-hand corner of the window to tell you if any syntax errors are present in the code currently in the window. When you have finished working in the Advanced Editor you can click the Done button to save your changes and close the window or Cancel to close the window without saving your changes.

Creating a Blank Query

The only option listed under the From Other Source button on the Power Query tab in the ribbon that has not already been mentioned is the last one: Blank Query. Clicking this option will create a new Power Query query with just one step in it, and no code for importing data from any data source. Once you have created a blank query you can write your own code in the Formula Bar or the Advanced Editor; you can still use all of the functionality of the Query Editor user interface, too, but you will not be able to automatically generate any code to import data from external data sources. This is useful in situations where you want to copy the M code from a query in another workbook, or from an article or blog post on the Internet, into a new query.

M Language Concepts

Microsoft provides two very detailed documents that describe the M language: the Power Query Formula Language Specification and the Power Query Formula Library Specification. These documents can be found on the Microsoft web site here: http://tinyurl.com/PQSpecs. They provide an essential guide to the language, and anyone learning M will need to have both of them at hand while they work for reference purposes, but they are long and complex. This chapter does not attempt to replace these documents, but rather acts as a companion to teach you the important features of M in a way that is, hopefully, easier to digest.

Expressions, Values, and Let statements

The two fundamental concepts in the M language are those of expressions and values. These concepts aren't hard to grasp. Values are values like the number 1 or the text "Hello World" or more complex objects like tables. M expressions return values when they are evaluated, so for example the expression 10+10 returns the value 20. What isn't so obvious is that each Power Query query is in fact a single M expression, and the value that this expression returns is the output of your query.

How can a Power Query query be a single M expression, though, when it is made up of multiple steps? This is possible through the Let statement, which allows a single expression to be broken up into multiple smaller expressions. Consider the simple Excel table shown in Figure 5-3 for example.

Month	Sales
January	2
February	3
March	5
April	3
May	6
June	8
July	7
August	6
September	6
October	9
November	8
December	5

Figure 5-3. A simple Excel table

If you imported this table into Power Query, then filtered it so you were left with rows where Sales is greater than 5, and then sorted the table in descending order by the Sales column, you would have a query with three steps, the names of which can be seen in Figure 5-4.

◢ APPLIED STEPS

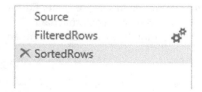

Source
FilteredRows
✕ SortedRows

Figure 5-4. A query with three steps

If you go to the Advanced Editor window, you will see the M code for the entire query consists of a single Let statement, given in Listing 5-1.

Listing 5-1. An example of a Let statement

```
let
    Source = Excel.CurrentWorkbook(){[Name="SalesTable"]}[Content],
    FilteredRows = Table.SelectRows(Source, each [Sales] > 5),
    SortedRows = Table.Sort(FilteredRows,{{"Sales", Order.Descending}})
in
    SortedRows
```

The names of the three steps in the query (Sources, FilteredRows, and SortedRows) are clearly visible in the code, as you can see. Each step in a query is in fact one of a comma-delimited list of variables defined in the let clause of a Let statement, where each variable returns the result of the M expression for that step. Variables can access the values returned by other variables, and in the example in Listing 5-1 you can see that SortedRows references the value returned by FilteredRows, and FilteredRows in turn references the value returned by Source (in this case all three variables return values that are tables). The Let statement returns the value of the expression given in the in clause, which in this case is just the name of the last variable in the list.

Interestingly, a Let statement can return the result of any expression: it can return the result of any variable in its list of variables, or it can return the result of an expression that references none of the variables. Also, variables can reference any other variable in the list, not just the variable declared immediately before it, including variables declared later on in the list. However, it's advisable to keep variables in the list in some kind of meaningful order for the sake of readability. More importantly, if you move your variables around too much, the Query Editor will no longer be able to display the individual steps in the Applied Steps (although the query itself will still work). It is also worth noting that a step is only evaluated if the value it returns is used by another step or is the final output of the query.

Writing M

While M syntax is fairly straightforward, there are a few features of the language that are worth highlighting before you start learning it.

The Standard Library

M comes with a large number of built-in functions for you to use, called the Standard Library. These functions are all listed in the Power Query Formula Library Specification document mentioned under "M Language Concepts." Going back to Listing 5-1, Excel.CurrentWorkbook(), Table.SelectRows(), and Table.Sort() are all examples of functions from the Standard Library. More functions are being added with each release of Power Query.

You can see some help text and examples for functions in the Standard Library by creating a step in your query that returns that function. For example, if you create a step with the following expression (notice that there are no brackets on the end of the function name here):

```
Table.SelectRows
```

then, as shown in Figure 5-5, Power Query will display help and examples for the Table.SelectRows() function. This is not the same as calling or invoking the function—the step is returning the function itself. If you do decide to invoke the function you can click the Invoke button underneath the help listing, or the Invoke Function button on the Query Editor toolbar.

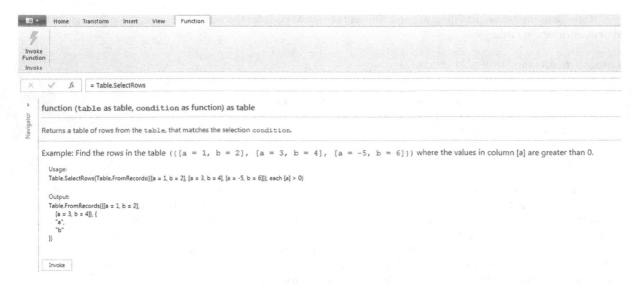

Figure 5-5. *Displaying help for the* `Table.SelectRows()` *function*

Case Sensitivity

Unlike some other languages you may be familiar with, M is case sensitive—something that may cause you a lot of frustration when you start to write your own expressions. This means that while Power Query recognizes `Excel.CurrentWorkbook()` as a function in the Standard Library, `Excel.Currentworkbook()` will not be recognized because the letter *w* is not capitalized. As a result, you need to be extremely careful when writing M code to avoid errors caused by case sensitivity.

Types

You have already seen in Chapter 3 that each column in a query is of a particular data type. In fact, every value in M has a type, whether it is a primitive type like a Number or a structured type like a table; this includes the variables in the variable list of the Let statement. You don't have to declare the type of a value—M will dynamically determine that.

M is strongly typed, which means that while the expression

```
"The number " & "1"
```

works fine and returns the text

```
"The number 1"
```

the expression

```
"The number " & 1
```

throws an error because the & operator (which concatenates two text values) cannot be used with a text value and a number. There are a lot of functions available in the Standard Library to convert one type to another, and in this case the function `Number.ToText` can be used to cast a number to text as follows:

```
"The number " & Number.ToText(1)
```

You can check to see whether a value is a particular type using the is operator. For example the expression

```
1 is number
```

returns the value TRUE, whereas

```
1 is text
```

returns the value FALSE.

Declaring dates, times, datetimes, datetimezones, and durations

If you need to declare values of type date, datetime, datetimezone, or duration in an expression, you can use the intrinsic functions #date(), #datetime(), #datetimezone(), and #duration(). For example, the signature of #datetime() is as follows:

```
#datetime(year, month, day, hour, minute, second)
```

If you use #datetime(2014,2,28,13,48,46) in an M expression it will return the datetime value containing the date February 28, 2014 and the time 13:48:46. Similarly, #date(2014,1,1) returns the date January 1, 2014 and #duration(1,0,0,0) returns a duration equivalent to one day.

Comments

Doubtless you already know that it is important to add comments to any code you write, and M code is no exception. There are two ways of adding comments to your code in M: single-line comments are preceded by // and multi-line comments begin with /* and end with */. Listing 5-2 shows the same query as Listing 5-1 but with added comments:

Listing 5-2. An example of commented code

```
/* This query loads data from the Content table on the worksheet
   and then filters and aggregates it */
let
    //Load data from Content table
    Source = Excel.CurrentWorkbook(){[Name="SalesTable"]}[Content],
    //Filter where Sales>5
    FilteredRows = Table.SelectRows(Source, each [Sales] > 5),
    //Sort in descending order by Sales
    SortedRows = Table.Sort(FilteredRows,{{"Sales", Order.Descending}})
in
    SortedRows
```

Unfortunately, although comments are always visible in the Advanced Editor, in most cases they are not displayed in expressions in the Formula Bar. You can add comments to the beginning or end of the expression used for a step in the Formula Bar, but when you click to another step and then return, the comments are filtered out. Only comments embedded inside an expression will be displayed, as in this example:

```
Table.Sort( /* this is a comment*/ FilteredRows,{{"Sales", Order.Descending}})
```

Trapping Errors

As you saw in Chapter 3, it is possible to filter out rows in a table that contain error values. However it's much better to trap errors at the expression level and you can do that using a try...otherwise expression.

For example, Figure 5-6 shows a table where one column contains numbers and one column contains a mixture of numbers and text.

NumberColumn ▾	TextColumn ▾
1	4
2	Apples
3	Oranges
4	1

Figure 5-6. *A table containing numbers and text*

If you import this table into Power Query, then explicitly set the type of the column TextColumn to text, you can then create a custom column using the following expression to try to sum the values in NumberColumn and TextColumn:

```
[NumberColumn] + Number.FromText([TextColumn])
```

The Number.FromText() function attempts to take a text value and convert it to a number (also known as "casting" the text value to a number); if the text value cannot be converted the function returns an error, so in this case the second and third rows in the table will contain error values as shown in Figure 5-7.

⊞▾	NumberColumn ▾	TextColumn ▾	Custom ▾
1	1	4	5
2	2	Apples	Error
3	3	Oranges	Error
4	4	1	5

Figure 5-7. *A custom column containing error values*

One way of preventing the errors from appearing would be to change the expression to the following:

```
[NumberColumn] + (try Number.FromText([TextColumn]) otherwise 0)
```

The output of the query now will be as shown in Figure 5-8.

⊞▾	NumberColumn ▾	TextColumn ▾	Custom ▾
1	1	4	5
2	2	Apples	2
3	3	Oranges	3
4	4	1	5

Figure 5-8. *A custom column where errors have been trapped*

The try expression evaluates the expression that is passed to it, and if no error is raised then the value returned by that expression is returned; if an error is raised, however, then the value specified in the otherwise clause is returned instead.

Conditional Logic

Conditional logic in M can be implemented using an if...then...else expression. It works exactly as you would expect: the Boolean expression in the if clause is evaluated, and if the result is true then the result of the expression in the then clause is returned; otherwise the result of the expression in the else clause is returned.

Taking the data shown in the table in Figure 5-6 as a starting point, if you import that data into a new Power Query query and create a custom column using the following expression:

```
if [NumberColumn]>2 then "More than 2" else "2 or less"
```

then the output will be as shown in Figure 5-9.

▦▾	NumberColumn ▾	TextColumn ▾	Custom ▾
1	1	4	2 or less
2	2	Apples	2 or less
3	3	Oranges	More than 2
4	4	1	More than 2

Figure 5-9. *A custom column using an if...then...else expression*

There is no equivalent of the Case statement as found in other languages, but you can nest multiple if expressions together, as in the following example:

```
if [NumberColumn]>3 then "More than 3" else if [NumberColumn]>2 then "More than 2" else "2 or less"
```

Lists, Records, and Tables

You have already learned about the primitive data types—numbers, dates, text, and so on—that describe the values you usually see inside cells in a table. When you saw how to navigate through a SQL Server database or an XML file you also saw different types of values appear in cells: tables and records. These are structured types: objects that contain many values bound together in a particular way.

Lists

A list is an ordered sequence of values, similar in some ways to an array in other programming languages. Items in a list can be of any type, though, and you can even have lists of lists. Lists are useful as a means to an end: you will use them when you are writing more complex calculations, but it's unlikely that the final output of a query will be a list. Many of the more complex M examples from this point on will feature lists in some capacity.

Defining Lists Manually

Lists can be defined manually as a comma-delimited list of values surrounded by braces. For example, {1,2,3} defines a list with the values 1, 2, and 3 in in that order; {"A", "B", "C"} defines a list with the values "A", "B", and "C" in it. You can define a continuous list of whole numbers using the syntax x..y, which will return a list of numbers from x to y inclusive; for example, {1..4} returns the list {1,2,3,4}. It is possible to have an empty list with no items in it, which is written as {}. Each item in a list can itself be a list, so {{1,2},{3,4}} defines a list containing two items, each of which is a list containing two items.

Working with Lists in the Query Editor

When you click a step in a query that returns a list, the Query Editor will show the contents of that list and a new List tab will appear on the ribbon, as shown in Figure 5-10.

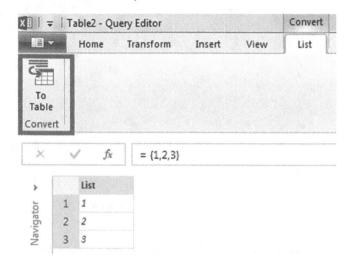

Figure 5-10. *A list shown in the Query Editor*

Clicking the To Table button on the List tab will create a new step in your query that converts the list into a table.

Functions That Generate Lists

To generate more complex number sequences you can use the List.Numbers() function, the signature for which is:

```
List.Numbers(start as number, count as number, optional increment as nullable number)
```

The start parameter is the number to start at, count is the number of values in the list to return, and increment is the difference between each value in the list, so the expression List.Numbers(5,4,3) returns the list {5,8,11,14}. Similarly, List.Dates() returns a range of dates starting from a given date, so List.Dates(#date(2014,1,1), 3,#duration(1,0,0,0)) returns a list containing the first three dates in January 2014.

Many other functions in the Standard Library are able to convert values of other types to lists, such as Table.ToList(), which converts a table into a list, and Table.Column(), which returns all of the values in a column in a table as a list.

Aggregating Values in Lists

One of the main reasons you will want to store a sequence of numbers in a list is to be able to aggregate those values in some way. All of the basic aggregation methods you would expect are supported through functions in the standard library. List.Count() returns the number of items in a list, so List.Count({1,2,3}) returns the value 3 because there are three numbers in the list {1,2,3}, and List.Sum({1,2,3}) returns the value 6, the sum of the numbers in the list. Other aggregation functions include List.Product(), List.Average(), List.Mode(), List.StandardDeviation(), List.Max(), and List.Min(). Some of these functions work with lists containing other data types, too, so List.Sum(), for example, will also sum up a list of values of type duration.

Sorting Lists

The List.Sort() function can be used to sort the items in a list. Its signature is:

```
List.Sort(list as list, optional comparisonCriteria as any )
```

The first parameter is the list to be sorted and the second parameter controls how the sorting takes place. In most cases all you will need to state in the second parameter is Order.Descending or Order.Ascending, although it is possible to specify more complex ordering criteria. For example List.Sort({1,2,3,4,5}, Order.Descending) returns the list {5,4,3,2,1} and List.Sort({"Helen", "Natasha", "Mimi", "Chris"}, Order.Ascending) returns the list {"Chris", "Helen", "Mimi", "Natasha"}. List.Reverse() reverses the order of items in a list, so that List.Reverse({3,5,4}) returns {4,5,3}.

Filtering Lists

There are several functions that can be used to filter the items in a list. List.First() and List.Last() return the first and last items in a list, while List.FirstN() and List.LastN() return lists that are a given number of values from the beginning and end of a list. List.Distinct() returns a list of all of the distinct values from a list.

More complex filtering scenarios can be handled with the List.Select() function. The signature of this function is:

```
List.Select(list as list, condition as function)
```

The first parameter is the list to be filtered; the second is something new: you need to write an expression that is a function. This topic will be covered in depth later in this chapter but for now you will be pleased to know that the basic syntax for doing this is quite straightforward. For example:

```
List.Select({1,2,3,4,5}, each _>2)
```

returns the list {3,4,5}. The each expression seen in this example is a way of defining an untyped, unnamed function whose only parameter is represented by the underscore character _. Therefore each _>2 is a function that returns TRUE when the value passed to it is greater than 2 and FALSE otherwise, and when it is used in the second parameter of List.Select(), each item in the list is passed to it, and only the items where the function returns true are returned.

Records

You can think of a record as being like a table with only one row in it. It is an ordered sequence of fields, where each field has a name and a single value (of any type) associated with it. Records can be defined manually as a comma-delimited list of field/value pairs surrounded by square brackets. For example, the following defines a record with four fields called firstname, lastname, gender, and town:

```
[firstname="Chris", lastname="Webb", gender="Male", town="Amersham"]
```

As with a list, when you view a step that returns a record in the Query Editor you can see each field in the record, as shown in Figure 5-11.

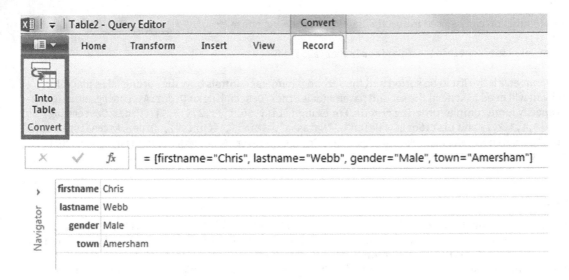

Figure 5-11. *A record shown in the Query Editor*

Clicking the Into Table button on the toolbar converts the record into a table with one row for each field, as shown in Figure 5-12.

▦▾	Name ▾	Value ▾
1	firstname	Chris
2	lastname	Webb
3	gender	Male
4	town	Amersham

Figure 5-12. *A table created from a record*

Tables

The table is the most important of all structured types. In most cases the data you import into a query is in table form; most steps in a query return tables; and you almost always return tables from queries. A table consists of data organized into rows and columns, where each column has a unique name and contains data of a particular type.

Creating Tables

If you look at the M code for the first step in most queries in the Formula Bar, you will see an expression that returns a table of data from a data source outside Power Query. For example, in Listing 5-1 the Source step uses the expression `Excel.CurrentWorkbook(){[Name="SalesTable"]}[Content]` to return the contents of the table called SalesTable in the current Excel workbook. The Standard Library contains many similar functions that allow you to retrieve tables of data from different data sources, and they are used in the M expressions generated by all of the functionality you saw in Chapter 2.

It is also possible to create tables without an external data source in a number of different ways. First of all you can use the `#table()` intrinsic function, which takes two parameters: a list containing the column headers and a list (or list of lists) containing the rows for the tables. For example, the following expression:

```
#table({"Fruit", "Sales"}, {{"Apples", 1}, {"Oranges", 2} })
```

returns the table shown in Figure 5-13.

⊞▾	Fruit ▾	Sales ▾
1	Apples	1
2	Oranges	2

Figure 5-13. *A table created using the #table intrinsic function*

Columns in tables created in this way all have the type any; you can specify types for columns by specifying a record in the first parameter instead of a list, as in the following example:

```
#table(type table [Fruit = text, Sales = number], {{"Apples", 1},{"Oranges", 2}})
```

Other functions can also be used to create tables, such as `Table.FromRows()`:

```
Table.FromRows({ {"Apples", 1}, {"Oranges", 2} }, {"Fruit", "Sales"} )
```

and `Table.FromRecords()`:

```
Table.FromRecords({[Fruit="Apples", Sales=1], [Fruit="Oranges", Sales=2]})
```

Aggregating Data in Tables

In Chapter 3 you saw a lot of examples of how to aggregate data from tables through the user interface using the Group By button, and this will be good enough for most of your needs. If you are curious about the M code generated for these operations, you can of course see the M code that the user interface generates in the Formula Bar or the Advanced Editor, and this is a good way of learning about the functions that are available for this purpose. Let's look at how some of these aggregation functions work using the sample data seen in Figure 5-14.

Quarter ▼	Month ▼	Sales ▼
Q1	January	2
Q1	February	3
Q1	March	5
Q2	April	3
Q2	May	6
Q2	June	8
Q3	July	7
Q3	August	6
Q3	September	6
Q4	October	9
Q4	November	8
Q4	December	5

Figure 5-14. *Sample data table for aggregation*

To find the number of rows in this table you can use the `Table.RowCount()` function. Listing 5-3 shows a query that loads data from the Excel table and counts the number of rows in it.

Listing 5-3. Counting rows in a table with `Table.RowCount()`

```
let
    //Load data from source table
    Source = Excel.CurrentWorkbook(){[Name="SalesTable"]}[Content],
    //Count rows
    CountRowsInTable = Table.RowCount(Source)
in
    CountRowsInTable
```

It's worth pointing out that this query returns the value 12 as a number, as shown in Figure 5-15, and not a table with one cell containing the value 12, although if the output of the query is loaded into the worksheet or the Excel Data Model it will nevertheless be treated as a table with one row and one column.

Figure 5-15. *The output of* `Table.RowCount` *in the Query Editor*

To get an output of type table and to perform other types of aggregation you will need to use the Table.Group() function instead of Table.RowCount(). The signature of Table.Group() is as follows:

```
Table.Group(table as table, key as any, aggregatedColumns as list,
optional groupKind as nullable number, optional comparer as nullable function)
```

The first parameter is the table to be aggregated, the second parameter is a list containing the columns to group by, and the third parameter specifies the way to aggregate the data. To count the number of rows in the sample table, the code for the whole M query is shown in Listing 5-4.

Listing 5-4. Counting rows in a table with Table.Group()

```
let
    //Load data from source table
    Source = Excel.CurrentWorkbook(){[Name="SalesTable"]}[Content],
    //Count rows and return a table
    GroupedRows = Table.Group(Source, {}, {{"Count of Rows", each Table.RowCount(_), type number}})
in
    GroupedRows
```

In this example the first parameter used by Table.Group() is Source, the output of the first step. The second parameter is an empty list, because in this case you are not grouping by any column in the table. The third parameter is a list containing one item that is itself a list, and that list contains three items: the name of the column in the output table, Count of Rows; an each expression that calls Table.RowCount() to get the count; and the type number, which specifies the type of this column. The output of this query is shown in Figure 5-16.

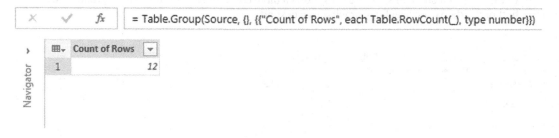

Figure 5-16. The output of Table.Group() in the Query Editor

Listing 5-5 shows a more complex example that groups by the Quarter column and not only counts rows but also sums the values in the Sales column.

Listing 5-5. Grouping by Quarter with Table.Group

```
let
    //Load data from source table
    Source = Excel.CurrentWorkbook(){[Name="SalesTable"]}[Content],
    //Group by Quarter, count rows and sum sales
    GroupedRows = Table.Group(
                        Source,
                        {"Quarter"},
```

```
                        {{"Count of Rows", each Table.RowCount(_), type number},
                        {"Sum of Sales", each List.Sum([Sales]), type number}}
                        )
in
    GroupedRows
```

In this example you can see that the second parameter is now a list with one item in it, "Quarter", the name of the column that is used in the Group by operation), and there is now a second list in the second parameter that uses List.Sum() to sum up all of the values in the sales column. The output is shown in Figure 5-17.

▦▾	Quarter ▾	Count of Rows ▾	Sum of Sales ▾
1	Q1	3	10
2	Q2	3	17
3	Q3	3	19
4	Q4	3	22

Figure 5-17. *Counting and Summing by Quarters using* Table.Group()

One last thing to mention about Table.Group() is the fourth parameter, which controls the type of grouping. The default value for this is GroupKind.Global, and this means that when you group by a column, the sort order of the table is not relevant: all rows related to a distinct value in a column are aggregated together. GroupKind.Local, the other possible value, means that Table.Group() does take table sort order into account and only groups by continuous ranges of values. To illustrate this, Figure 5-18 shows a table containing sales and units by date with a column showing whether the date was a weekday or fell on a weekend.

Date ▾	WeekdayOrWeekend ▾	Sales ▾	Units ▾
01-Jan-14	Weekday	5	2
02-Jan-14	Weekday	4	1
03-Jan-14	Weekday	2	1
04-Jan-14	Weekend	6	1
05-Jan-14	Weekend	8	5
06-Jan-14	Weekday	6	3
07-Jan-14	Weekday	4	2
08-Jan-14	Weekday	5	1
09-Jan-14	Weekday	5	2
10-Jan-14	Weekday	2	3
11-Jan-14	Weekend	1	1
12-Jan-14	Weekend	3	1

Figure 5-18. *Sales table showing weekdays and weekends*

The following expression uses `Table.Group()` to find the count of rows grouped by the WeekdayOrWeekend column; the default value for the fourth parameter, `GroupKind.Global`, is explicitly set for the sake of clarity:

```
Table.Group(Source, {"WeekdayOrWeekend"},
{{"Count of Rows", each Table.RowCount(_), type number}}, GroupKind.Global)
```

The output of this expression is shown in Figure 5-19.

▦▾	WeekdayOrWeek... ▾	Count of Rows ▾
1	Weekday	8
2	Weekend	4

Figure 5-19. `Table.Group()` output using `GroupKind.Global`

If you instead use `GroupKind.Local` in the fourth parameter, as follows:

```
Table.Group(Source, {"WeekdayOrWeekend"},
{{"Count of Rows", each Table.RowCount(_), type number}}, GroupKind.Local)
```

the output will be as shown in Figure 5-20. The reason that there are now four rows instead of two is that `Table.Group()` has only aggregated the sequences of rows that have the same values in the WeekdayOrWeekend column: the first three rows of the original table are weekdays, then the next two rows are weekends, then the next five rows are weekdays and the last two rows are weekends.

▦▾	WeekdayOrWeek... ▾	Count of Rows ▾
1	Weekday	3
2	Weekend	2
3	Weekday	5
4	Weekend	2

Figure 5-20. `Table.Group()` output using `GroupKind.Local`

Sorting Tables

As with a list, the rows in a table are inherently sorted even if the order of the rows is just the order that they arrived from the data source. The options for sorting a table are very similar to the options for sorting a list, so `Table.ReverseRows()` reverses the rows in a table and `Table.Sort()` sorts the rows in a table in either ascending or descending order by one or more columns.

Using the data shown in Figure 5-18 as an example, the following expression first sorts this table in descending order by the WeekdayOrWeekend column, then in ascending order by the Sales column:

```
Table.Sort(Source,{{"WeekdayOrWeekend", Order.Descending}, {"Sales", Order.Ascending}})
```

Notice how, in the second parameter, a list of lists is used to pass the combinations of columns and sort orders used. The output of this expression is shown in Figure 5-21.

⊞▾	Date ▾	WeekdayOrW... ₁⬇	Sales ₂⬇	Units ▾
1	11/01/2014 00:00:00	Weekend	1	1
2	12/01/2014 00:00:00	Weekend	3	1
3	04/01/2014 00:00:00	Weekend	6	1
4	05/01/2014 00:00:00	Weekend	8	5
5	03/01/2014 00:00:00	Weekday	2	1
6	10/01/2014 00:00:00	Weekday	2	3
7	07/01/2014 00:00:00	Weekday	4	2
8	02/01/2014 00:00:00	Weekday	4	1
9	01/01/2014 00:00:00	Weekday	5	2
10	09/01/2014 00:00:00	Weekday	5	2
11	08/01/2014 00:00:00	Weekday	5	1
12	06/01/2014 00:00:00	Weekday	6	3

Figure 5-21. A table sorted with `Table.Sort()`

Filtering Tables

Again, the functions for filtering tables are similar to the functions available for filtering lists. `Table.First()` and `Table.Last()` return the first and last rows from a table; `Table.FirstN()` and `Table.LastN()` return the first and last N rows from a table. `Table.SelectRows()` works in a similar way to `List.Select()`, although in the second parameter you can refer to the value in a column in the table without using the _ notation. For example, using the data from the table shown in Figure 5-18, to remove all rows where the Sales column contain values less than 6, you can use the expression:

```
Table.SelectRows(Source, each [Sales] > 5)
```

In this case you can use [Sales] to refer to the value in the Sales column for the current row as the function iterates over the table. The output of this expression is shown in Figure 5-22.

⊞▾	Date ▾	WeekdayOrWeek... ▾	Sales ▾	Units ▾
1	04/01/2014 00:00:00	Weekend	6	1
2	05/01/2014 00:00:00	Weekend	8	5
3	06/01/2014 00:00:00	Weekday	6	3

Figure 5-22. A table filtered with `Table.SelectRows()`

Pivoting and Unpivoting Tables

You saw in Chapter 3 how to unpivot the data in a table in the user interface. The M functions behind this feature are `Table.UnPivot()`, which unpivots a given list of columns in a table, and `Table.UnPivotOtherColumns()`, which unpivots all but a given list of columns in a table. The signatures for these functions are:

```
Table.Unpivot(table as table, pivotColumns as list, attributeColumn as text,  valueColumn as text)
Table.UnpivotOtherColumns(table as table, pivotColumns as list, attributeColumn as text, valueColumn
as text)
```

Again, taking the table shown in Figure 5-18 as a starting point, the expression

```
Table.UnpivotOtherColumns(Source,{"Date", "WeekdayOrWeekend"},"Attribute","Value")
```

unpivots the table so that instead of two columns for Sales and Units, you have a single column that contains the values for both and two rows in the output table for each row in the original table, as shown in Figure 5-23.

▦	Date	WeekdayOrWeek...	Attribute	Value
1	01/01/2014 00:00:00	Weekday	Sales	5
2	01/01/2014 00:00:00	Weekday	Units	2
3	02/01/2014 00:00:00	Weekday	Sales	4
4	02/01/2014 00:00:00	Weekday	Units	1
5	03/01/2014 00:00:00	Weekday	Sales	2
6	03/01/2014 00:00:00	Weekday	Units	1
7	04/01/2014 00:00:00	Weekend	Sales	6
8	04/01/2014 00:00:00	Weekend	Units	1
9	05/01/2014 00:00:00	Weekend	Sales	8
10	05/01/2014 00:00:00	Weekend	Units	5
11	06/01/2014 00:00:00	Weekday	Sales	6
12	06/01/2014 00:00:00	Weekday	Units	3
13	07/01/2014 00:00:00	Weekday	Sales	4
14	07/01/2014 00:00:00	Weekday	Units	2
15	08/01/2014 00:00:00	Weekday	Sales	5
16	08/01/2014 00:00:00	Weekday	Units	1
17	09/01/2014 00:00:00	Weekday	Sales	5
18	09/01/2014 00:00:00	Weekday	Units	2
19	10/01/2014 00:00:00	Weekday	Sales	2
20	10/01/2014 00:00:00	Weekday	Units	3
21	11/01/2014 00:00:00	Weekend	Sales	1
22	11/01/2014 00:00:00	Weekend	Units	1
23	12/01/2014 00:00:00	Weekend	Sales	3
24	12/01/2014 00:00:00	Weekend	Units	1

Figure 5-23. *A table unpivoted with* `Table.UnPivotOtherColumns()`

What isn't possible in the user interface is the opposite of the above: the ability to pivot a table so rows become columns. You can do this using `Table.Pivot()`, the signature for which is:

```
Table.Pivot(table as table, pivotValues as list, attributeColumn as text, valueColumn as text,
optional aggregationFunction as nullable function)
```

Using the table in Figure 5-18 once again, the following expression pivots the table so that instead of one column for sales you have two: one for sales on a weekday and one for sales on a weekend:

```
Table.Pivot(Source, {"Weekday", "Weekend"}, "WeekdayOrWeekend", "Sales", List.Sum)
```

The output of this expression is shown in Figure 5-24. Notice how the Units column is unaffected by the pivot operation, and how it was necessary to supply a list of values in the WeekdayOrWeekend column—rather than hard-coding this list, a combination of the `Table.Column()` function (which returns a list of values from a column in a table) and `List.Distinct()` (which returns only the distinct values from a list) could be used instead:

```
Table.Pivot(Source, List.Distinct(Table.Column(Source, "WeekdayOrWeekend")), "WeekdayOrWeekend",
"Sales", List.Sum)
```

▦▾	Date ▾	Units ▾	Weekday ▾	Weekend ▾
1	01/01/2014 00:00:00	2	5	null
2	02/01/2014 00:00:00	1	4	null
3	03/01/2014 00:00:00	1	2	null
4	04/01/2014 00:00:00	1	null	6
5	05/01/2014 00:00:00	5	null	8
6	06/01/2014 00:00:00	3	6	null
7	07/01/2014 00:00:00	2	4	null
8	08/01/2014 00:00:00	1	5	null
9	09/01/2014 00:00:00	2	5	null
10	10/01/2014 00:00:00	3	2	null
11	11/01/2014 00:00:00	1	null	1
12	12/01/2014 00:00:00	1	null	3

Figure 5-24. *A table pivotted with* `Table.Pivot()`

The final parameter to `Table.Pivot()`, which in this example is the `List.Sum()` function, is used if the pivot operation needs to aggregate any values. In this example it is not necessary, but if there were multiple rows in the table with the same combination of values in the Date and WeekdayOrWeekend columns, then the values in these rows would need to be aggregated, because the resulting table contains just one row for each date.

Tables and Keys

Although this fact is well-hidden, tables in Power Query can have primary and foreign keys defined for them. Tables imported from data sources such as relational databases will have keys defined for them automatically and you can define your own key columns on any table you create.

The user interface does not display which columns on a table are key columns, but you can use the Table.Keys() function to return a list of the key columns on a table. For example if you import the DimDate table in the SQL Server Adventure Works database used in Chapter 2, and then use the Table.Keys() function on the resulting table in your query, it will return a list containing two records: one for the DateKey column, the primary key; and one for the FullDateAlternateKey column, which is a foreign key. Figure 5-25 shows the result of expanding this list of records into a table:

⊞▾	Column1.Columns ▾	Column1.Primary ▾
1	FullDateAlternateKey	FALSE
2	DateKey	TRUE

Figure 5-25. *The key columns on the DimDate table*

Keys can be added to a table that has none defined using the Table.AddKey() function. Using the data from the table in Figure 5-18, Listing 5-6 shows how to define a primary key based on the Date column after the table has been imported.

Listing 5-6.

```
let
    //Load data from source table
    Source = Excel.CurrentWorkbook(){[Name="DailySales"]}[Content],
    //Define a primary key on the Date column
    DefineDateKey = Table.AddKey(Source, {"Date"}, true)
in
    DefineDateKey
```

Note that using Table.AddKey() does not actually check whether the columns being used to define the key contain distinct values, so it is up to you to ensure that they do in some other way.

Performing some other types of operation on a table also has the side effect of defining a primary key on a table, such as selecting a column in the Query Editor and clicking the Remove Duplicates button from the toolbar—which in fact generates an expression using the Table.Distinct() function to remove all the rows in the table that have duplicated values in the selected column, and which in turn defines a primary key on the selected column.

Defining keys on a table has few benefits that are immediately obvious. Certain functions, such as those that aggregate data in a table, may perform better when keys are defined on a table, and keys are used when importing multiple tables from a relational database along with the relationships between them. That said, the keys defined on a table will affect how you can reference individual rows in a table, as you will find out in the next section.

Selections and Projections

Individual values in tables, records, or lists can be referenced using the selection and projection operators.

Referencing Items in Lists

Bearing in mind that a list is inherently ordered, you can reference an item in a list using a zero-based index. For example, if you take the list {"A", "B", "C"}, then the expression {"A", "B", "C"}{0} returns "A" and the expression {"A", "B", "C"}{2} returns "C". If you use an index that does not exist in the list, as in {"A", "B", "C"}{4}, by default an error will be returned; but if you add the ? operator onto the end of the expression, as in {"A", "B", "C"}{4}?, you will get a null value returned instead of an error.

Referencing Rows in Tables

Rows in tables can be referenced by index in the same way as items in a list, although instead of individual values being returned, a record representing that row is returned instead. Figure 5-26 shows a simple table that can be used to illustrate this.

Fruit	Sales	Units
Apples	10	7
Oranges	20	8
Pears	30	9

Figure 5-26. *A simple table*

Listing 5-7 shows how the first row of the table can be referenced: the expression Source{0} returns the record shown in Figure 5-27 containing the values from the first row of the table.

Listing 5-7.

```
let
    //Load data from source table
    Source = Excel.CurrentWorkbook(){[Name="FruitSales"]}[Content],
    //Returns first row of the table
    FirstRow = Source{0}
in
    FirstRow
```

Fruit	Apples
Sales	10
Units	7

Figure 5-27. *Record representing the first row of a table*

The same row in the table can be referenced in a different way using the expression Source{[Fruit="Apples"]}. This searches the table for the row where the Fruit column contains the value "Apples"; if no row is found, or if multiple rows are found, an error is returned. Therefore in the current example the expression Source{[Fruit="Grapes"]} would return an error, but adding the ? operator at the end of an expression, as in Source{[Fruit="Grapes"]}?, returns a null instead of an error. If the column being searched in the expression is a primary key of the table, then there should be no risk of rows containing duplicate values and therefore no risk of errors.

Referencing Fields in Records

Values from fields in a record can be referenced using the name of the field. Listing 5-8 builds on the query shown in listing 5-7 to return the value from the field called "Fruit" in the first row of the table using the expression FirstRow[Fruit], which is the value "Apples".

Listing 5-8.

```
let
    //Load data from source table
    Source = Excel.CurrentWorkbook() {[Name="FruitSales"]}[Content],
    //Returns first row of the table
    FirstRow = Source{0}?,
    //Returns value from first column of first row, called Fruit
    FirstColumn = FirstRow[Fruit]
in
    FirstColumn
```

Rather than return an individual value, it is also possible to return a record containing only some of the fields from a larger record by passing a record containing column names rather than just one column name. For example, changing the last line of Listing 5-7 to use the expression FirstRow[[Fruit],[Sales]] would return the record shown in Figure 5-28.

Fruit	Apples
Sales	10

Figure 5-28. Record representing the values from the first two columns of a row

Referencing Values in Tables

Putting together what you have learned so far, it becomes very easy to reference an individual value in a table by selecting a row and then a column in the same expression. Listing 5-9 demonstrates how to retrieve the value from the Fruit column of the first row of the example table in a single expression.

Listing 5-9.

```
let
    //Load data from source table
    Source = Excel.CurrentWorkbook(){[Name="FruitSales"]}[Content],
    //Returns value from first column of first row, called Fruit
    FirstValue = Source{0}[Fruit]
in
    FirstValue
```

The important expression here—the one that returns the value that you want—is Source{0}[Fruit]. The pattern of TableName{RowIndex|KeyMatch}[ColumnName] to retrieve a single value from a table is very common in M, and in fact it appears in the first step in the query shown in Listing 5-9, too. The Excel.CurrentWorkbook() function returns a table containing all of the Excel tables in the current workbook, and Excel.CurrentWorkbook() {[Name="FruitSales"]}[Content] returns the value from the [Content] column from the row in that table where the Name column contains the value "FruitSales".

It is also possible to use the user interface to select an individual value in a table. To do this you must right-click in a table and then choose Drill Down from the right-click menu as shown in Figure 5-29.

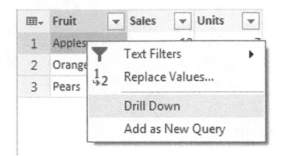

Figure 5-29. *The Drill Down right-click menu option*

It is important to understand, however, that the references generated using this method will vary depending on whether a primary key has been defined for that table. If no primary key has been defined, then the reference will be based on row index, for example Source{0}[Fruit]. If a primary key has been defined, however, the reference will use a value from the primary key columns instead of the row index, for example Source {[Fruit="Apples"]} [Fruit]. The two are subtly different: the first expression will always return the value from the Fruit column for the first row in the table, whereas the second will return whichever row from the table contains the value "Apples" in the Fruit column.

Functions

As well as the ability to use all of the functions in the Standard Library, M allows you to define and use your own functions. These functions can be defined inside a query or even as separate queries, and are a very useful way of sharing business logic between different steps in a query or between multiple queries.

Defining Functions Inside a Query

Listing 5-10 shows how a function can be defined as a step within a query.

Listing 5-10.

```
let
    //Define a function that multiplies two numbers then adds one
    ExampleFunction = (x,y) => (x * y) +1,
    //Call the function and pass 3 and 4 as parameters
    QueryOutput = ExampleFunction(3,4)
in
    QueryOutput
```

In this query the first step defines a function called ExampleFunction that takes two parameters, x and y, and returns the value of (x * y) + 1. The next step, QueryOutput, calls this function with the values 3 and 4, and returns the value of (3 * 4) + 1, which is 13.

The parameters of a function can be specified to be a particular type, and it is also possible to specify the type of the value that the function returns. Parameters may be marked as being optional, in which case they need not be passed when the function is called; if they are not passed then the parameter value will be null. Optional parameters must be listed after all required parameters in the parameter list of a function. Listing 5-11 shows another query that declares a function, this time with three parameters x, y, and z of type number of which z is optional. If the parameter z is passed then the function returns the value (x * y) + z; if z is not passed it returns the value of (x * y) + 1.

Listing 5-11.

```
let
    //Define a function that multiplies two numbers then adds either the third number or 1
    ExampleFunction = (x as number,y as number, optional z as number)
                    as number =>
                    (x * y) + (if z=null then 1 else z),
    //Call the function and pass 3 and 4 as parameters
    QueryOutput = ExampleFunction(3,4)
in
    QueryOutput
```

each Expressions

You saw earlier, in the "Filtering Lists" section, an example of how an each expression can be used to define an unnamed function with a single parameter for use with functions like List.Select(). The each expression can be used anywhere a function declaration is required, and is shorthand for a function that takes a single, untyped parameter that is named _. Listing 5-12 shows an example of a function declaration that uses an each expression.

Listing 5-12.

```
let
    //Define a function that multiplies a number by 2
    ExampleFunction = each _ * 2,
    //Call the function and pass 3 as a parameter
    QueryOutput = ExampleFunction(3)
in
    QueryOutput
```

In this example the expression each _ * 2 is directly equivalent to the expression (_) => _ * 2. The output of the query is the value 6.

Mostly, however, each expressions are used when passing parameters to other functions. Many functions other than List.Select() take functions as parameters; a slightly more complex example is Table.TransformColumns() whose signature is:

```
Table.TransformColumns(table as table, transformOperations as list,
optional defaultTransformation as nullable function, optional missingField as nullable number)
```

Listing 5-13 shows an example of how an each expression can be used with Table.TransformColumns() to multiply all of the values in the Sales column of the table shown in Figure 5-26 by two.

Listing 5-13.

```
let
    //Load data from source table
    Source = Excel.CurrentWorkbook(){[Name="FruitSales"]}[Content],
    //Multiply each value in the Sales column by 2
    SalesTimesTwo = Table.TransformColumns(Source, {"Sales", each _ * 2})
in
    SalesTimesTwo
```

In this example, the first parameter passed to `Table.TransformColumns()` is the source table, and the second parameter is a list where the first item is the name of the column whose values are to be altered and the second item is the function to apply to each value in the column. The `Table.TransformColumns()` function passes each value in the Sales column to the _ parameter of the function defined by each _ * 2. The output of this query is shown in Figure 5-30.

▦▾	Fruit	▾	Sales	▾	Units	▾
1	Apples		20		7	
2	Oranges		40		8	
3	Pears		60		9	

Figure 5-30. Output of the `Table.TransformColumns()` function

Queries As Functions

As well as defining functions within queries, it is also possible to define a query as a function. Doing this will allow you to use this function in any other query in your workbook, which means that you can share business logic between multiple queries. The reason this works is because a function is a data type in Power Query, just like the types Table, Number, or Text, so your query can return a value of type Function.

To define a query that returns a function you will need to create a new query using the Blank Query option in the Power Query ribbon and then use the Advanced Editor to write the M code for your query. Listing 5-14 shows an example of a query that returns a function that takes two numbers and returns the value of them multiplied together plus 1:

Listing 5-14.

```
let
    MyFunction = (x,y) => (x * y) + 1
in
    MyFunction
```

Once you have entered this code in the Advanced Editor and clicked OK, you will see the function listed as a step in your query and a new tab will appear in the Query Editor: the Function tab, as shown in Figure 5-31. On this tab is the Invoke Function button, which, if you click it, will prompt you to enter values for the function parameters and call the function (there is also a button in the body of the Query Editor window that does the same thing)—but in this case you do not want to do this, of course; you want to return the function itself.

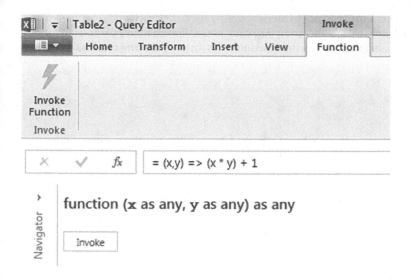

Figure 5-31. *A function shown in the Query Editor*

The name you give to this query will be the name of the function created; in this case the name of the query is MultiplyThenAddOne. You'll see that both the `Load to Worksheet` and `Load to Data Model` check boxes are disabled because a function does not return any data until it is invoked; you can now click the `Apply and Close` button and exit the Query Editor.

To use this function in another query, you create another query as normal and you can invoke the new function in the same way that you would invoke any other function. Listing 5-15 shows the M code for a query that calls the `MultiplyThenAddOne()` function inside a custom column using the Sales and Units columns from the table shown in Figure 5-26 as parameters. The output is shown in Figure 5-32.

Listing 5-15.

```
let
    //Load data from source table
    Source = Excel.CurrentWorkbook(){[Name="FruitSales"]}[Content],
    //Call function in a custom column
    InsertedCustom = Table.AddColumn(Source, "FunctionCallExample",
each MultiplyThenAddOne([Sales],[Units]))
in
    InsertedCustom
```

⊞▾	Fruit ▾	Sales ▾	Units ▾	FunctionCallExample ▾
1	Apples	10	7	71
2	Oranges	20	8	161
3	Pears	30	9	271

Figure 5-32. *Output of a query using the* `MultiplyThenAddOne()` *function*

The function can also be invoked directly from the Workbook Queries pane by right-clicking it and selecting Invoke, as shown in Figure 5-33. When you do this, a dialog will appear prompting you to enter the function's parameters, and once you have done this a new query will be created that invokes the functions with these values and returns the result.

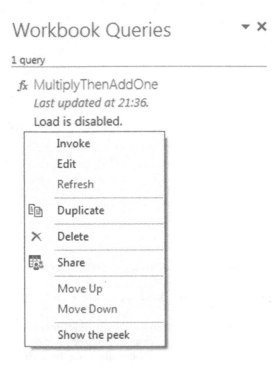

Figure 5-33. *A function in the Workbook Queries pane*

`let` Expressions in Function Definitions

More complex function definitions will require more than a single line of code for their definition, so you will need to use a let expression inside the function definition to allow this. Listing 5-16 shows the function from listing 5-15 rewritten so that the operations of multiplying the two parameters and then adding 1 are accomplished in two separate steps in an inner let expression.

Listing 5-16.

```
let
    //define function that will return the value of the inner let expression
    MyFunction = (x,y) =>
      let
          //multiply x and y
          Step1 = x * y,
          //add one to the result
          Step2 = Step1 + 1
      in
          Step2
in
    MyFunction
```

Remember that a let expression is simply a way of breaking up an operation into several steps and returning a value—and that that value can be a function. If you use a let expression inside a function definition, the Query Editor will only be able to show a single step for the entire function definition and you will not see all of the M code for it in the Formula Bar.

Recursive Functions

A recursive function is a function that calls itself within its own definition. To avoid having the function being caught in an infinite loop where it keeps calling itself forever, a recursive function must only call itself if a certain condition is met.

Listing 5-17 shows an example of a function that takes a single parameter, and if that parameter is greater than or equal to 100, then it returns the parameter value, but if it is less than 100 it calls the function recursively with the original parameter value multiplied by 2.

Listing 5-17.

```
let
    //define a recursive function with one parameter
    DoubleToOneHundred = (x) =>
      //if the parameter is greater than one hundred, return the parameter
      if x > 100
      then x
      //otherwise call the function again with the original parameter
      //multiplied by two
      else @DoubleToOneHundred(x*2),
    //call the function with the value 4
    //the output is 128
    FunctionOutput = DoubleToOneHundred(4)
in
    FunctionOutput
```

From a language point of view the only new thing to notice here is that when the DoubleToOneHundred() function calls itself recursively, it has to use the @ operator before its name as follows: @DoubleToOneHundred().

Functions Imported from Data Sources

Certain types of objects in external data sources, such as user-defined functions in a SQL Server database and OData Service Operations, are treated as functions when you import them into Power Query. Once they have been imported they behave like any other Power Query function, although of course there is no M definition that you can see.

Working with Web Services

One important type of data source that you will need to use M to work with is web services. Power Query is able to call a RESTful web service using the Web.Contents() function, and while there is a working example of how to use this function to retrieve data from the Bing Maps web service in Chapter 8, there are a few features of this function that are worth highlighting.

The Web.Contents() function takes two parameters. The first parameter is the URL of the web service that you want to call, while the second, optional parameter takes a record containing additional properties. Consider an imaginary web service that can be called from the following URL:

```
http://www.mywebservice.com/GetData
```

This web service could be called from Power Query using the expression:

```
Web.Contents("http://www.mywebservice.com/GetData")
```

Normally a web service returns data in the form of an XML or JSON document and Power Query will recognize the format used automatically and open it so that you can see the contents.

Many web services also require you to add parameters to the URL; something like this:

```
http://www.mywebservice.com/GetData?search=somedata&results=10
```

While you could construct the entire URL yourself and pass it to the first parameter of Web.Contents(), there is an easier way. In the second parameter of Web.Contents() you can use the Query field to construct a query string such as the following:

```
Web.Contents("http://www.mywebservice.com/GetData",
[Query=[#"search"="somedata", #"results"="10"] ])
```

If you need to pass custom HTTP headers you can do so in a similar way, using the Headers field:

```
Web.Contents("http://www.mywebservice.com/GetData",  [
Query=[#"search"="somedata", #"results"="10"],
Headers=[#"HeaderName"="ValueToPass"]
])
```

In some cases a web service will require you to pass a key or token through a custom HTTP header. While you can do this, it would force you to hard-code the value of this key or token inside the code of your query, which would not be secure. Instead you can use the ApiKeyName field to specify the name of the custom HTTP header that contains the key or token, like so:

```
Web.Contents("http://www.mywebservice.com/GetData",  [
Query=[#"search"="somedata", #"results"="10"],
Headers=[#"HeaderName"="ValueToPass"],
ApiKeyName="APIToken"
])
```

When you do this, the first time the query executes the Power Query credentials dialog will appear and prompt you to enter the key or token value. After this the key or token will be stored in Power Query's secure credentials store, as described in Chapter 2.

Finally, although Web.Contents() generates a GET request by default, you can make it generate a POST request instead by specifying the Content field, as in this example:

```
Web.Contents("http://www.mywebservice.com/SendData",
[Content=Text.ToBinary("Text content to send in POST request")])
```

In this case the value of the Content field contains the binary data that is to be used as the content of the POST request; the Text.ToBinary() function must be used to convert the text value to be sent to a value of type Binary.

Query Folding

Something that is not immediately obvious about Power Query is where all of the hard work that it does actually takes place: when a query connects to a data source and applies a series of transformations to your data, where possible Power Query will try to push as much of the work as possible back to the data source, where (or so it assumes) it can be done more efficiently. This behavior is called *query folding*. Whether Power Query is able to do this or not depends on the type of data source you are using and the type of transformations in your query. With a relational database like SQL Server, Power Query will attempt to translate all of the logic in the query to a SQL SELECT statement, and with an OData data source it will attempt to translate all of the logic into a single OData URL. However, for data sources like text files, Power Query has no option but to load all of the data into its own engine and perform all of the transformations in the query internally.

As you can probably guess, whether Power Query can push an operation back to the data source can have a big impact on the performance of that operation. It will be much more efficient for SQL Server to aggregate data from a large table than for Power Query to download all of the data to the desktop and perform the aggregation there. In general, therefore, query folding is a good thing and you will want it to happen in your queries. On the other hand, there may be occasions where Power Query is the more efficient option, or where your data source changes so frequently that you have to prevent query folding from taking place so that you have a stable snapshot of data to work with.

If query folding is a good thing, then the obvious next question is: how do you construct your query to make sure query folding happens? Unfortunately there are no easy answers. At the time of writing query folding is limited to four types of data source: relational databases, OData data sources, Exchange, and Active Directory. This could change in the future, though. Furthermore, there are a lot of other factors that determine whether query folding can take place, such as certain types of transformation, and again these factors will almost certainly change in the future. As a result only very general recommendations can be given about how to ensure query folding takes place; if performance is a problem, then you should monitor the queries Power Query executes against your data source and experiment to see whether making changes within Power Query alters the queries that are generated.

Monitoring Query Folding in SQL Server

There is no indication in the Power Query user interface as to whether query folding is taking place or not, unfortunately—you have to use other tools to monitor the communication between Power Query and your data source.

If you are using SQL Server as a data source, you can quite easily see it taking place by running a SQL Server Profiler trace while your query executes. The query in Listing 5-18 connects to the DimProductCategory table in the Adventure Works DW database in SQL Server, filters it so only the rows where the ProductCategoryKey column is less than 4, and then counts the number of rows after the filter has taken place.

Listing 5-18.

```
let
    //connect to SQL Server
    Source = Sql.Database("localhost", "Adventure Works DW"),
    //connect to the DimProductCategory table
    dbo_DimProductCategory = Source{[Schema="dbo",Item="DimProductCategory"]}[Data],
    //filter the table where ProductCategoryKey is less than 4
    FilteredRows = Table.SelectRows(dbo_DimProductCategory, each [ProductCategoryKey] < 4),
    //count the number of rows in the resulting table
    GroupedRows = Table.Group(FilteredRows, {}, {{"Count", each Table.RowCount(_), type number}})
in
    GroupedRows
```

If you open SQL Server Profiler and start a new trace running against the Adventure Works DW database using the Standard template while refreshing the Power Query query, you will see the SQL shown in Listing 5-19 in a SQL:BatchCompleted event, as shown in Figure 5-34. This SQL query contains all of the logic in the Power Query query and returns a table containing a single value—the same table that the Power Query query itself returns. In this case query folding has clearly taken place.

Listing 5-19.

```
select count(1) as [Count]
from
(
    select [_].[ProductCategoryKey],
        [_].[ProductCategoryAlternateKey],
        [_].[EnglishProductCategoryName],
        [_].[SpanishProductCategoryName],
        [_].[FrenchProductCategoryName]
    from [dbo].[DimProductCategory] as [_]
    where [_].[ProductCategoryKey] < 4
) as [rows]
```

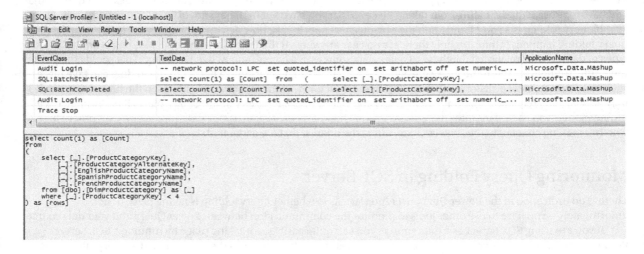

Figure 5-34. A SQL Server Profiler trace showing query folding in action

Preventing Query Folding in Code

There are two functions that can be used if you want to prevent query folding from taking place: List.Buffer() and Table.Buffer(). Both functions work in the same way, taking a list or a table and loading all its data into Power Query, then returning the list or table unchanged.

Listing 5-20 shows how the Power Query query shown in Listing 5-18 in the previous section can be modified using Table.Buffer() to turn off query folding. Running a Profiler trace when this query refreshes shows only the SQL SELECT statement to retrieve all of the data in the DimProductCategory table—there is no filtering in the Where clause and there is no Group By.

Listing 5-20.

```
let
    //connect to SQL Server
    Source = Sql.Database("localhost", "Adventure Works DW"),
    //connect to the DimProductCategory table
    dbo_DimProductCategory = Source{[Schema="dbo",Item="DimProductCategory"]}[Data],
    //buffer table
    BufferedTable = Table.Buffer(dbo_DimProductCategory),
    //filter the table where ProductCategoryKey is less than 4
    FilteredRows = Table.SelectRows(BufferedTable, each [ProductCategoryKey] < 4),
    //count the number of rows in the resulting table
    GroupedRows = Table.Group(FilteredRows, {}, {{"Count", each Table.RowCount(_), type number}})
in
    GroupedRows
```

Other Operations That May Prevent Query Folding

As mentioned earlier in the "Query Folding" section, the scenarios where query folding is unable to take place will change with each new release of Power Query. In this section you'll see a number of scenarios where query folding is prevented in the version of Power Query used for writing this book, but please do not assume that same behavior applies to whatever version of Power Query you are using. Instead, take the following list as indicative of the kind of operation to watch out for.

Custom SQL Statements

The use of a custom SQL statement with any relational database data source (i.e. the scenario where you enter your own SQL query as the starting point for a query, instead of selecting a table from the Navigator pane and then filtering it in the Query Editor) automatically prevents query folding. As a result, if you do need to use custom SQL and you are worried about performance you could do one of two things: either create a view using the custom SQL instead, and point Power Query at the view; or alternatively try to do as little work as possible in Power Query and as much work as possible in the SQL query itself.

Removing rows with errors

Using the Remove Rows With Errors option in the Query Editor toolbar or the `Table.RemoveRowsWithErrors()` function in a step prevents query folding from taking place. Therefore if you need to remove rows from a table that contain error values, this should be one of the last things you do in a query. The query shown in Listing 5-21 shows an example of this: it contains a step that returns an error in one row, which is then filtered out using `Table.RemoveRowsWithErrors()` in the next step. As a result, the filter in the last step to remove rows where the ProductCategoryKey column is less than 4 is not seen in the SQL generated by Power Query.

Listing 5-21.

```
let
    //connect to SQL Server
    Source = Sql.Database("localhost", "Adventure Works DW"),
    //connect to the DimProductCategory table
    dbo_DimProductCategory = Source{[Schema="dbo",Item="DimProductCategory"]}[Data],
    //insert custom column that returns an error in one row
```

```
    InsertedCustom = Table.AddColumn(dbo_DimProductCategory, "DivideByZero", each if
[ProductCategoryKey]=1 then xyz else null),
    //remove error row
    RemovedErrors = Table.RemoveRowsWithErrors(InsertedCustom, {"DivideByZero"}),
    //filter table by ProductCategoryKey < 4
    FilteredRows = Table.SelectRows(RemovedErrors, each [ProductCategoryKey] < 4)
in
    FilteredRows
```

Switching the order of the last two steps, so that errors are removed last of all as shown in Listing 5-22, means that query folding does now take place and the filter on ProductCategoryKey does appear in the SQL that Power Query generates.

Listing 5-22.

```
let
    //connect to SQL Server
    Source = Sql.Database("localhost", "Adventure Works DW"),
    //connect to the DimProductCategory table
    dbo_DimProductCategory = Source{[Schema="dbo",Item="DimProductCategory"]}[Data],
    //insert custom column that returns an error in one row
    InsertedCustom = Table.AddColumn(dbo_DimProductCategory, "DivideByZero", each if
[ProductCategoryKey]=1 then xyz else null),
    //filter table by ProductCategoryKey < 4
    FilteredRows = Table.SelectRows(InsertedCustom , each [ProductCategoryKey] < 4),
    //remove error row
    RemovedErrors = Table.RemoveRowsWithErrors(FilteredRows , {"DivideByZero"})

in
    RemovedErrors
```

Complex Operations

Unfortunately, many of the advanced features in M discussed in this chapter can also prevent query folding. For example, pivoting and unpivoting a table using the Table.Pivot() and the Table.UnPivot() functions prevent query folding, and indeed it is probably fair to say that any transformation where the equivalent SQL might be a challenge to write will also suffer from the same problem. Similarly if you define and use functions inside your queries—even if the function is trivial—this also can prevent query folding. Therefore you should always try to apply simple filters and aggregations (the kind of thing that can be accomplished using just the user interface) in the first few steps of your query, where possible, and leave the more advanced operations until last.

Summary

In this chapter you have learned about the M language behind Power Query and seen how you can use it to create calculations and transformations that you cannot create using just the user interface. The M language is indeed powerful, but, like all programming languages, it does require some effort to learn and you will need to invest some time to become competent with it. You should also bear in mind that the more custom M code you write in your queries, the harder it will be for other users to understand how they work and alter or update them. You should always try to solve a problem using the functionality available in the user interface unless there is no other alternative to writing M.

In the next chapter you will see how to work with multiple queries and combine data from them in different ways. This will provide many more opportunities for you to practice your M language skills!

CHAPTER 6

■ ■ ■

Working with Multiple Queries

So far the focus of this book has been on what you can achieve within an individual Power Query query. In many real-world scenarios, however, a single Excel workbook will contain multiple queries connecting to different data sources, and you may want to combine the data from these queries somehow. In this chapter you'll learn about the various ways you can do this and about some of the data privacy issues that you will encounter when doing this.

Using One Query as a Source for Another

In Chapter 2 you saw how you could use the Reference option to use the output of one query as the data source for another. Now that you have learned a little bit of M, it's time to revisit that concept and see how the code behind this functionality actually works, and how you can adapt it to create parameterized queries.

Referencing Queries in Code

Figure 6-1 shows an Excel worksheet with two tables on it. On the left there is a table called Sales, and on the right a table with one column and one row called Product.

Month	Product	Sales		Product
January	Apples	1		Apples
February	Apples	2		
March	Apples	3		
January	Oranges	10		
February	Oranges	12		
March	Oranges	14		
January	Pears	20		
February	Pears	23		
March	Pears	26		

Figure 6-1. Two tables in an Excel worksheet

149

If you create a Power Query query that uses the right-hand table, Product, as a data source using the From Table option on the ribbon, and you call that query ProductQuery, then the code for that query will be as shown in Listing 6-1.

Listing 6-1.

```
let
    Source = Excel.CurrentWorkbook(){[Name="Product"]}[Content]
in
    Source
```

If you then right-click that query in the Workbook Queries pane and select Reference (as shown in Chapter 2), a new query will be created with code shown in Listing 6-2 that uses the output of the original query as its data source and itself returns that same table unchanged.

Listing 6-2.

```
let
    Source = ProductQuery
in
    Source
```

In this very simple example, you can see that the table returned by the first query, called ProductQuery, can be referenced directly in the definition of the second query simply by using the first query's name. All queries in the same worksheet can reference each other in this way. One thing to point out here is that ProductQuery does not need to load its data into either the worksheet or the Excel Data Model for this to work—both of the boxes in the Load Settings section in the Query Editor can be left unchecked.

Creating Parameterized Queries

If you have very large amounts of data in a data source, then it's a good idea to filter that data so you only load what you need into the Excel Data Model. You have already seen lots of examples of how Power Query can help you do this. But what happens if you need to load a different subset of data at different times? Instead of having to edit your query manually to change the filter (which you may be capable of doing, but other users may not be comfortable with), you can create a parameterized query. A parameterized query is a query with two data sources; one data source contains the data you want to load into Excel, while the second data source contains information on how you want the data from the first data source to be filtered.

Going back to Figure 6-1, let's say that you want to import data from the Sales table on the left of the screenshot into the Excel Data Model, but you only want to load data for one product at any given time. If you create a Power Query query that uses the Sales table as a data source, and then filters the table so that the query only returns the rows where the Product column contains the value Apples, the code would look something like what is shown in Listing 6-3.

Listing 6-3.

```
let
    Source = Excel.CurrentWorkbook(){[Name="Sales"]}[Content],
    FilteredRows = Table.SelectRows(Source, each ([Product] = "Apples"))
in
    FilteredRows
```

The output of this query is shown in Figure 6-2.

⊞▾	Month ▾	Product ▾	Sales ▾
1	January	Apples	1
2	February	Apples	2
3	March	Apples	3

Figure 6-2. *The Sales table filtered by the Product "Apples"*

It's very easy to see here where the value that is being filtered on, "Apples," is hard-coded. Remember also that you have a query from the other table on the worksheet, the Product table, which also returns the value "Apples." Therefore you can rewrite the query in Listing 6-3 to parameterize it so that it filters on the name of the Product given in the Product table. Listing 6-4 shows how this can be achieved.

Listing 6-4.

```
let
    Source = Excel.CurrentWorkbook(){[Name="Sales"]}[Content],
    FilteredRows = Table.SelectRows(Source, each ([Product] = ProductQuery[Product]{0}))
in
    FilteredRows
```

As you learned in Chapter 5, you can reference an individual cell in a table by its column name and its row, and the expression ProductQuery[Product]{0} returns the value from the first row in the Product column, which at the moment is "Apples." However, each time this query is run, the ProductQuery query is also run to return the contents of the Product table, so if you change the contents of the Product table so that it contains "Oranges" rather than "Apples," as shown in Figure 6-3, you will now find the output of the query given in Listing 6-4 is as shown in Figure 6-4—only the rows from the Sales table where the Product is "Oranges" are now returned.

Month ▾	Product ▾	Sales ▾		Product ▾
January	Apples	1		Oranges
February	Apples	2		
March	Apples	3		
January	Oranges	10		
February	Oranges	12		
March	Oranges	14		
January	Pears	20		
February	Pears	23		
March	Pears	26		

Figure 6-3. *The Product table changed to contain the value "Oranges"*

⊞▾	Month	▾	Product	▾	Sales	▾
1	January		Oranges		10	
2	February		Oranges		12	
3	March		Oranges		14	

Figure 6-4. *The Sales table filtered by the Product "Oranges"*

This is an example of a parameterized query, a query that filters the rows returned from one data source by a value (the parameter) returned from a second data source.

Working with Data from Different, External Data Sources

In the last section you saw an example of a parameterized query where all of the data was sourced from Excel. A more practical application for parameterized queries would be if you wanted to filter the data in a large table stored in a relational database such as SQL Server by a value stored in a table in Excel—but this raises issues about data privacy and performance that require quite a lot of explanation.

Data Privacy Settings

Listings 6-5 and 6-6 contain the code for two queries that do something very similar to the queries shown in the previous section, but which in this case take data from the DimDate table in the Adventure Works DW SQL Server database and filter it by a value taken from a table in Excel called Weekday. The Weekday table, like the Product table in the previous section, has just one row and one column, and you can assume its single cell always contains the name of a day of the week.

Listing 6-5.

```
//Code for the query Weekday
Let
    //Get data from the Weekday table in the Excel worksheet
    Source = Excel.CurrentWorkbook(){[Name="Weekday"]}[Content]
in
    Source
```

Listing 6-6.

```
//Code for the query DimDate
Let
    //Connect to the Adventure Works DW SQL Server database
    Source = Sql.Database("localhost", "adventure works dw"),
    //Connect to the DimDate table
    dbo_DimDate = Source{[Schema="dbo",Item="DimDate"]}[Data],
    //Filter the rows by the weekday name from the Weekday query above
    FilteredRows = Table.SelectRows(dbo_DimDate,
                    each ([EnglishDayNameOfWeek] = Weekday[Weekday]{0}))
in
    FilteredRows
```

This second query is almost identical to the one shown in Listing 6-4 except that in this case the two data sources being used are different: they are Excel and SQL Server. The first time the DimDate query shown in Listing 6-6 is executed in the Query Editor, you will see a warning prompt like the one shown in Figure 6-5.

Figure 6-5. *A Data Privacy prompt in the Query Editor*

Clicking the Continue button here will open the Privacy levels dialog shown in Figure 6-6, where you will be asked to set one of three different privacy levels for both of the data sources in the workbook.

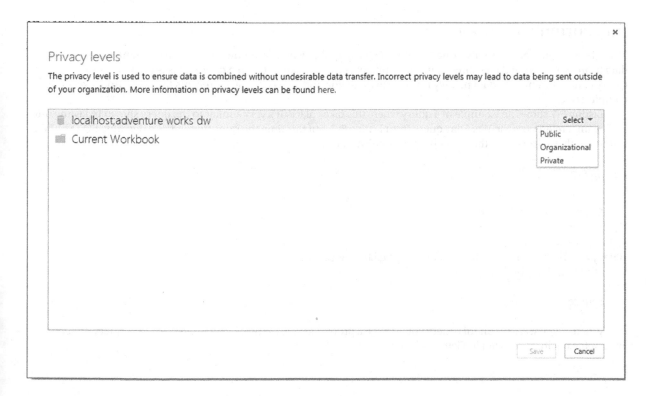

Figure 6-6. *The Privacy levels dialog*

The three privacy levels that can be used are:

- *Public*, for data sources where there are no data privacy concerns and where you don't mind anyone seeing the data.

- *Organizational*, for data that can only be shared among a trusted group of people, such as your coworkers.

- *Private*, for data that is confidential or in some way sensitive.

At this point you are probably still wondering what this all means! The privacy levels here control which data sources are allowed to be combined with other data sources during query evaluation—for example, when you are working with parameterized queries. In Chapter 5 you learned about query folding and how Power Query always tries to push work back to the data source where possible. In some cases, however, doing this could represent a data privacy risk. In Listing 6-6, if Power Query was able to translate the entire query into a single SQL SELECT statement, this would result in a value from your Excel worksheet (the weekday name) being incorporated into the text of the query and being sent to SQL Server where a DBA running a Profiler trace would be able to see it.

As a result, Power Query takes data privacy settings into account when deciding whether to perform query folding or not. Data from public data sources can be passed to any other data source; data from organizational data sources can be passed to other organizational data sources, but not public data sources; and data from private data sources cannot be shared with any other data source, including other private data sources. These data privacy levels can therefore affect the performance of queries, and in some cases they may even prevent a query from executing.

In this particular case, query folding cannot take place, so your choice of privacy level for the two data sources makes no difference to how the query executes—it will work whichever privacy levels you choose. However, as you will see next, there will be cases where choosing the correct privacy level will be very important, and on top of that there are other privacy rules that Power Query applies.

The Formula Firewall

There is another, more restrictive rule that Power Query applies when combining data from different data sources: data from two different data sources cannot be referenced in the same step in a query. This is because Power Query cannot evaluate its data privacy rules in this situation and so, to be safe, it prevents the query from executing completely.

Listing 6-7 shows an example of a query where this takes place. It's very similar to the query shown in Listing 6-6, and again it references the Weekday query from Listing 6-5, but this time the query generates a dynamic SQL SELECT statement that selects all of the data from the DimDate table.

Listing 6-7.

```
let
    Source = Sql.Database(
"localhost",
"adventure works dw",
[Query="select * from DimDate where EnglishDayNameOfWeek='"
& Weekday[Weekday]{0} & "'" ])
in
    Source
```

When you first try to run this query you will see a prompt asking for permission to run the SQL query directly against the database, as seen in Figure 6-7.

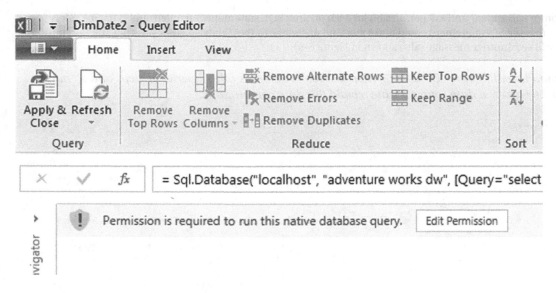

Figure 6-7. Prompt for permission to run a native database query

Clicking Edit Permission shows the Native Database Query dialog, seen in Figure 6-8.

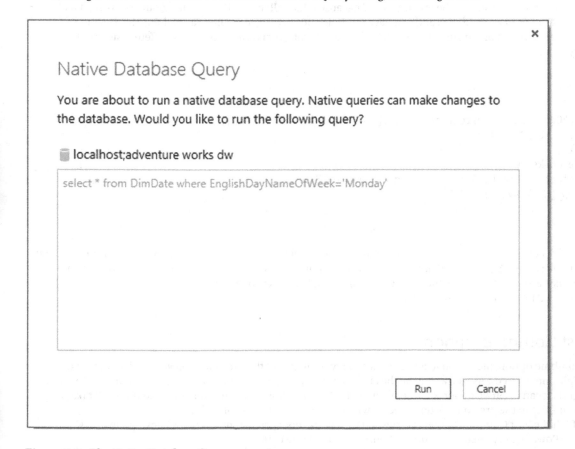

Figure 6-8. The Native Database Query prompt

This prompt will appear and ask permission for each distinct SQL statement generated, and is itself a safety feature, given that the SQL statement could make any kind of change to the database. After you click the Run button, though, you will see another message (also shown in Figure 6-9):

Formula.Firewall: Query 'DimDate2' (step 'Source') references other queries or steps and so may not directly access a data source. Please rebuild this data combination.

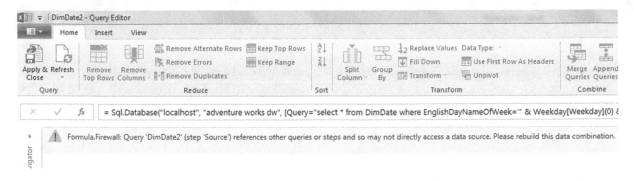

Figure 6-9. *The Formula Firewall error*

At this point the query cannot be executed at all because it has fallen afoul of the rule about accessing data from different data sources in a single step, and you have no choice but to rewrite it. One way of doing this is shown in Listing 6-8 where, instead of returning the weekday from a separate query, this is done in a different step in the same query.

Listing 6-8.

```
let
    GetWeekDay = Excel.CurrentWorkbook(){[Name="Weekday"]}[Content],
    Source = Sql.Database(
"localhost",
"adventure works dw",
[Query="select * from DimDate where EnglishDayNameOfWeek='"
& GetWeekDay[Weekday]{0} & "'"])
in
    Source
```

The single-step rule has now been avoided, and the query will now run if the data privacy settings for the current Excel workbook and the SQL Server database are both set to Public or both set to Organizational. However if one of the data sources is set to Public and one is set to Organizational, the firewall error will reappear, and the same will happen if either data source is set to Private.

The Fast Combine Option

The Fast Combine option allows you to ignore data privacy settings and the firewall when you are combining data from multiple data sources. As well as having the effect of turning off all those nagging prompts and restriction, as its name suggests it can improve performance of your query by increasing the chance that query folding will take place. All of the examples in the previous section execute with Fast Combine turned on.

By default the Fast Combine option is turned off for a workbook; you can turn it on by clicking the Fast Combine button in the Power Query tab on the Excel ribbon, shown in Figure 6-10.

Figure 6-10. *The Fast Combine button on the Power Query tab in the ribbon*

Clicking this button opens the dialog shown in Figure 6-11, which asks you to confirm whether you want to enable Fast Combine.

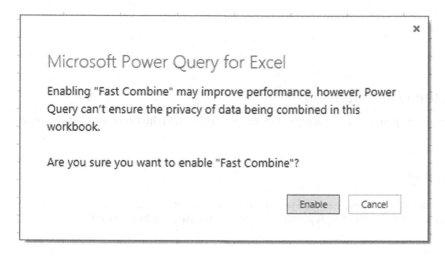

Figure 6-11. *The Fast Combine dialog*

Fast Combine can be enabled or disabled for individual Excel workbooks. The setting is saved when you save your workbook, so you don't have to re-enable it when you reopen a workbook.

■ **Note**   It is all too easy to enable Fast Combine without thinking every time you encounter a data privacy prompt or a firewall error. However, it is your responsibility to take data privacy issues seriously; if you do not, you may leave your employer liable to criminal charges (especially if you work in a highly regulated sector like financial services or healthcare) and as a result you will put your own job and career at risk.

Appending Data from One Query onto Another

Another way that you may want to combine data from multiple queries is by appending the data from one query to another, rather like a union in SQL. This is very easy to achieve through the user interface as well as in M code.

Figure 6-12 shows an Excel worksheet with four tables in, and these tables will be used for the examples in this section and the following section on merging queries. Their names are shown above the tables and you can assume that four Power Query queries have been created to load data from each of these tables and that each query has the same name as the table it uses as a data source.

Apples		
Month ▼	Product ▼	Sales ▼
January	Apples	1
February	Apples	2
March	Apples	3

Oranges		
Month ▼	Product ▼	Sales ▼
January	Oranges	5
February	Oranges	7
March	Oranges	9

Pears		
Month ▼	Product ▼	Sales ▼
January	Pears	20
February	Pears	23
March	Pears	26

ApplesProfit		
Month ▼	Product ▼	Profit ▼
January	Apples	100
February	Apples	200
March	Apples	300

Figure 6-12. *Data for appending*

Appending Queries in the User Interface

There are two ways that one query can be appended to another: in the Power Query tab in the Excel ribbon and inside the Query Editor.

Appending Queries in the Ribbon

In the Power Query tab on the Excel ribbon it is possible to take two already-created Power Query queries and append one to the other to create a third, new query. This is possible by clicking the Append button in the ribbon, shown in Figure 6-13.

Figure 6-13. *The Append button in the ribbon*

Once you have clicked this button the Append dialog appears, as shown in Figure 6-14, and you can choose the query you want to use as your starting point and the query to append to this first query.

Append

Select the primary table to which you want to append more data.

Apples

Select the table to append with the primary table.

Oranges

OK   Cancel

Figure 6-14. *The Append dialog*

Once you have chosen your two queries (in this case the queries Apples and Oranges) and clicked OK, a new query will be created and the Query Editor window will open to show the combined data, as shown in Figure 6-15.

▦▾	Month ▾	Product ▾	Sales ▾
1	January	Apples	1
2	February	Apples	2
3	March	Apples	3
4	January	Oranges	5
5	February	Oranges	7
6	March	Oranges	9

Figure 6-15. *Appended data in the Query Editor window*

Appending Queries in the Query Editor

When you are editing an existing query in the Query Editor window, you can append the data from another query to the query you are currently editing as a new step by clicking the Append Queries button on the Home tab of the toolbar (shown in Figure 6-16).

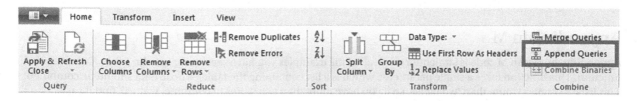

Figure 6-16. *The Append Queries button in the Query Editor*

When you click this button the Append dialog opens again, as shown in Figure 6-17, but this time you can only select one query: the query whose data you want to append to the current query.

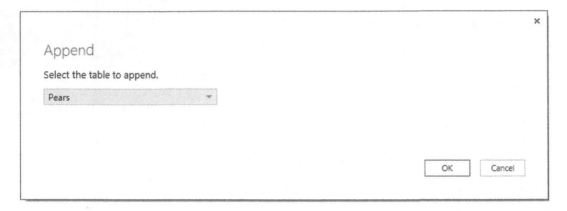

Figure 6-17. *The Append dialog*

Taking the query created in the last section, the output of whose first step is shown in Figure 6-15, if you append the query Pears, then the output of the new step will be as shown in Figure 6-18.

⊞▾	Month	▾	Product	▾	Sales	▾
1	January		Apples			1
2	February		Apples			2
3	March		Apples			3
4	January		Oranges			5
5	February		Oranges			7
6	March		Oranges			9
7	January		Pears			20
8	February		Pears			23
9	March		Pears			26

Figure 6-18. *The output of the new step appending Pears to the query in Figure 6-15*

Appending in M

Appending queries in M code is straightforward: all of the examples you have seen so far use the Table.Combine() function. This function takes a single parameter, which is a list containing the tables whose data should be combined. This list can contain more than two tables, so if you have more than two tables to combine, you will find it easier to write some code to do this than clicking the Append button multiple times in the user interface. For example, the following expression combines the data from the tables Apples, Oranges, and Pears in a single operation and returns the same result that is seen in Figure 6-18:

```
Table.Combine({Apples, Oranges, Pears})
```

The Table.Combine() function will not return an error if the tables in the list you pass to it do not contain the same columns. Taking the Apples and ApplesProfit queries as an example, these tables both have columns called Month and Product, but Apples has a third column called Sales whereas ApplesProfit has a third column called Profit. Combining these two tables, as in the following expression, returns the output shown in Figure 6-19, a table with four columns: Month, Product, Sales and Profit.

```
Table.Combine({Apples, ApplesProfit})
```

▦▾	Month ▾	Product ▾	Sales ▾	Profit ▾
1	January	Apples	1	null
2	February	Apples	2	null
3	March	Apples	3	null
4	January	Apples	null	100
5	February	Apples	null	200
6	March	Apples	null	300

Figure 6-19. *Output of* Table.Combine() *on tables with different columns*

Merging Two Queries

Whereas an append operation involves adding the data from one query onto the bottom of another, a merge involves joining two queries together, rather like a join in SQL. Once again you can merge two queries together either in the user interface or in code using a variety of M functions.

Merging Queries in the User Interface

As with append operations, you can merge two queries either from the Power Query tab in the Excel ribbon or within the Query Editor.

Merging Queries in the Ribbon

To merge two queries from the ribbon, you need to click the Merge button as shown in Figure 6-20.

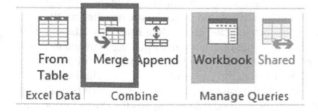

Figure 6-20. *The Merge button on the ribbon*

When you click the Merge button, the Merge dialog appears, as shown in Figure 6-21.

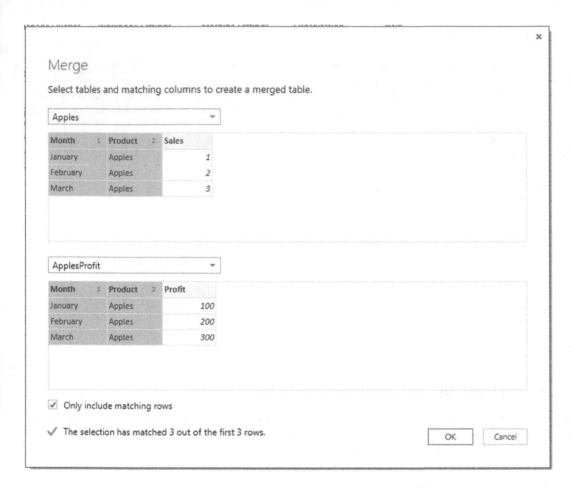

Figure 6-21. *The Merge dialog*

In this dialog, the first thing you have to do is to select the two tables you want to work with in the drop-down boxes. Once this has been done, you have to select the column or columns containing the values to match in each table by clicking them—you can select more than one column by holding down the Shift or Ctrl keys on the keyboard and then clicking. The order that you select each column is important and is indicated by numbers that appear in the column headers after they have been selected; columns with the same numbers are matched to each other.

In the example shown in Figure 6-21, the queries Apples and ApplesProfit are selected and the result is a new query containing all of the rows from Apples where there is a matching row in ApplesProfit based on the Month and Product columns containing the same two values. The values in the Month column in Apples are matched to the values in the Month column in ApplesProfit because both columns were selected first in their respective tables and have the number 1 displayed next to them. Likewise, the values in the Product column in Apples are matched to the values in the Product column in ApplesProfit because they were selected second and have the number 2 displayed next to them; it is the numbers in the columns that determine how the matching takes place, not the column names. Because the Only include matching rows check box is checked, only the rows where these two columns contain matching values are returned. Clicking OK creates a new query with the merged data and opens the Query Editor, and you can see the output of the merge operation in Figure 6-22.

⊞▾	Month	▾	Product	▾	Sales	▾	NewColumn	⬌
1	January		Apples		1		Table	
2	February		Apples		2		Table	
3	March		Apples		3		Table	

Figure 6-22. *Output of the Merge operation*

As you can see, the table returned from the merge operation is the same as the Apples table, the table selected in the upper drop-down box in the Merge dialog. However, it has an extra column, NewColumn, containing values of type Table; clicking the Expand icon in the column header allows you to add some or all of the matched columns from the table selected in the lower drop-down box in the Merge dialog, ApplesProfit. After doing this, the output of the query will be as shown in Figure 6-23.

⊞▾	Month	▾	Product	▾	Sales	▾	NewColumn.Month	▾	NewColumn.Product	▾	NewColumn.Profit	▾
1	January		Apples		1		January		Apples		100	
2	February		Apples		2		February		Apples		200	
3	March		Apples		3		March		Apples		300	

Figure 6-23. *The output of the Merge operation with columns expanded*

Those of you familiar with relational databases and SQL will recognize what has happened here as being something like an inner join between the two queries. In this example, each row of the Apples query can be matched to a row in the ApplesProfit query, but if this is not the case and if the Only include matching rows check box is checked, then some rows of data will be lost. To illustrate this, alter the ApplesProfit table so the third row contains the month April instead of March, as shown in Figure 6-24.

	ApplesProfit		
Month ▼	Product ▼	Profit ▼	
January	Apples	100	
February	Apples	200	
April	Apples	300	

Figure 6-24. *Altered version of the ApplesProfit table*

The Merge operation, after the columns have been expanded, will return the table shown in Figure 6-25—only two rows are returned now, because only two rows in Apples and ApplesProfit contain matching combinations of values in the Month and Product columns.

Month	Product	Sales	NewColumn.Month	NewColumn.Product	NewColumn.Profit
1 January	Apples	1	January	Apples	100
2 February	Apples	2	February	Apples	200

Figure 6-25. Output of the Merge operation showing only matched rows

If, however, the Only include matching rows check box on the Merge dialog is not checked, with this new version of the ApplesProfit table all three rows from the Apples table are returned from the Merge (rather like a left outer join in SQL), and null values are used in cells where no matching took place, as shown in Figure 6-26. Note that the values from the April row in ApplesProfit are not returned anywhere.

Month	Product	Sales	NewColumn.Month	NewColumn.Product	NewColumn.Profit
1 January	Apples	1	January	Apples	100
2 February	Apples	2	February	Apples	200
3 March	Apples	3	null	null	null

Figure 6-26. Output of the Merge operation with non-matching rows returned

Merging Queries in the Query Editor

Merging queries in the Query Editor works in exactly the same way as merging queries in the ribbon. In this case there is a Merge Queries button on the toolbar in the Query Editor, shown in Figure 6-27, that generates a new step in your query: merging the table returned by the previous step (automatically selected in the Merge dialog) with the selected query.

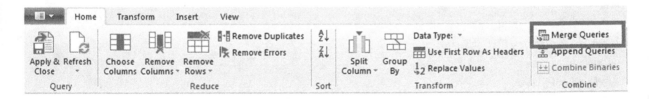

Figure 6-27. The Merge Queries button in the Query Editor toolbar

Merging in M

There are several functions in M that can be used to merge two tables of data. All of the examples you've seen so far use the Table.NestedJoin() function, whose signature is:

```
Table.NestedJoin(table1 as table, key1 as any, table2 as any, key2 as any, newColumnName as text,
optional joinKind as nullable number)
```

The M expression generated by the Merge dialog to join Apples and ApplesProfit together and only include matching rows, as shown in Figure 6-22, is as follows:

```
Table.NestedJoin(
Apples,{"Month", "Product"},
ApplesProfit,{"Month","Product"}
,"NewColumn",JoinKind.Inner
)
```

Table.NestedJoin() returns a table with a single extra column containing values of type Table; the first four parameters define the two tables used in the merge and the columns on which to join. The final parameter allows you to specify what kind of join to perform:

- JoinKind.Inner performs an inner join, where only the rows from both tables that match are returned.

- JoinKind.LeftOuter performs a left outer join, where all rows from the table in the first parameter are returned but only matching rows from the table in the third parameter are returned.

- JoinKind.RightOuter performs a right outer join, where all rows from the table in the third parameter are returned but only matching rows from the table in the first parameter are returned.

- JoinKind.FullOuter performs a full outer join where all rows from both tables are returned.

- JoinKind.LeftAnti performs a left anti join, where only the rows from the table in the first parameter that do not match any rows in the table in the third parameter are returned.

- JoinKind.RightAnti performs a right anti join, where only the rows from the table in the third parameter that do not match any rows in the table in the first parameter are returned.

The Table.AddJoinColumn() function does exactly the same as Table.NestedJoin() function, only it does not allow you to specify the kind of join it does and only performs left outer joins.

The Table.Join() function is very similar to Table.NestedJoin() but instead of returning joined rows as a value of type Table, it returns a flattened table with the joined rows already expanded. For example, the following expression returns the table shown in Figure 6-28:

```
Table.Join(
Apples,{"Month", "Product"},
ApplesProfit,{"Month","Product"}
,JoinKind.Inner
)
```

▦▾	Month ▾	Product ▾	Sales ▾	Profit ▾
1	January	Apples	1	100
2	February	Apples	2	200

Figure 6-28. *Output of the* Table.Join() *function*

Summary

In this chapter you have moved beyond the individual query and seen how data from multiple queries can be combined in different ways. You have also learned that this raises important concerns about data privacy that must be addressed. In the next chapter these two themes will be continued as you learn how you can share data and queries with other users in your organization.

■ ■ ■

CHAPTER 7

Power Query and Power BI for Office 365

So far in this book we have concentrated on what can be achieved with Power Query in the context of a single Excel workbook. Once you have built a Power Query query, though, often the natural next step is to share it, either so you can use it in other Excel workbooks you build, or with your colleagues so that they can use it in their Excel workbooks. You could do this by just copying the M code from the Advanced Editor window and pasting it into a new query in a new workbook, but there is a better way: if you have a Power BI for Office 365 subscription, you can share your queries through the Power BI Data Catalog. In this chapter you will learn how to do this and about how these shared queries should be managed. You will also learn about how Excel workbooks containing Power Query queries can be refreshed once they have been published to SharePoint Online.

Sharing and Using Shared Queries in Power Query

The process of sharing a query in Power Query, and then reusing that shared query elsewhere, is relatively straightforward and can be achieved with a few clicks. At a high level, what happens is this: a user can select any Power query query and share it, which means that the query definition and some other metadata is uploaded to the Power BI Data Catalog. Once that has happened it can be found by other users through the Online Search functionality in Power Query, and these other users can then download a copy of the query to use in their own workbooks.

■ **Note**   It is important to emphasize that when you share a Power Query query via the Power BI Data Catalog, you are only sharing the definition of that query and some other metadata. You are not sharing the data that the query returns or credentials to access any data sources.

Sharing queries

Before you can share a query, you first have to ensure that your organization has a Power BI for Office 365 subscription and that a license has been assigned to you (this is something that whoever manages your Office 365 and Power BI subscriptions will have to do). If that is the case, you then have to sign in to Power BI from Power Query. Excel 2013 allows you to sign in to a Microsoft organizational account from the Account page in the File menu, but unfortunately this is not enough for Power Query—you have to click the Sign In button on the Power Query tab in the Excel ribbon, as shown in Figure 7-1.

When you click this button the Sign In dialog will appear, as shown in Figure 7-2, and you will need to click the Sign in button here. At this point you may need to enter your e-mail address and password, or Power Query may be able to sign you in automatically from credentials already held in Excel.

Figure 7-2. The Power BI Sign In dialog

You can then share any query from the Workbook Queries pane in Excel either by right-clicking it and selecting Share (as shown in Figure 7-3) or by clicking the Share option in the fly-out window that appears when you hover over a query, or by clicking the Share button on the Power Query Query pane that appears in the Excel ribbon after a query's results has been loaded into the worksheet.

Workbook Queries ▾ ✕

1 query

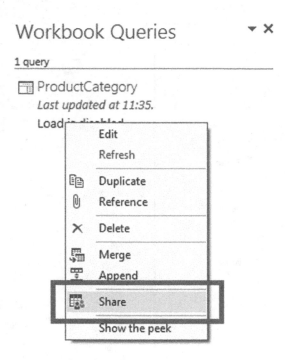

Figure 7-3. *The Share menu option in the Workbook Queries pane*

When you do this, the Share Query dialog opens as shown in Figure 7-4.

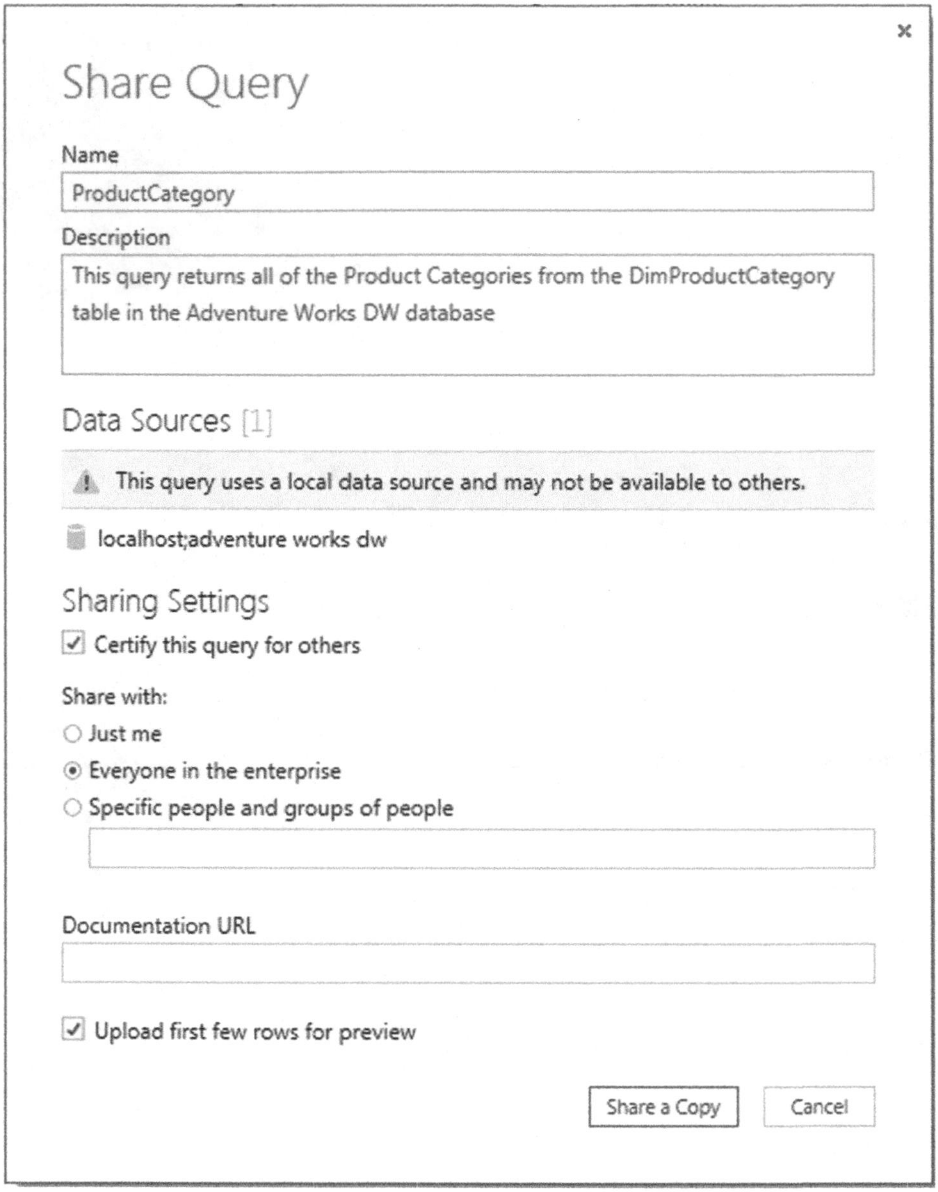

Figure 7-4. *The Share Query dialog*

In the Share Query dialog you can edit the name of the query, add a text description, and specify a documentation URL (most likely the URL of a Word document stored in a SharePoint document library in SharePoint Online) for users to visit to get more information about your query. It's a good idea to fill in as much detail as possible here because it will help other users to understand what your query does; also the text here is indexed by the Power BI Data Catalog, so more detail will also increase the chance of your query being found when users search online for queries.

By default a snapshot of the first few rows of data will also be included with the shared query so that potential users can see a sample of the data the query returns, but if your query returns sensitive data you should uncheck the Upload first few rows for preview box.

You can also choose who to share your query with here: either just with yourself, with everyone else in your organization (that's to say everyone else who uses the same tenant as your Power BI for Office 365 subscription), or with specific people or groups of people. If this last option is selected then you can type the name of specific Windows users or Active Directory Security Groups (although not Active Directory Distribution Groups) and a drop-down box will appear with names you can select. Whatever you select here, you will always have access to queries you have shared. It may seem obvious but it's worth pointing out that if you share a query with other users, it must use a data source that these users have access to (or can be granted access to). If your query uses a CSV file on your local hard drive as a data source, that is unlikely to be the case.

Finally, if you are a member of the Data Steward group in Power BI, a checkbox will be visible in the middle of the dialog allowing you to certify this query. You'll learn more about what a data steward is, and what certification means, later on in this chapter.

Clicking the Share a Copy button on the bottom of the dialog will upload the definition of your query to your Power BI site.

Consuming Shared Queries

There are two places you can find shared queries so that you can reuse them in new Excel workbooks. First, you can find queries that you have yourself shared by clicking the Shared button in the Power Query tab on the Excel ribbon; second, you can find queries that you and other people have shared via the Power BI Data Catalog using the Online Search option. Full details about both of these options were given in Chapter 2.

When you use a shared query in a new workbook, it is important to understand exactly what is happening behind the scenes. If your shared query simply imports data directly from a data source and doesn't apply any transformations to it (e.g., if your query imports an entire table from a SQL Server database), then when you edit your shared query you will see that you have a copy of the original query. However, if the shared query was more complex than that, then when you open the Query Editor after referencing your shared query, you will see it has a single step and looks something like the query shown in Listing 7-1.

Listing 7-1.

```
let
    Source = Embedded.Value("ceecf637-e800-400d-a5c8-422f95e38800")
in
    Source
```

What has happened in this case is the definition of the shared query you selected is copied into the current workbook, but it is not visible anywhere and cannot be edited. The M function Embedded.Value() returns the result of this query, where the embedded query is referenced by the GUID you can see here. This means that if the definition of the shared query changes, then that change will not be reflected in your workbook—you have taken a copy of the query that was shared, and no link is maintained between this copy and the shared query in the Power BI Data Catalog. On one hand this is a good thing because there is no chance that a change to the original query can break your current Excel workbook; on the other, it is bad because you can't benefit from bug fixes or alterations by the original author.

With this in mind, a good practice to follow when using shared queries is this: immediately after you have imported your shared query, create a second query that references the shared query and use that for any further transformation work and to load data into the Excel Data Model. Then, if the definition of the shared query changes, you can easily delete the shared query from your workbook (leaving the second query unchanged) and then reimport it with the same name to get the updated version, without needing to make any other changes to your workbook.

Updating Queries That Have Been Shared

After you have shared a query you can update either the metadata associated with a shared query (the description, the documentation URL, the people it is shared with, and so on) or the definition of the query itself.

To update the metadata associated with a query, in the Shared Queries pane either right-click the query and select Edit Settings from the right-click menu, or hover over the query until the fly-out window appears and select Edit Settings from the bottom of that. When you do that the Update Query dialog appears, which is almost identical to the Share Query dialog shown in Figure 7-4, except that instead of having a Share a Copy button at the bottom, it has an Update button. Clicking that Update button will update the metadata of the shared query in the Power BI Data Catalog.

To update the definition of the query itself, you need to open the Excel workbook that contained the original Power Query query. You can then make any changes that are necessary in the Query Editor in the usual way, and to update it you need to select the Share right-click menu item or click the Share button again (as you did when you originally shared the query); when you do this the Share Query dialog box will reappear. This time, as well as having a Share a Copy button at the bottom of the screen, it will have an Update button, too. Clicking the Update button will update the existing shared query definition.

■ **Tip** Since you can only update a shared query from the workbook it was originally created it, it is important that you keep the workbook in a safe place. You may want to create an otherwise empty workbook to hold each shared query you create, and then store each of these empty workbooks in a dedicated folder or SharePoint document library.

To delete a shared query from the Power BI Data Catalog, you need to go to the Shared Queries pane in Excel and either right-click the query and select Delete, or hover over the query with your mouse until the fly-out window appears and click Delete there. Note that this will not affect the query in your Excel workbook; it will only mean that that query is no longer shared.

Managing Shared Queries in the Power BI Data Catalog

You can also see a list of queries that have been shared to the Power BI Data Catalog by going to your My Power BI site. On this page you can also manage access to the data sources uses by these queries and see reports showing who has been using them.

Finding Your My Power BI page

All users with a Power BI for Office 365 subscription have their own My Power BI site in SharePoint Online. You can find your My Power BI site by going to the main Power BI page and clicking the My Power BI link in the top right-hand corner of the page, as highlighted in Figure 7-5.

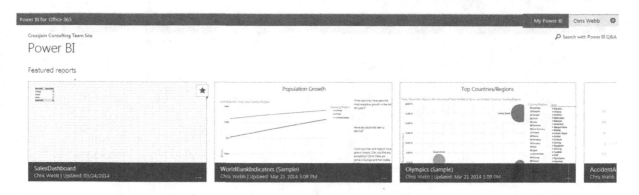

Figure 7-5. *The My Power BI site link*

The My Power BI site serves two functions: it allows you to find all of your favorited reports easily, and it allows you to manage your shared queries and data sources. When you first open it you will see the favorite reports tab displayed, as in Figure 7-6; to be able to manage your data sources, you need to click the data link highlighted in the figure.

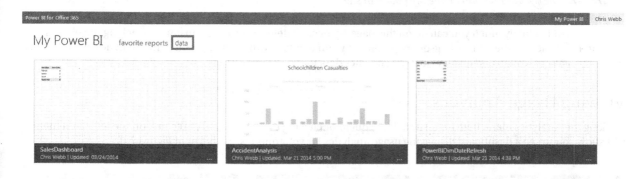

Figure 7-6. *The favorite reports tab on a My Power BI site*

Viewing Shared Queries

Once you have moved to the data tab in your My Power BI site, you can see a list of your shared queries by clicking the my queries option in the menu on the left-hand side of the screen, as shown in Figure 7-7.

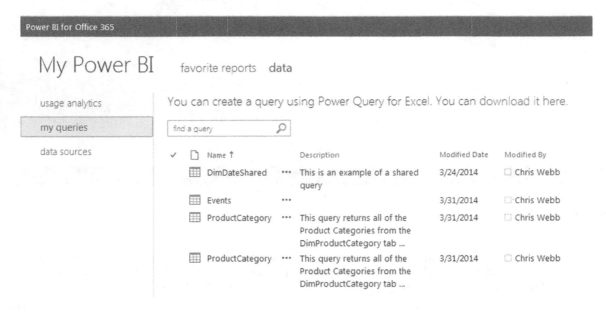

Figure 7-7. *The my queries tab on the My Power BI site*

There isn't actually much you can do on this page—you can't delete queries, for instance. Clicking the ellipsis (the three dots next to the name of the query) opens a fly-out window with a single menu item, Analytics, which opens the usage analytics tab and displays just the analytics data for the selected query.

Viewing Usage Analytics

Clicking the Analytics menu item for an individual query or clicking the usage analytics link on the left-hand menu will allow you to see a dashboard displaying usage analytics for your queries, as shown in Figure 7-8.

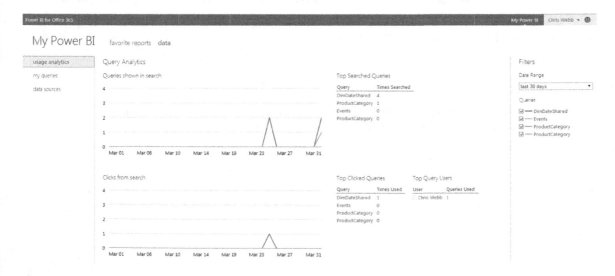

Figure 7-8. *The usage analytics tab*

The two graphs on this page tell you how often a given query has appeared in the results returned for the Online Search functionality, and how often a query has been clicked on in those search results. On the right-hand side of the screen you can select or deselect individual queries and choose the timeframe to display.

Managing data sources

Every time you create a query that connects to an external data source in Power Query in Excel (that's to say, a data source that appears to Power Query as if it is not on your local PC and therefore one to which other users might want to connect) and you are signed in to Power Query, some metadata about that data source will be sent to the Power BI Data Catalog. It should be stressed that this happens every time you use an external data source—not just when you share a query! The full connection string details are not shared, however, and neither are any usernames or passwords. You can see this metadata on the data sources tab of your My Power BI site, as shown in Figure 7-9.

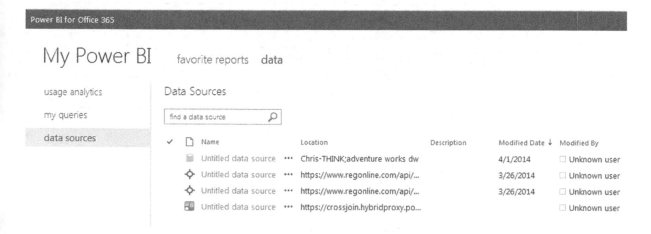

Figure 7-9. *The data sources tab*

Clicking the ellipsis next to each data source's name opens a fly-out window with a single menu option: Edit. Clicking this will allow you to edit the metadata for that query as shown in Figure 7-10.

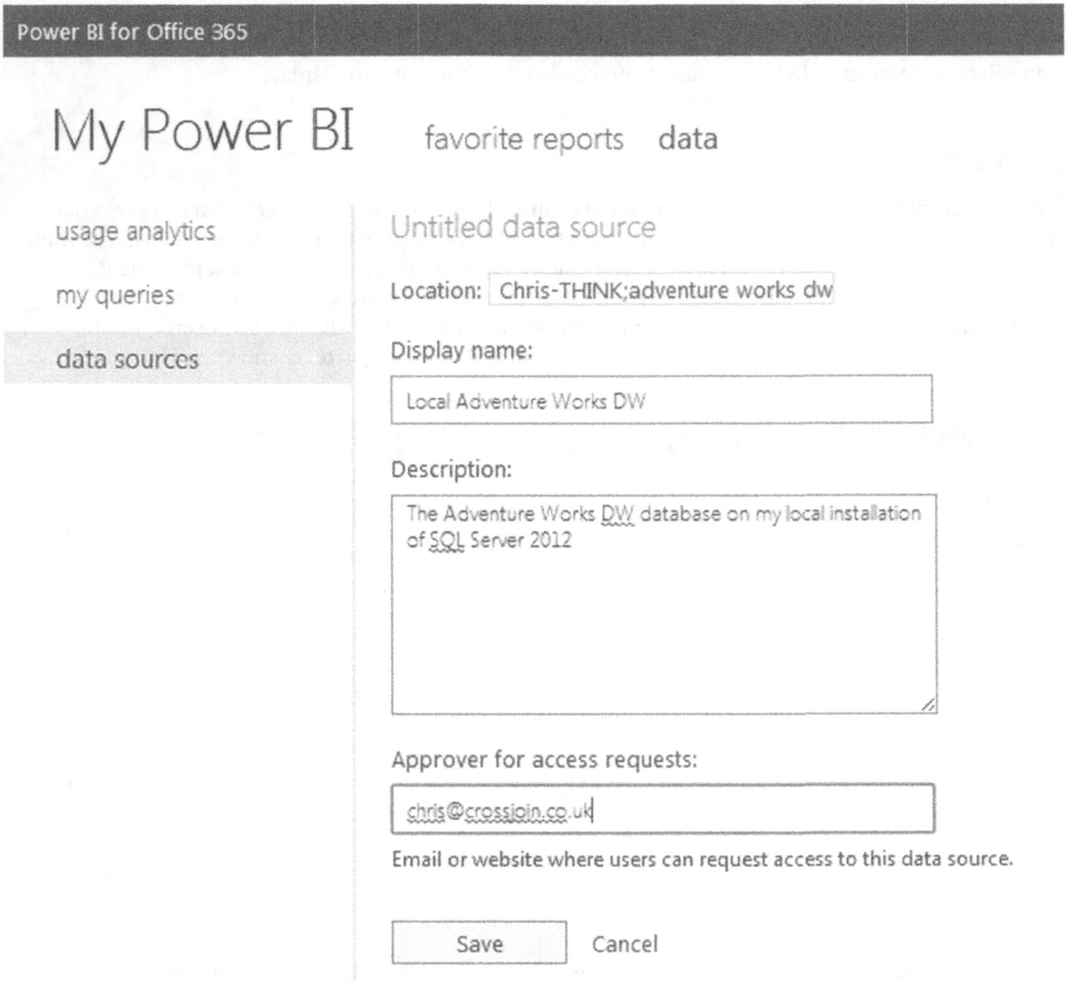

Power BI for Office 365

My Power BI   favorite reports   data

usage analytics

my queries

data sources

Untitled data source

Location: Chris-THINK;adventure works dw

Display name:

Local Adventure Works DW

Description:

The Adventure Works DW database on my local installation of SQL Server 2012

Approver for access requests:

chris@crossjoin.co.uk

Email or website where users can request access to this data source.

Save   Cancel

Figure 7-10. Editing the metadata for a data source

On this screen you can enter a friendly display name for the data source, a description, and the e-mail address of someone who can grant a user permission to access this data source.

This information is used when you share a query (either through the Power BI Data Catalog or any other way—e.g., by emailing them a workbook) with someone who does not have access to the data source that it uses. When this happens and the other user opens the query in Excel, they will be prompted to enter credentials to access the data source as shown in Figure 7-11.

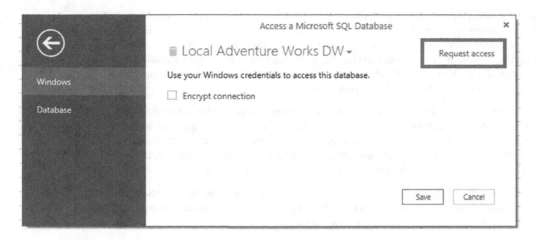

Figure 7-11. *Accessing a data source with extra metadata defined for it*

There are some subtle differences between what you can see in Figure 7-11 and the same dialog shown in Figure 2-3 in Chapter 2, now that extra metadata has been entered for this data source in the My Power BI site. First of all you see the display name of the data source at the top of the dialog, and there is an arrow next to the name that, if you click it, displays the description. Second, in the top right-hand corner of the screen there is a Request access link that, if clicked, generates an e-mail to the approver whose e-mail address is given in the My Power BI site, requesting access to this data source. This means that if the user does not currently have access to the data source in question, it is easy for them to contact someone who can grant them access.

The Data Steward

While the ability to share queries from Power Query is very useful, you can probably appreciate that it could also cause a lot of confusion if not managed properly: you would end up with lots of duplicated queries pointing to the same data source, mysterious queries with no documentation that do things no one quite understands, and broken queries that no longer work for one reason or another. This is where the Data Steward comes in: this person's job is to organize, maintain, and even create the majority of shared queries.

Who Is the Data Steward?

The Data Steward has a very important role in any self-service BI implementation, and their responsibilities extend well beyond Power Query's functionality. The Data Steward sits somewhere between the IT department and the business users—although they should probably be closer to the latter group—and acts as the main point of contact between the two. In large organizations there will be enough work for the Data Steward for this to be a full-time role; in smaller organizations the Data Steward is likely to be the most technically minded of all of the business users.

As far as Power Query is concerned, the Data Steward's job will involve the following tasks:

- Identifying as many of the data sources as possible within the organization that Power Query users will need to access. While the nature of self-service BI is such that it will never be possible to identify and manage all the data sources that will be used, there will be data sources like the corporate data warehouse that are used very frequently.

- Having identified these data sources, the Data Steward should determine which users have access to them and work with the IT department to manage the granting and revoking of permissions. It should be the Data Steward's name in the Approver for access requests box in the dialog shown in Figure 7-10.

- The Data Steward should also ensure that users have access to clean, conformed data. While a data warehouse and formal master data-management initiatives should provide this, not all organizations have a data warehouse; even where they do exist, not all data is stored in the data warehouse. In these cases the Data Steward must try to ensure data quality and consistency using whatever methods they can, and create and share queries to make this cleaned and conformed data available to everyone.

- The Data Steward should try to make access to data as easy as possible for the users. This will involve creating simplified views on relational data sources, creating OData feeds from applications or other non-relational data sources, or even just creating a central repository in SharePoint for all the CSV or Excel files that are used for BI purposes. These data sources should be made available via the Power BI Data Catalog where possible.

- Monitoring usage of data sources after they have been created will also be necessary, so that unused or out-of-date data sources can be retired. This can be achieved in part by looking at the data source usage dashboards in the Power BI site.

- Where direct access to clean, conformed data sources is not possible, the Data Steward should ensure that Power Query queries that clean and conformed data from these sources are available in the Power BI Data Catalog.

- Since creating Power Query queries can be quite a technically challenging task, the Data Steward will probably end up creating a lot of these queries on behalf of other users.

- The Data Steward should also be on hand to help other users create their own queries, encourage these users to store their query definitions in the Power BI Data Catalog, and try to formulate and enforce M coding standards.

- It should be the Data Steward's job to ensure that the definitions of the most important shared queries (whether they are created by the Data Steward or by other users) are kept somewhere central where they can be found easily and be backed up. Ideally this would be in a dedicated SharePoint document library.

- As the number of queries in the Power BI Data Catalog grows, so will the importance of things like the creation and enforcement of naming conventions to ensure that these queries are properly organized. Again, this should be the Data Steward's responsibility.

- Finally, it should be the Data Steward's job to evangelize the use of Power Query, the rest of the Power BI stack, and the data that is available for use with it throughout the organization.

Certifying Queries

One way that a Data Steward can help guide users towards Power Query queries that have been properly tested and that use validated data sources is to certify them. To certify a query, a user first has to be a member of the data steward group in your organization's Power BI site. Only a Power BI administrator can add a user to this group, and to do this the administrator has to go to the Power BI admin center site, choose the role management option from the left-hand menu, and then go to the data steward group tab, as shown in Figure 7-12.

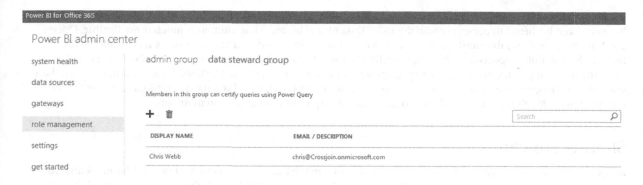

Figure 7-12. *Adding a user to the Data Steward group in the Power BI admin center*

If a user has been made a member of the Data Steward group, when they share a query in Power Query the Share Query dialog will have an extra option to certify the query (this can be seen in the middle of the dialog in Figure 7-4). Certified queries appear with a small seal icon next to them in the Online Search pane and in the Shared Queries pane, as shown in Figure 7-13.

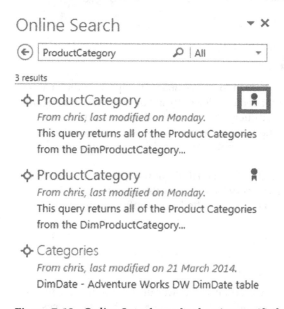

Figure 7-13. *Online Search results showing certified queries*

Which Queries Should Be Shared?

Broadly speaking there are two types of query that you should be sharing in Power Query: those that expose clean, conformed, low-level, detailed data for loading into the worksheet or the Excel Data Model, where it can be used as the basis of many reports; and queries that take data, aggregate it, transform it, and perform calculations on it for the purposes of a specific report.

A Data Steward will end up creating and sharing both types of query, but the first is the most important. Trying to second-guess your users' reporting requirements is unlikely to succeed, and it is always better to give them the raw data so that they can build whatever they want with it. It's certainly true that some types of calculation or transformation will be easier to achieve in Power Query and M than in the Excel Data Model, Power Pivot, and DAX, but even then it's better to persevere with the Excel Data Model because it is ultimately much more flexible. Once you have modeled your data and created any DAX calculations you need, you and your users will be able to take that model and build reports from it using PivotTables, Excel Cube Formulas, and Power View sheets very easily. In contrast, if you give them a Power Query query that returns exactly the data they need for a particular report, then you will need to give them another query for the next report they build, and if you have to build one Power Query query for every single report you will end up with too many queries to manage and maintain.

Sharing Functions

Staying on the subject of queries for loading detailed data into the Excel Data Model, you saw in Chapter 5 how you can create Power Query queries that return functions. A Data Steward might decide that sharing queries that return functions is better for this purpose than sharing queries that return tables of data, for a number of reasons. For example, a Power Query function that filtered a fact table to only return rows in a given date range would allow users to select only the data they needed to load into the Excel Data Model rather than the whole fact table. Similarly, if users wanted to build a report showing the top 10 products based on a variety of criteria, the Data Steward could share a Power Query function that took a date and a country as parameters and returned the top 10 products for whatever date and country the user selected.

Consuming a shared query that returns a function works in exactly the same way as consuming a regular shared query.

Power BI for Office 365 Data Refresh

Apart from the ability to share queries, the other major benefit of a Power BI for Office 365 subscription is that it allows you to refresh the data stored in Excel workbooks that have been uploaded to a Power BI site on a schedule. What this means is that you can upload a workbook that contains a Power Query query to your Power BI site, and then have it automatically refresh at a set time every day or week. The Power Query query in the workbook, even though it is stored in the cloud in your Power BI site, will be able to connect back to your on-premises data source and execute just the same as it does in Excel on your desktop.

At the time of writing this functionality had just been released and had several limitations. You will also see from the following section that it is relatively complex to set up. However, it is very likely that by the time you read this, many improvements will have been made in this area, limitations will have been lifted, and configuration will be much easier.

Supported Data Sources

The main limitation for Power Query users when publishing an Excel workbook to a Power BI site is that you will only be able to set up scheduled data refresh if your Power Query queries use either SQL Server or Oracle data sources. To a certain extent Power Query queries that use no external data sources and generate all data within the query itself also work, although you do need to include a reference to a SQL Server or Oracle data source in the query even if data from that data source is not actually output from the query. The only way to access other data sources is by using a Linked Server in SQL Server, although it is probable that support for other data sources will be available in the future.

Enabling Scheduled Refresh

These are the steps you must follow to enable scheduled data refresh of an Excel workbook that contains a Power Query query:

- Before you start, ensure that you have a Power BI Data Management Gateway installed on your local server, that it is registered in your Power BI Admin Center, and that it is version 1.1 or greater.

- Create your Power Query query in an Excel workbook on the desktop. Make sure your query only uses a SQL Server or an Oracle data source.

- Save the workbook direct to your Power BI site. If you do not do this and you save it to a regular SharePoint Online document library, you will also have to enable the workbook for Power BI inside the Power BI site—to do this, find your workbook in the Power BI site, click the ellipsis at the bottom right-hand corner, and select Enable, as shown in Figure 7-14.

Figure 7-14. *Enabling a workbook for Power BI*

- Go to the Power BI Admin Center site and to the data sources tab. Click the new data source link, as shown in Figure 7-15, and then click the Power Query option.

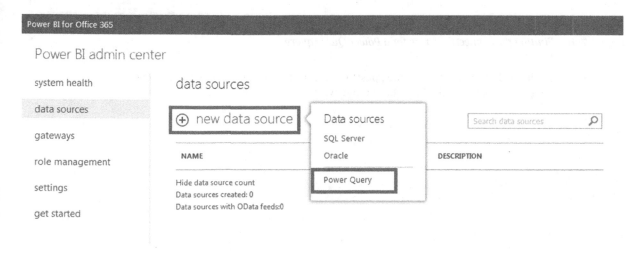

Figure 7-15. *Creating a new data source in the Power BI Admin Center*

- Next, go back to Excel and in the Data tab of the Excel ribbon, click the Connections button. The Workbook Connections dialog will appear, as shown in Figure 7-16, and you will see the connection relating to your Power Query query. Select that connection and click the Properties... button, and the Connection Properties dialog will appear. Go to the Definition tab and copy all of the text in the Connection String box to the clipboard. This is the connection string used by the Power Query query, which you will need to use for your new data source in the Power BI Admin Center.

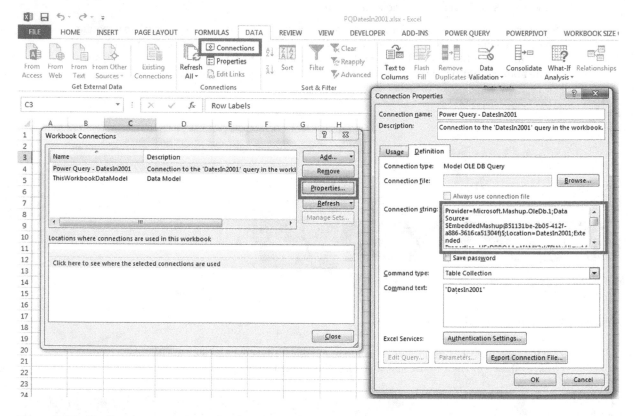

Figure 7-16. *Finding the connection string for a Power Query query*

- Back in the Power BI Admin Center, paste the connection string text into the Connection String box on Step 1 of the New Data Source wizard, as shown in Figure 7-17. Click Next.

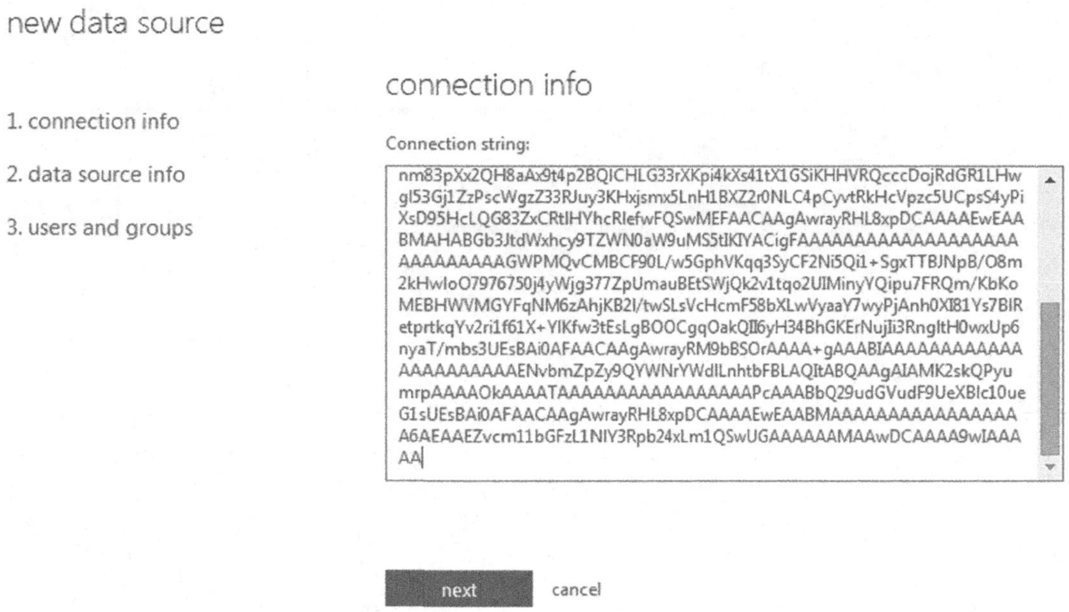

new data source

1. connection info

2. data source info

3. users and groups

connection info

Connection string:

nm83pXx2QH8aAx9t4p2BQICHLG33rXKpi4kXs41tX1GSiKHHVRQcccDojRdGR1LHw
gl53Gj1ZzPscWgzZ33RJuy3KHxjsmx5LnH1BXZ2r0NLC4pCyvtRkHcVpzc5UCpsS4yPi
XsD95HcLQG83ZxCRtIHYhcRIefwFQSwMEFAACAAgAwrayRHL8xpDCAAAAEwEAA
BMAHABGb3JtdWxhcy9TZWN0aW9uMS5tMS5tMS5tMS5tIKIYACigFAAAAAAAAAAAAAAAAAA
AAAAAAAAAGWPMQvCMBCF90L/w5GphVKqq3SyCF2Ni5Qi1+SgxTTBJNpB/O8m
2kHwloO7976750j4yWjg377ZpUmauBEtSWjQk2v1tqo2UIMinyYQipu7FRQm/KbKo
MEBHWVMGYFqNM6zAhjKB2I/twSLsVcHcmF58bXLwVyaaY7wyPjAnh0XI81Ys7BIR
etprtkqYv2ri1f61X+YIKfw3tEsLgBOOCgqOakQIl6yH34BhGKErNujIi3RngItH0wxUp6
nyaT/mbs3UEsBAi0AFAACAAgAwrayRM9bBSOrAAAA+gAAABIAAAAAAAAAAAAA
AAAAAAAAAAENvbmZpZZy9QYWNrYWdlLnhtbFBLAQItABQAAgAIAMK2skQPyu
mrpAAAAOkAAAATAAAAAAAAAAAAAAAAAAPcAAABbQ29udGVudF9UeXBlc10ue
G1sUEsBAi0AFAACAAgAwrayRHL8xpDCAAAAEwEAABMAAAAAAAAAAAAAAAAAA
A6AEAAEZvcm11bGFzL1NIY3Rpb24xLm1QSwUGAAAAAAMAAwDCAAAA9wIAAA
AA

next   cancel

Figure 7-17. *Step One of the New Data Source wizard*

- On Step 2 of the wizard, all of the data sources used by the Power Query connection must be configured. Click the data source and fill in a name and a description, as shown in Figure 7-18. You must also choose the Data Management Gateway you wish to use and select a Privacy level (which is the same thing as the privacy levels discussed in Chapter 6). Clicking the Credentials button will allow you to enter the credentials you wish to use to connect back to the data source. Finally, click the Save button. If your data source has been configured successfully, its status will change to Configured. Click Next.

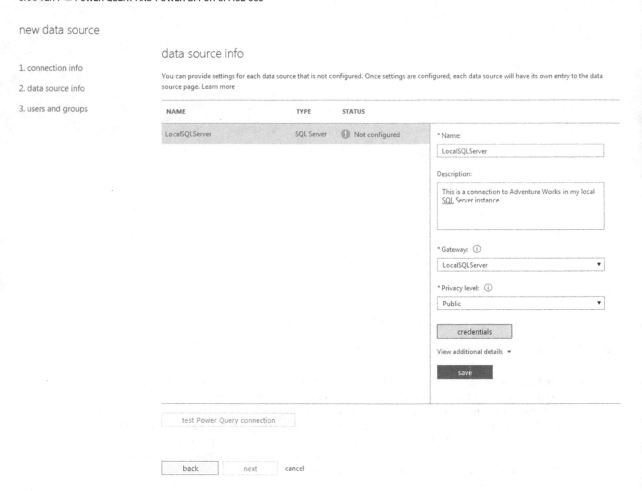

Figure 7-18. *Configuring a Power Query data source*

- On Step 3 of the wizard, add the users who will have access to this data source by clicking the + button shown in Figure 7-19. Click Save to finish the wizard.

Figure 7-19. *Adding users to the data source*

- If everything has been successful, your new data source should be displayed in the Power BI Admin Center and its status should be Ready, as shown in Figure 7-20.

Figure 7-20. *A successfully configured data source in the Power BI Admin Center*

- Now go back to your Power BI site, click the ellipsis at the bottom right-hand corner of the workbook, and select Schedule Data Refresh, as shown in Figure 7-21.

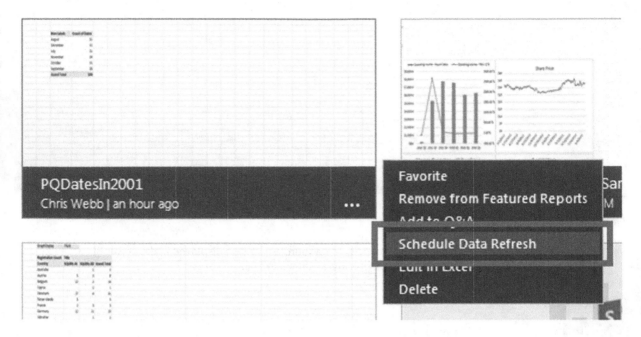

Figure 7-21. *The Schedule Data Refresh option*

- Finally, in the settings tab of the data refresh page, you can set up the refresh schedule for your workbook in the same way that you can for any other workbook, as shown in Figure 7-22. Click either Save and Refresh Report or Save Settings to finish.

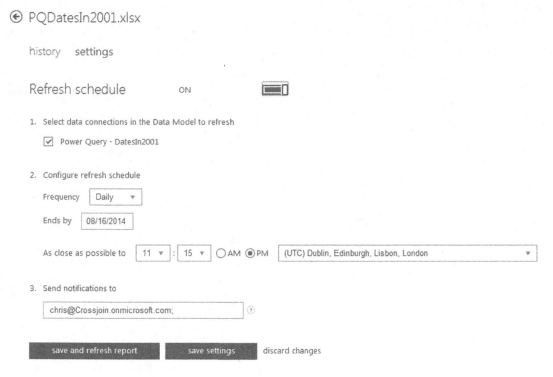

Figure 7-22. *Setting up a refresh schedule for a workbook*

Summary

Sharing queries through the Power BI Data Catalog is a very important feature of Power Query. It allows users to share their work with each other, meaning that there is greater consistency and less duplication of effort, and it allows the Data Steward in an organization to share certified queries so that all users can be sure they are using clean, trustworthy data. Data refresh is equally important but, at the time of writing, less mature. They are the last pieces of Power Query functionality to be introduced in this book: the final chapter, coming next, consists of a series of Power Query worked examples that will help you consolidate your knowledge.

■ ■ ■

CHAPTER 8

Power Query Recipes

You have now learned all about the functionality of Power Query, but when you are learning about a new tool it isn't enough to know what each button does when you press it, or what each function returns when you call it. You also need to know how to solve problems with Power Query. In this final chapter you will see a number of reasonably complex examples that demonstrate how to solve some common problems with Power Query. The purpose of this is twofold: to provide a number of ready-made queries that you can adapt for your own purposes, and to show you how to "think" in Power Query and M. By following a recipe you learn to cook the exact dish that the author set out to describe when he or she wrote the recipe down, and at the same time you are learning cooking skills that will allow you to make up your own recipes later on. The same is true with Power Query.

The layout of this chapter is as follows. There are three main sections covering calculations, table transformations and retrieving data from the web. Each section is then split up into a number of clearly defined problems where you will be shown the input data, the output data, and the steps you need to follow to get from the input to the output. In all cases the examples will attempt to solve the problem using only the functionality exposed in the user interface and with as little custom M code as possible. More elegant solutions may be possible by using more custom code, but that would make the examples much harder to understand!

Calculations

Let's start by seeing how you can implement a number of common types of calculation as custom columns using Power Query.

Percentage Share of Grand Total
Objective

Using the data from the Excel table (called PercentageShareOfTotalInput) shown in Figure 8-1, add a column that shows the sales value for each product as a percentage of the grand total of sales for all the products shown.

Product	Sales
Apples	5
Oranges	7
Pears	8
Grapes	3

Figure 8-1. *Input data for the percentage share of grand total sales calculation*

Steps

1. Click inside the table in the Excel worksheet, then click the From Table button on the Power Query tab in Excel to create a new Power Query query. The Query Editor window will open.

2. Click the Group By button on the Home tab in the Query Editor toolbar to open the Group By dialog. Click the minus button so that no columns are shown in the Group By section. Enter the text **GrandTotal** in the New Column Name box, select Sum in the Operation drop-down box, and select Sales in the Column drop-down box. The dialog should be as shown in Figure 8-2. Click OK to close the dialog.

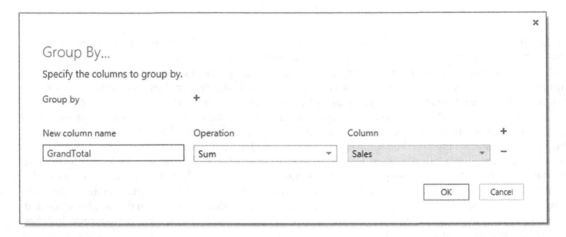

Figure 8-2. Configuration for the Group By dialog

3. The Query Editor will now show a table containing a single column called GrandTotal and a single value, 23, which is the sum of all of the values in the Sales column in the original table. Right-click this value and select Drill Down, as shown in Figure 8-3, and a new step will be created that shows this grand total as just a value and not a value in a table.

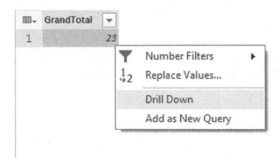

Figure 8-3. Drilling down on the grand total value

4. The output of the previous step will be as shown in Figure 8-4, and this will be the grand total value you need to divide all of the original sales values by to calculate the percentage.

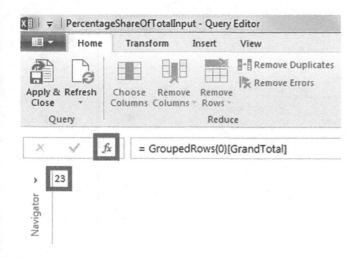

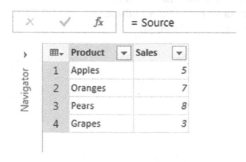

Figure 8-4. *The grand total value shown in the Query Editor*

5. You now need to retrieve the original sales values to perform the calculation. Click the *ƒx* button next to the formula bar (highlighted in Figure 8-4) to create a new step and delete all of the code to the right of the equals sign in the formula bar; replace it with the name of the first step in your query, which should be Source. This means the step will return the original table of data loaded from Excel, as shown in Figure 8-5.

Figure 8-5. *The original source data in a new step*

6. Click the Insert Custom Column button on the Insert tab in the Query Editor toolbar and the Insert Custom Column dialog will appear. Call the new column Share. Double-click the Sales column to add it to the `Custom column formula` box and then divide that value by the GrandTotal value returned by the result of the drilldown. The `Custom column formula` box should contain the following code:

```
[Sales]/GrandTotal
```

The full configuration can be seen in Figure 8-6.

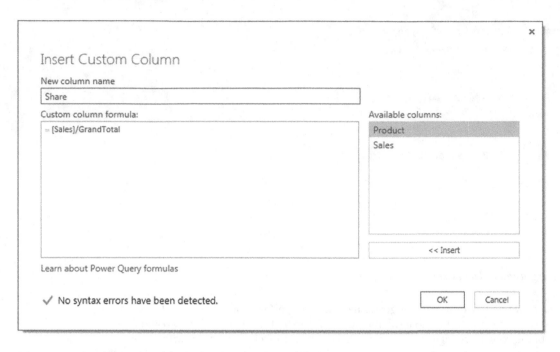

Figure 8-6. Configuration of the Insert Custom Column dialog

7. You will now have a custom column containing the raw percentage values, as shown in Figure 8-7. Remember that you cannot format values as percentages in the Query Editor, so make sure that the Load to Worksheet check box is checked and click the Apply & Close button to close the Query Editor.

▦▾	Product ▾	Sales ▾	Share ▾
1	Apples	5	0.217391
2	Oranges	7	0.304348
3	Pears	8	0.347826
4	Grapes	3	0.130435

Figure 8-7. The raw, unformatted percentage values in the Query Editor

8. In the output table in the workbook you can format the values in the Share column as percentages in the usual way by selecting the column and selecting Format Cells from the right-click menu. The table will be as shown in Figure 8-8.

	A	B	C
1	Product	Sales	Share
2	Apples	5	21.74%
3	Oranges	7	30.43%
4	Pears	8	34.78%
5	Grapes	3	13.04%

Figure 8-8. *The final output table with formatted percentage values*

Code

The M code for the entire query is given in Listing 8-1.

Listing 8-1.

```
let
    //Load data from the Excel worksheet
    Source = Excel.CurrentWorkbook(){[Name="PercentageShareOfTotalInput"]}[Content],
    //Return a table containing the grand total of sales
    GroupedRows = Table.Group(Source, {}, {{"GrandTotal", each List.Sum([Sales]), type number}}),
    //Returns the grand total as a value on its own
    GrandTotal = GroupedRows{0}[GrandTotal],
    //Fetch the original input table
    Custom1 = Source,
    //Insert a custom column to calculate the percentage share
    InsertedCustom = Table.AddColumn(Custom1, "Share", each [Sales]/GrandTotal)
in
    InsertedCustom
```

Percentage Growth in Sales from the Previous Day
Objective

Using the data from the Excel table (called PercentageGrowthPrevDayInput) shown in Figure 8-9, add a column that shows the percentage growth in sales from the previous date.

Date	Sales
01 January 2014	1
02 January 2014	2
03 January 2014	2
04 January 2014	3
05 January 2014	5
06 January 2014	7

Figure 8-9. *Input data for the percentage growth in sales from the previous day calculation*

Steps

1. Click inside the table in the Excel worksheet, then click the From Table button on the Power Query tab in Excel to create a new Power Query query. The Query Editor window will open.

2. Since this data comes from an Excel table, you have to explicitly set the type of the Date column. Select the Date column in the Query Editor, and in the Data Type drop-down menu in the Query Editor toolbar, select Date.

3. Next, create a custom column that contains the date that is the day before the date in the Date column. Click the Insert Custom Column button on the Insert tab in the Query Editor toolbar and the Insert Custom Column dialog will appear. Enter the text **PreviousDate** in the New column name box, and in the Custom column formula box enter the following M expression to subtract a duration value of one day from the date in the Date column:

   ```
   [Date] - #duration(1,0,0,0)
   ```

   The Insert Custom Column dialog should be as shown in Figure 8-10. Click OK to close the dialog.

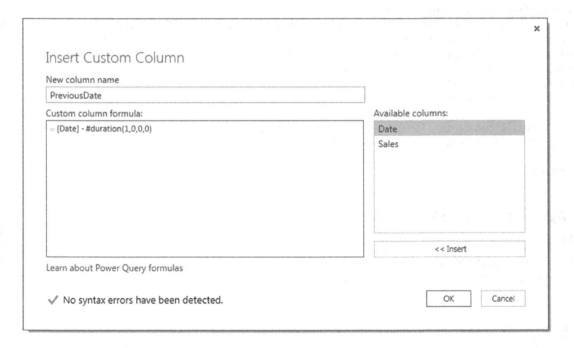

Figure 8-10. *Configuration of the Insert Custom Column dialog to find the previous date*

4. At this point you will have a new column in your original table, as shown in Figure 8-11 (Note that in this screenshot dates are shown in dd/mm/yyyy format).

⊞▾	Date	▾	Sales	▾	PreviousDate	▾
1	01/01/2014		1		31/12/2013	
2	02/01/2014		2		01/01/2014	
3	03/01/2014		2		02/01/2014	
4	04/01/2014		3		03/01/2014	
5	05/01/2014		5		04/01/2014	
6	06/01/2014		7		05/01/2014	

Figure 8-11. *Previous day dates shown in the Query Editor*

5. The next step is to look up the sales associated with the previous day's date and add those to the table. You can do that by merging the table with itself, joining the PreviousDate column to the Date column. Click the Merge Queries button on the Home tab in the Query Editor toolbar and the Merge Queries dialog will appear with the current table selected in the top half. In the drop-down box to select the table to merge with, select the current query again; its name should be something like PercentageGrowthPrevDayInput (Current). In the top table select the PreviousDate table; in the bottom table select the Date column. Leave the `Only include matching rows` box unchecked. The dialog should be as shown in Figure 8-12. Click OK to close the dialog.

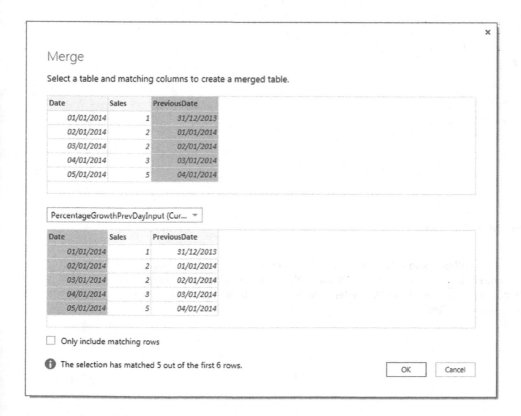

Figure 8-12. *Configuration of the Merge dialog*

195

6. Once you have closed the Merge dialog, the Query Editor will show a new column in the table containing table values, as shown in Figure 8-13.

▦▾	Date	▾	Sales	▾	PreviousDate	▾	NewColumn ᐪᐟᐣ
1	01/01/2014		1		31/12/2013		Table
2	02/01/2014		2		01/01/2014		Table
3	03/01/2014		2		02/01/2014		Table
4	04/01/2014		3		03/01/2014		Table
5	05/01/2014		5		04/01/2014		Table
6	06/01/2014		7		05/01/2014		Table

Figure 8-13. Output of the Merge operation

7. The next thing to do is to expand the column called NewColumn and return the Sales values from it. Click the expand icon in the column header for NewColumn and uncheck everything except the Sales column, as shown in Figure 8-14. Then click OK.

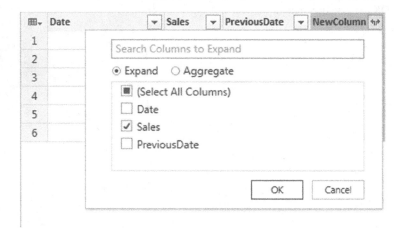

Figure 8-14. Expanding the Sales column

8. The Query Editor will now show the sales for the date shown in the PreviousDate column in a new column called NewColumn.Sales. Rename this column by double-clicking the column header and enter **PreviousDateSales** to be the new column name. The result should be as shown in Figure 8-15.

⊞▾	Date	▾	Sales	▾	PreviousDate	▾	PreviousDateSales	▾
1	02/01/2014		2		01/01/2014		1	
2	03/01/2014		2		02/01/2014		2	
3	04/01/2014		3		03/01/2014		2	
4	05/01/2014		5		04/01/2014		3	
5	06/01/2014		7		05/01/2014		5	
6	01/01/2014		1		31/12/2013		null	

Figure 8-15. *The PreviousDateSales column*

9. You now have two columns that contain the values you need to calculate the percentage growth value. Click the Insert Custom Column button on the Insert tab in the Query Editor toolbar once again. In the Insert Custom Column dialog, name your new column PercentageSalesGrowth and enter the following formula:

```
([Sales] - [PreviousDateSales]) / [PreviousDateSales]
```

The dialog will be as shown in Figure 8-16. Click OK to close.

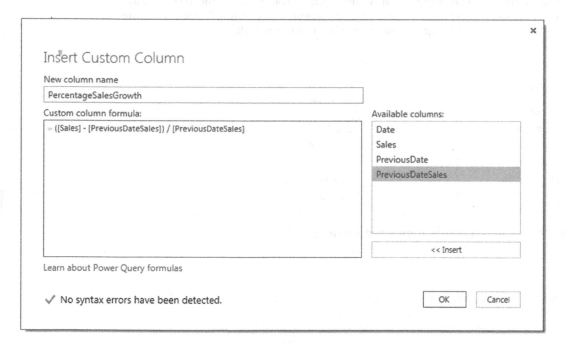

Figure 8-16. *Custom column definition to calculate the percentage growth*

10. At this point you will have the raw percentage sales growth values in a column in your table. You can now select the PreviousDate and PreviousDateSales columns, right-click them, and click Remove Columns to remove them from the table.

11. The table will also no longer be in date order, so select the Date column and click the Sort Ascending button on the Home tab in the Query Editor toolbar to sort the table by date. The table will be as shown in Figure 8-17.

▦▾	Date ▾↑	Sales ▾	PercentageSalesGrowth ▾
1	01/01/2014	1	null
2	02/01/2014	2	1
3	03/01/2014	2	0
4	04/01/2014	3	0.5
5	05/01/2014	5	0.666667
6	06/01/2014	7	0.4

Figure 8-17. *Unformatted percentage sales growth figures shown in the Query Editor*

12. At this point you can click the Apply & Close button to close the Query Editor, making sure that the Load to worksheet box is checked. Finally, in the output table in the Excel worksheet, you can format the values in the PercentageSalesGrowth column as percentages by selecting the column in the worksheet and selecting Format Cells from the right-click menu. The table will then be as shown in Figure 8-18.

◢	A	B	C
1	Date ▾	Sales ▾	PercentageSalesGrowth ▾
2	01 January 2014	1	
3	02 January 2014	2	100.00%
4	03 January 2014	2	0.00%
5	04 January 2014	3	50.00%
6	05 January 2014	5	66.67%
7	06 January 2014	7	40.00%

Figure 8-18. *The final output table with formatted percentage values*

Code

The M code for the entire query is given in Listing 8-2.

Listing 8-2.

```
let
    //Load data from Excel workbook
    Source = Excel.CurrentWorkbook(){[Name="PercentageGrowthPrevDayInput"]}[Content],
    //Set the type of the Date column to be date
    ChangedType = Table.TransformColumnTypes(Source,{{"Date", type date}}),
    //Calculate the date one day before the current date
    InsertedCustom = Table.AddColumn(ChangedType, "PreviousDate", each [Date] - #duration(1,0,0,0)),
```

```
    //Join the table to itself to look up the previous date value
    Merge = Table.NestedJoin(InsertedCustom,{"PreviousDate"},InsertedCustom,{"Date"},"NewColumn"),
    //Expand the Sales column from the joined table
    #"Expand NewColumn" = Table.ExpandTableColumn(Merge,
                            "NewColumn", {"Sales"}, {"NewColumn.Sales"}),
    //Rename the new column to PreviousDateSales
    RenamedColumns = Table.RenameColumns(#"Expand NewColumn",
                            {{"NewColumn.Sales", "PreviousDateSales"}}),
    //Calculate the percentage growth
    InsertedCustom1 = Table.AddColumn(RenamedColumns, "PercentageSalesGrowth",
                        each ([Sales] - [PreviousDateSales]) / [PreviousDateSales]),
    //Remove the PreviousDate and PreviousDateSales columns
    RemovedColumns = Table.RemoveColumns(InsertedCustom1,{"PreviousDate", "PreviousDateSales"}),
    //Sort the table in ascending order by the Date column
    SortedRows = Table.Sort(RemovedColumns,{{"Date", Order.Ascending}})
in
    SortedRows
```

Tied Ranks
Objective

Using the data from the Excel table (called TiedRanksInput) shown in Figure 8-19, add a column that shows the rank of each product by its sales value. The product that has the highest sales value should have the rank 1, and products that have the same sales should have the same rank.

Product	Sales
Apples	10
Oranges	30
Pears	30
Grapes	20
Pineapples	10
Bananas	50

Figure 8-19. Input data for the tied rank calculation

Steps

1. Click inside the table in the Excel worksheet, then click the From Table button on the Power Query tab in Excel to create a new Power Query query. The Query Editor window will open and the first step in the new query will be called Source.

2. Click the *f*x button next to the Formula Bar to add a new step to the query. Delete everything to the right of the equals sign and replace it with the following expression:

```
(SalesValue) =>
  Table.RowCount(
  Table.SelectRows(Source, each [Sales]>SalesValue)
  ) + 1
```

This expression declares a function to calculate the rank that can be called for each row on the original table. It works as follows: it takes a single argument, which is the sales value from the current row, and counts the number of rows in the table that have a sales value greater than the value passed in, then adds one to that number. The function will appear as shown in Figure 8-20.

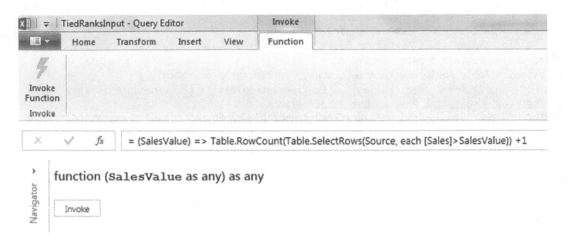

Figure 8-20. *The step containing the function to calculate the rank*

3. At this point the query will have two steps: one to load the data into the query, and one to declare the function. Since the name of the function is the name of the step it is declared in, you should rename that step to be something meaningful. To do this, right-click the name of the second step (which will at this point be called Custom1) in the Applied Steps pane and select Rename from the right-click menu, as shown in Figure 8-21. Rename the step Rank.

◢ APPLIED STEPS

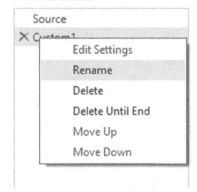

Figure 8-21. *Renaming the step containing the function*

4. Next, you need to click the *f*x button again to add yet another new step to the query. Once again, delete everything to the right of the equals sign and replace it with the name of the first step in the query, which should be called Source. This will create a new step that returns the original input table.

5. Click the Insert Custom Column button on the Insert tab of the Query Editor toolbar and the Insert Custom Column dialog will appear. Call the new custom column Rank and enter the following expression into the `Custom column formula` box to call the function you have just created for the each row:

    `Rank([Sales])`

    The dialog should be as shown in Figure 8-22. Click OK to close the dialog.

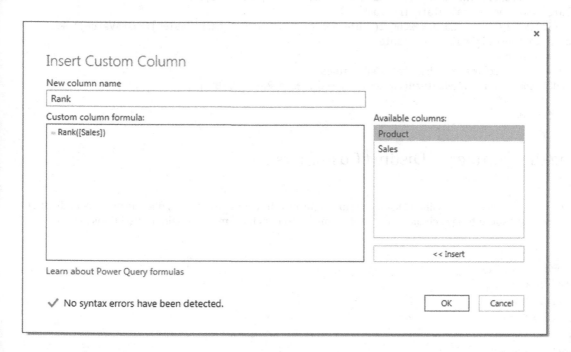

Figure 8-22. *The Insert Custom Column dialog showing a call to the Rank() function*

6. You will now see the ranks calculated correctly for each row in the table. Make sure that the Load to Worksheet box is checked and click the Apply & Close button to close the Query Editor. The output of the query will be as shown in Figure 8-23.

	A	B	C
1	Product	Sales	Rank
2	Apples	10	5
3	Oranges	30	2
4	Pears	30	2
5	Grapes	20	4
6	Pineapples	10	5
7	Bananas	50	1

Figure 8-23. *The final output table showing the rank values*

Code

The M code for the entire query is given in Listing 8-3.

Listing 8-3.

```
let
    //Load data from Excel worksheet
    Source = Excel.CurrentWorkbook(){[Name="TiedRanksInput"]}[Content],
    //Declare function to calculate the rank
    Rank = (SalesValue) => Table.RowCount(Table.SelectRows(Source, each [Sales]>SalesValue)) +1,
    //Go back to the original input table
    Custom1 = Source,
    //Add new custom column to show the rank values
    InsertedCustom = Table.AddColumn(Custom1, "Rank", each Rank([Sales]))
in
    InsertedCustom
```

Counting the Number of Distinct Customers
Objective

Using the data from the Excel table (called DistinctCustomersInput) shown in Figure 8-24, find the number of distinct customers that bought something each day. Notice that some customers have multiple sales transactions per day.

Date	Customer	Sales
01 January 2014	Chris	1
01 January 2014	Helen	2
01 January 2014	Chris	2
01 January 2014	Mimi	4
02 January 2014	Robert	7
02 January 2014	Chris	3
02 January 2014	Mimi	4
02 January 2014	Natasha	2
02 January 2014	Mimi	2
03 January 2014	Helen	6
03 January 2014	Natasha	4
03 January 2014	Natasha	3
03 January 2014	Helen	2
03 January 2014	Robert	4

Figure 8-24. *Input data for the distinct customers calculation*

Steps

1. Click inside the table in the Excel worksheet, then click the From Table button on the Power Query tab in Excel to create a new Power Query query. The Query Editor window will open.

2. Set the data type for the Date column by selecting it in the Query Editor and then, in the Data Type drop-down menu in the Query Editor toolbar, select Date.

3. Select both the Date and the Customer columns in the Query Editor by clicking each of them with the Shift or Control key held down. Next, click the Remove Duplicates button on the Home tab of the Query Editor toolbar, as shown in Figure 8-25.

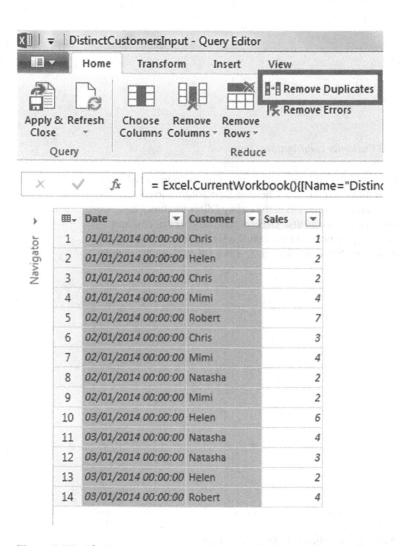

Figure 8-25. *The Remove Duplicates button in the Query Editor toolbar*

4. Once you have clicked the Remove Duplicates button, the table will be filtered so only the first row with each distinct combination of Date and Customer is returned, as shown in Figure 8-26. Notice how the table now has only 10 rows now, rather than 14.

▦▾	Date	▾	Customer	▾	Sales	▾
1	01/01/2014 00:00:00		Chris		1	
2	01/01/2014 00:00:00		Helen		2	
3	01/01/2014 00:00:00		Mimi		4	
4	02/01/2014 00:00:00		Robert		7	
5	02/01/2014 00:00:00		Chris		3	
6	02/01/2014 00:00:00		Mimi		4	
7	02/01/2014 00:00:00		Natasha		2	
8	03/01/2014 00:00:00		Helen		6	
9	03/01/2014 00:00:00		Natasha		4	
10	03/01/2014 00:00:00		Robert		4	

Figure 8-26. *The table with duplicate Date and Customer combinations removed*

5. You can now count the number of rows in the table for each date to find the number of distinct customers who bought something on that date. Click the Date column to select it and then click the Group By button on the Home tab of the Query Editor toolbar. The Group By dialog will appear. Change the text in the New column name box to read **Distinct Customers**, and ensure that in the Group By box the Date column is selected, and that in the Operation box Count Rows is selected, as shown in Figure 8-27. Click OK to close the dialog.

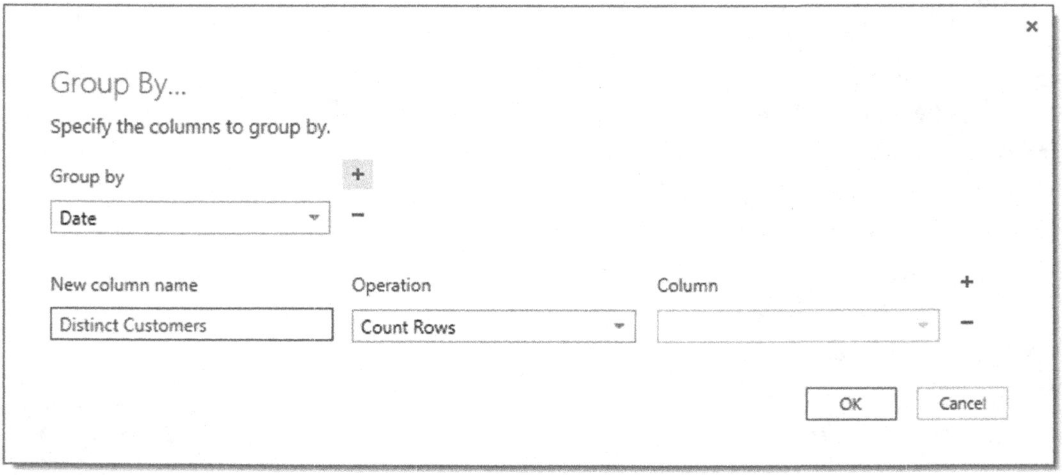

Figure 8-27. *The Group By dialog configured to count the number of rows per date*

6. You now have a table showing the number of distinct customers that bought something for each date. Ensure that the Load to worksheet box is checked and then click the Apply & Close button to close the Query Editor. The output of the query is shown in Figure 8-28.

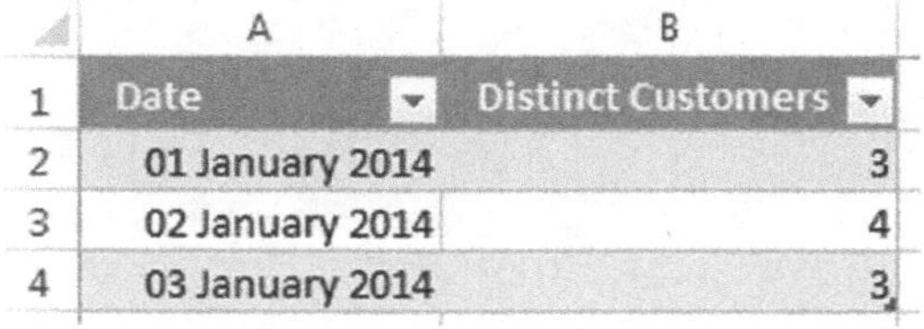

◢	A	B
1	Date ▼	Distinct Customers ▼
2	01 January 2014	3
3	02 January 2014	4
4	03 January 2014	3

Figure 8-28. Output of the distinct customers calculation

Code

The M code for the entire query is given in Listing 8-4.

Listing 8-4.

```
let
    //Load data from the Excel worksheet
    Source = Excel.CurrentWorkbook(){[Name="DistinctCustomersInput"]}[Content],
    //Set the data type of the Date column to date
    ChangedType = Table.TransformColumnTypes(Source,{{"Date", type date}}),
    //Remove all duplicate combinations of Date and Customer
    DuplicatesRemoved = Table.Distinct(ChangedType, {"Date", "Customer"}),
    //Find the count of rows per date
    GroupedRows = Table.Group(DuplicatesRemoved, {"Date"},
                    {{"Distinct Customers", each Table.RowCount(_), type number}})
in
    GroupedRows
```

Table Transformations

In this section you will see a number of examples of queries that perform more complex table transformations.

Converting a Single-Column Table to a Multiple-Column Table
Objective

The table of data shown in Figure 8-29 contains information about customers. Each customer's information is spread over three rows: the first row contains the customer's name, the second row contains the customer's gender, and the third row contains the customer's country.

Data
Chris
Male
UK
Bill
Male
USA
Helen
Female
Australia
Mimi
Female
UK

Figure 8-29. *A single-column table*

The aim in this exercise is to transform this table into one where there is one row for each customer and three columns, one each for the customer's name, gender, and country, as shown in Figure 8-30.

	A	B	C	D
1	RecordNumber	Name	Gender	Country
2	0	Chris	Male	UK
3	1	Bill	Male	USA
4	2	Helen	Female	Australia
5	3	Mimi	Female	UK

Figure 8-30. *A multiple-column table*

Steps

1. Click inside the table in the Excel worksheet, then click the From Table button on the Power Query tab in Excel to create a new Power Query query. The Query Editor window will open.

2. Go to the Insert tab in the Query Editor and click the Insert Index Column button. This will add a row number for each row in the table, starting at zero. The results will be as shown in Figure 8-31.

▦▾	Data	▾	Index	▾
1	Chris			0
2	Male			1
3	UK			2
4	Bill			3
5	Male			4
6	USA			5
7	Helen			6
8	Female			7
9	Australia			8
10	Mimi			9
11	Female			10
12	UK			11

Figure 8-31. *Table with index column added*

3. The next task is to identify the data held on each line. Since the data comes in a repeating pattern of name, gender, and country, you can do this by dividing the index value calculated in the previous step by 3 and finding the remainder (more formally, the modulo). To do this you must click the Insert Custom Column button on the Insert tab of the Query Editor toolbar to create a new custom column, call it RowType, and enter the following expression:

```
Number.Mod([Index],3)
```

4. The previous step returns either the value 0, 1, or 2. Rows with the value 0 contain names, rows with 1 contain genders, and rows with 2 contain countries. Next, you need to convert these numbers into these text values by again clicking the Insert Custom Column button, calling the new column RowTypeText, and entering the following expression:

```
if [RowType]=0 then "Name" else if [RowType]=1 then "Gender" else "Country"
```

The output of this step will be as shown in Figure 8-32.

▦▾	Data ▾	Index ▾	RowType ▾	RowTypeText ▾
1	Chris	0	0	Name
2	Male	1	1	Gender
3	UK	2	2	Country
4	Bill	3	0	Name
5	Male	4	1	Gender
6	USA	5	2	Country
7	Helen	6	0	Name
8	Female	7	1	Gender
9	Australia	8	2	Country
10	Mimi	9	0	Name
11	Female	10	1	Gender
12	UK	11	2	Country

Figure 8-32. Table with row types identified

5. The next thing to do is to identify each customer record. This is necessary because, although it is not true in this case, you may have multiple customers with the same name; if this is true, then later steps will return an error if you try to identify each unique customer by name. You can do this by dividing the index value by 3 and returning the integer part of the result (while discarding the remainder). Click the Insert Custom Column button once again, call the new custom column "CustomerID," then enter the following expression:

```
Number.IntegerDivide([Index], 3)
```

The output will be as in Figure 8-33.

▦▾	Data	▾	Index	▾	RowType	▾	RowTypeText	▾	CustomerID	▾
1	Chris		0		0		Name		0	
2	Male		1		1		Gender		0	
3	UK		2		2		Country		0	
4	Bill		3		0		Name		1	
5	Male		4		1		Gender		1	
6	USA		5		2		Country		1	
7	Helen		6		0		Name		2	
8	Female		7		1		Gender		2	
9	Australia		8		2		Country		2	
10	Mimi		9		0		Name		3	
11	Female		10		1		Gender		3	
12	UK		11		2		Country		3	

Figure 8-33. Table with CustomerID column added

6. You can now remove the columns you have no further use for. Select the Index and RowType columns in the Query Editor window, right-click, and select Remove Columns from the menu.

7. The final step is to pivot the table so that it is in the desired format. Click the *fx* button in the formula bar to add a new step to your query, then enter the following expression for that step (assuming that the previous step was called RemoveColumns) after the equals sign:

```
Table.Pivot(
 RemovedColumns,
 {"Name", "Gender", "Country"},
 "RowTypeText",
 "Data"
)
```

The output will be a pivoted table as shown in Figure 8-34.

▦▾	CustomerID	▾	Name	▾	Gender	▾	Country	▾
1	0		Chris		Male		UK	
2	1		Bill		Male		USA	
3	2		Helen		Female		Australia	
4	3		Mimi		Female		UK	

Figure 8-34. The pivoted table

Code

The M code for the entire query is given in Listing 8-5.

Listing 8-5.

```
let
    //Load data from the Excel worksheet
    Source = Excel.CurrentWorkbook(){[Name="ListData"]}[Content],
    //Add index column
    InsertedIndex = Table.AddIndexColumn(Source,"Index"),
    //Calculate row type as a number
    InsertedCustom = Table.AddColumn(InsertedIndex, "RowType", each Number.Mod([Index],3)),
    //Convert the row type number to a text value
    InsertedCustom1 = Table.AddColumn(InsertedCustom, "RowTypeText",
                        each if [RowType]=0 then "Name"
                        else if [RowType]=1 then "Gender"
                        else "Country"),
    //Identify each customer record
    InsertedCustom2 = Table.AddColumn(InsertedCustom1, "CustomerID",
                        each Number.IntegerDivide([Index], 3)),
    //Remove columns not needed for output
    RemovedColumns = Table.RemoveColumns(InsertedCustom2,{"Index", "RowType"}),
    //Pivot the table
    Custom1 = Table.Pivot(RemovedColumns, {"Name", "Gender", "Country"}, "RowTypeText", "Data")
in
    Custom1
```

Finding New, Lost, and Returning Customers
Objective

The two tables shown in Figure 8-35 contain lists of customers: one is a list of customers that have bought something from a company in the current year, and the other is a list of customers that bought something from the same company in the previous year.

Customers This Year ▼		Customers Last Year ▼
Chris		Chris
Natasha		Helen
Helen		Mimi
Louisa		Robert
Victoria		Barbara
Robert		

Figure 8-35. *Two tables containing lists of customers to compare*

The objective here is to divide the customers into three groups: those that bought something this year and last year (returning customers), those that bought something last year but not this year (lost customers), and those that bought something this year but not last year (new customers).

Steps

1. For both tables, click inside the table in the Excel worksheet, then click the From Table button on the Power Query tab in Excel to create a new Power Query query. The two queries should be called ThisYearCustomers and LastYearCustomers.

2. Then, in the Power Query tab on the Excel ribbon, click the Append button and select these two queries in the drop-down boxes, as shown in Figure 8-36, then click OK.

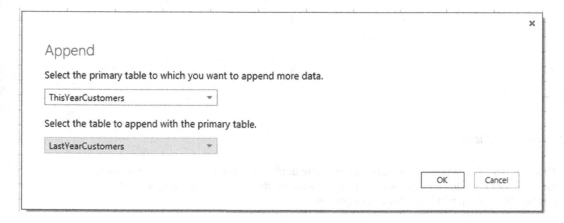

Figure 8-36. Appending one table of customers to another

3. A new query will be created and the Query Editor will open. Call the new query Customers. The query will show the result of the append operation, as shown in Figure 8-37.

▦▾	Customers This Year ▾	Customers Last Year ▾
1	Chris	*null*
2	Natasha	*null*
3	Helen	*null*
4	Louisa	*null*
5	Victoria	*null*
6	Robert	*null*
7	*null*	Chris
8	*null*	Helen
9	*null*	Mimi
10	*null*	Robert
11	*null*	Barbara

Figure 8-37. Output of the append operation

4. The next thing to do is to turn this table into a single list of customers. Select both columns in the table in the Query Editor, then right-click and select Merge Columns from the right-click menu. Leave the drop-down box containing the separator value at the default of None, and then click OK. The output will be as shown in Figure 8-38.

	Merged
1	Chris
2	Natasha
3	Helen
4	Louisa
5	Victoria
6	Robert
7	Chris
8	Helen
9	Mimi
10	Robert
11	Barbara

Figure 8-38. *A merged table of customers*

5. This merged table of customers still contains some duplicated customer names. To remove these duplicates, click the Remove Duplicates button on the Home tab in the Query Editor toolbar. The output will be as shown in Figure 8-39.

	Merged
1	Chris
2	Natasha
3	Helen
4	Louisa
5	Victoria
6	Robert
7	Mimi
8	Barbara

Figure 8-39. *A table containing distinct customers*

6. Rename the column in your table from Merged to Customer by double-clicking the column header and entering the new name.

7. Now that you have a complete list of customers, you need to find which of them appear in the list of this year's customers. To do this you can merge the current query with the query called ThisYearCustomers. Click the Merge Queries button on the Home tab in the Query Editor toolbar and select ThisYearCustomers in the drop-down box of the Merge dialog, select the Customer column and the CustomersThisYear column as shown in Figure 8-40, then click OK.

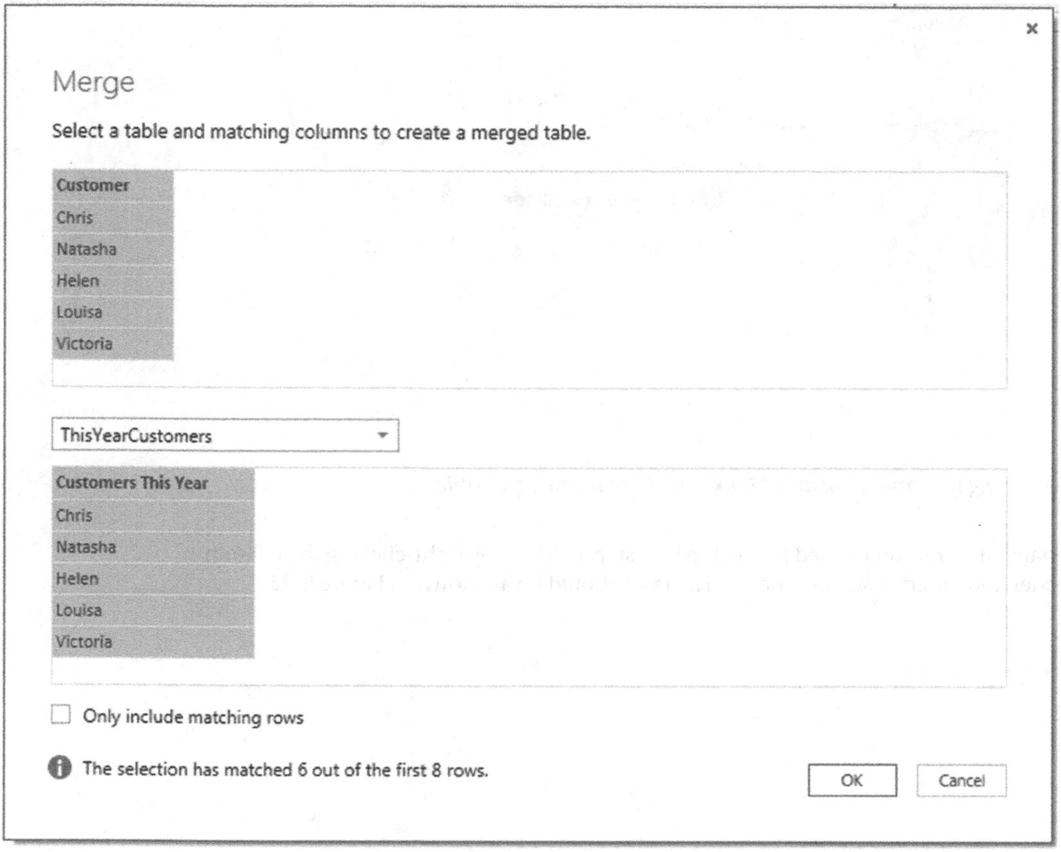

Figure 8-40. *Merging the complete list of customers with this year's customers*

8. The previous step adds a new column to the table containing the merged rows from the CustomersThisYear query. Click the Expand icon in the new column, select the Aggregate radio button, and then click the drop-down box next to the column name to select the Count (Not Blank) option, as shown in Figure 8-41. Click OK. This will replace the new column with a column containing the number of rows in CustomersThisYear that matched the current row—that is, it will contain the value 1 when the customer bought something in the current year and 0 if the customer did not buy anything.

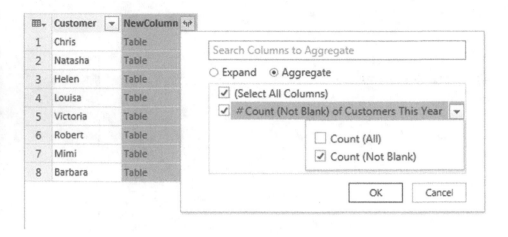

Figure 8-41. *Returning the number of non-blank rows from the merged table*

9. Rename the column created in the previous step ThisYear by right-clicking the column header and entering the new name. The table should be as shown in Figure 8-42.

⊞▾	Customer ▾	ThisYear ▾
1	Chris	1
2	Natasha	1
3	Helen	1
4	Louisa	1
5	Victoria	1
6	Robert	1
7	Mimi	0
8	Barbara	0

Figure 8-42. *The ThisYear column*

10. Repeat steps 7 to 9, but use the LastYearCustomer query and call the new column created LastYear. The output should be as shown in Figure 8-43.

⊞▾	Customer ▾	ThisYear ▾	LastYear ▾
1	Chris	1	1
2	Natasha	1	0
3	Helen	1	1
4	Louisa	1	0
5	Robert	1	1
6	Victoria	1	0
7	Mimi	0	1
8	Barbara	0	1

Figure 8-43. *The LastYear column*

11. You now have columns telling you whether each customer bought something in the current year and in the previous year. To classify each customer, click the Insert Custom Column button on the Insert tab in the Query Editor toolbar, call the new column Classification, and enter the following expression, as shown in Figure 8-44:

```
if [ThisYear]=1 and [LastYear]=1 then "Returning"
else if [ThisYear]=1 and [LastYear]=0 then "New"
else "Lost"
```

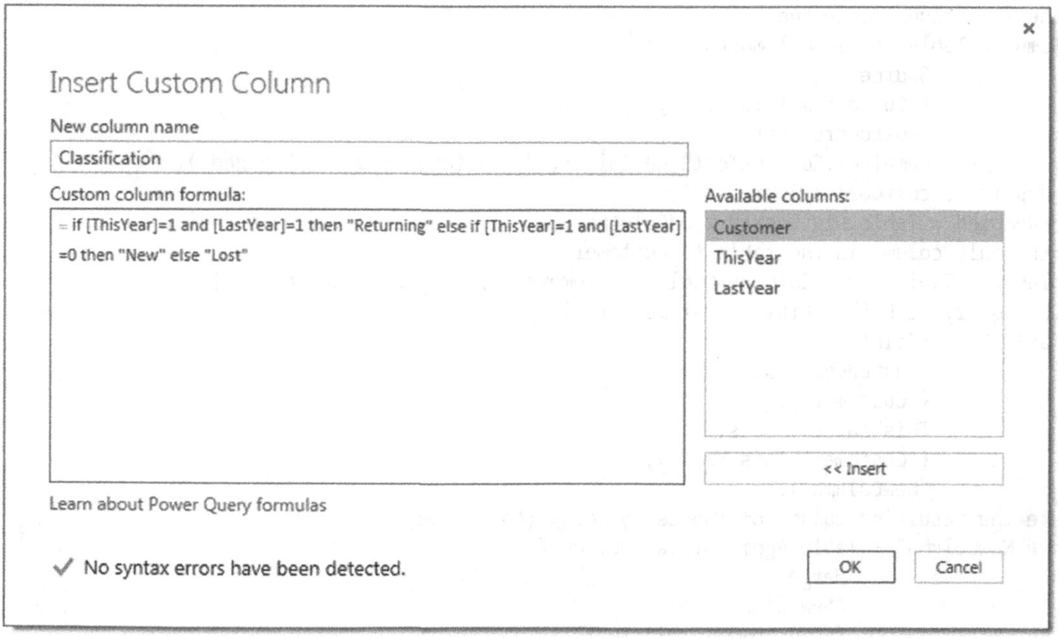

Figure 8-44. *Custom column expression to classify customers*

12. Finally, select the ThisYear and LastYear columns, right-click, and select Remove Columns. The final output of the query should be as shown in Figure 8-45.

▦▾	Customer	▾	Classification	▾
1	Chris		Returning	
2	Natasha		New	
3	Helen		Returning	
4	Louisa		New	
5	Robert		Returning	
6	Victoria		New	
7	Mimi		Lost	
8	Barbara		Lost	

Figure 8-45. *The final output of the query*

Code

The M code for the entire query is given in Listing 8-6.

Listing 8-6.

```
let
    //Append the LastYearCustomers table to the ThisYearCustomers table
    Source = Table.Combine({ThisYearCustomers,LastYearCustomers}),
    //Merge the two columns into one
    MergedColumns = Table.CombineColumns(
                    Source,
                    {"Customers This Year",
                    "Customers Last Year"},
                    Combiner.CombineTextByDelimiter("", QuoteStyle.None),"Merged"),
    //Remove duplicate customers
    DuplicatesRemoved = Table.Distinct(MergedColumns),
    //Rename the only column in the table to Customer
    RenamedColumns = Table.RenameColumns(DuplicatesRemoved,{{"Merged", "Customer"}}),
    //Merge this query with the ThisYearCustomers table
    Merge = Table.NestedJoin(
                    RenamedColumns,
                    {"Customer"},
                    ThisYearCustomers,
                    {"Customers This Year"},
                    "NewColumn"),
    //Aggregate the resulting column of tables by Count (Not Blank)
    #"Aggregate NewColumn" = Table.AggregateTableColumn(
                        Merge,
                        "NewColumn",
                        {{"Customers This Year",
                        List.NonNullCount,
                        "Count (Not Blank) of NewColumn.Customers This Year"}}),
```

```
    //Rename the new column to ThisYear
    RenamedColumns1 = Table.RenameColumns(
                        #"Aggregate NewColumn",
                        {{"Count (Not Blank) of NewColumn.Customers This Year",
                        "ThisYear"}}),
    //Merge this query with the LastYearCustomers table
    Merge1 = Table.NestedJoin(
                    RenamedColumns1,
                    {"Customer"},
                    LastYearCustomers,
                    {"Customers Last Year"},
                    "NewColumn"),
    //Aggregate the resulting column of tables by Count (Not Blank)
    #"Aggregate NewColumn1" = Table.AggregateTableColumn(
                        Merge1,
                        "NewColumn",
                        {{"Customers Last Year",
                        List.NonNullCount,
                        "Count (Not Blank) of NewColumn.Customers Last Year"}}),
    //Rename the new column to LastYear
    RenamedColumns2 = Table.RenameColumns(
                        #"Aggregate NewColumn1",
                        {{"Count (Not Blank) of NewColumn.Customers Last Year",
                        "LastYear"}}),
    //Use the ThisYear and LastYear columns to classify each customer
    InsertedCustom = Table.AddColumn(
                        RenamedColumns2,
                        "Classification",
                        each
                        if [ThisYear]=1 and [LastYear]=1 then "Returning"
                        else if [ThisYear]=1 and [LastYear]=0 then "New"
                        else "Lost"),
    //Remove unwanted columns
    RemovedColumns = Table.RemoveColumns(InsertedCustom,{"ThisYear", "LastYear"})
in
    RemovedColumns
```

Generating a Date Table
Objective

When you are building models with Power Pivot and the Excel Data Model, you will almost certainly need a Date table—a table where each row contains a date, with columns containing values derived from each date such as the day name, month, and year. Although many data sources contain a pre-built Date table, the objective of this section is to dynamically generate a Date table in Power Query.

Steps

1. Unlike all of the previous recipes in this chapter, this query has no external data source—all of the data that the query returns is generated in the table itself. Therefore, to create a new query you need to click the Blank Query button on the From Other Sources drop-down on the Power Query tab in the Excel ribbon.

2. Once you have done this, the Query Editor will open with your new query. In the Formula Bar, enter the following expression for the first step of the new query:

   `= List.Dates(#date(2014,1,1), 365, #duration(1,0,0,0) )`

   This expression uses the `List.Dates()` function to return a list of 365 dates starting from January 1, 2014, at increments of one day. The output will be as shown in Figure 8-46.

Figure 8-46. *Output of the* `List.Dates()` *function*

3. Click the To Table button on the List tab in the Query Editor toolbar (also shown in Figure 8-46) to convert the list to a table. In the To Table dialog that appears, leave the default selections of None for the delimiter and Show as errors for How to handle extra columns, as shown in Figure 8-47. Click OK.

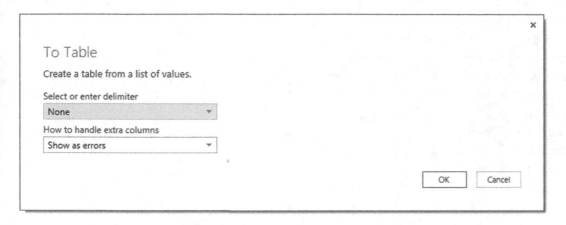

Figure 8-47. *The To Table dialog*

4. Rename the column in the resulting table Date.

5. Select the Date column in the table and then, in the Data Type drop-down box at the top of the Home tab in the Query Editor toolbar, select Date to convert the data in this column to the data type Date.

6. Select the Date column again, then right-click and select Duplicate Column to create a copy of the Date column. Double-click the header of the new column and rename it Year.

7. Right-click the Year column, then select Transform ➤ Year, as shown in Figure 8-48, to replace the date values in that column with just the years.

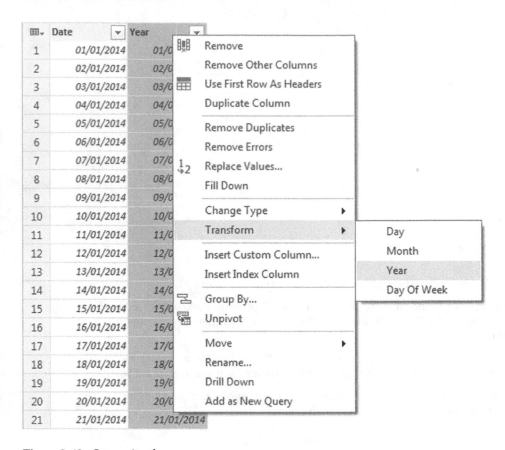

Figure 8-48. *Converting dates to years*

8. Click the Insert Custom Column button on the Insert tab of the Query Editor toolbar. Call the new column Month and enter the following expression into the formula text box, as shown in Figure 8-49:

```
Date.ToText([Date], "MMMM")
```

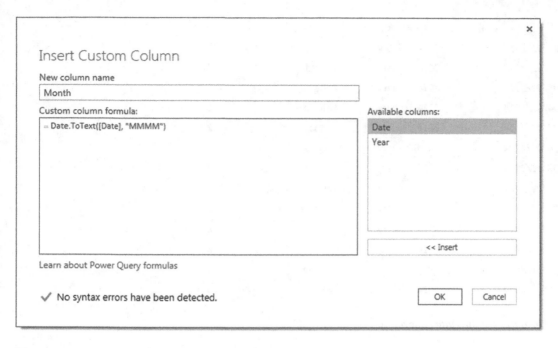

Figure 8-49. *A custom column expression to return the month name*

9. Click the Insert Custom Column button again to create another new column. Call the column DayName and use the following expression:

```
Date.ToText([Date], "DDDD")
```

10. Click the Insert Custom Column button again to create another new column. Call the column Week and use the following expression:

```
Date.WeekOfYear([Date])
```

11. The final output of the query will be as shown in Figure 8-50.

⊞▾	Date ▾	Year ▾	Month ▾	DayName ▾	Week ▾
1	01/01/2014	2014	January	Wednesday	1
2	02/01/2014	2014	January	Thursday	1
3	03/01/2014	2014	January	Friday	1
4	04/01/2014	2014	January	Saturday	1
5	05/01/2014	2014	January	Sunday	2
6	06/01/2014	2014	January	Monday	2
7	07/01/2014	2014	January	Tuesday	2
8	08/01/2014	2014	January	Wednesday	2
9	09/01/2014	2014	January	Thursday	2
10	10/01/2014	2014	January	Friday	2
11	11/01/2014	2014	January	Saturday	2
12	12/01/2014	2014	January	Sunday	3
13	13/01/2014	2014	January	Monday	3

Figure 8-50. *The output of the Date table query*

Code

The M code for the entire query is given in Listing 8-7.

Listing 8-7.

```
let
    //Create a list of 365 dates starting from January 1st 2014
    Source = List.Dates(#date(2014,1,1), 365, #duration(1,0,0,0) ),
    //Turn the list into a table
    TableFromList = Table.FromList(
                        Source,
                        Splitter.SplitByNothing(),
                        null,
                        null,
                        ExtraValues.Error),
    //Rename the only column in the table to Date
    RenamedColumns = Table.RenameColumns(TableFromList,{{"Column1", "Date"}}),
    //Change the type of the column to Date
    ChangedType = Table.TransformColumnTypes(RenamedColumns,{{"Date", type date}}),
    //Duplicate the Date column
    DuplicatedColumn = Table.DuplicateColumn(ChangedType, "Date", "Copy of Date"),
    //Rename the duplicated column to Year
    RenamedColumns1 = Table.RenameColumns(DuplicatedColumn,{{"Copy of Date", "Year"}}),
    //Convert the dates in the Year column to years
    TransformedColumn = Table.TransformColumns(RenamedColumns1,{{"Year", Date.Year}}),
    //Add a custom column containing month names
    InsertedCustom = Table.AddColumn(TransformedColumn, "Month", each Date.ToText([Date], "MMMM")),
    //Add a custom column containing day names
```

```
    InsertedCustom1 = Table.AddColumn(InsertedCustom, "DayName", each Date.ToText([Date], "dddd")),
    //Add a custom column containing week numbers
    InsertedCustom2 = Table.AddColumn(InsertedCustom1, "Week", each Date.WeekOfYear([Date]))
in
    InsertedCustom2
```

This query can be turned into a function with two parameters, start date and end date, so that you can generate a table containing all of the dates between the start date and the end date. Listing 8-8 shows an example of this.

Listing 8-8.

```
let
    DateFunction = (StartDate as date, EndDate as date) as table =>
let
    //Find the number of dates between the start date and end date
    NumberOfDays = Duration.Days(EndDate-StartDate)+1,
    //Create a list of dates starting from the start date
    Source = List.Dates(StartDate, NumberOfDays, #duration(1,0,0,0) ),
    //Turn the list into a table
    TableFromList = Table.FromList(
                        Source,
                        Splitter.SplitByNothing(),
                        null,
                        null,
                        ExtraValues.Error),
    //Rename the only column in the table to Date
    RenamedColumns = Table.RenameColumns(TableFromList,{{"Column1", "Date"}}),
    //Change the type of the column to Date
    ChangedType = Table.TransformColumnTypes(RenamedColumns,{{"Date", type date}}),
    //Duplicate the Date column
    DuplicatedColumn = Table.DuplicateColumn(ChangedType, "Date", "Copy of Date"),
    //Rename the duplicated column to Year
    RenamedColumns1 = Table.RenameColumns(DuplicatedColumn,{{"Copy of Date", "Year"}}),
    //Convert the dates in the Year column to years
    TransformedColumn = Table.TransformColumns(RenamedColumns1,{{"Year", Date.Year}}),
    //Add a custom column containing month names
    InsertedCustom = Table.AddColumn(TransformedColumn, "Month", each Date.ToText([Date], "MMMM")),
    //Add a custom column containing day names
    InsertedCustom1 = Table.AddColumn(InsertedCustom, "DayName", each Date.ToText([Date], "dddd")),
    //Add a custom column containing week numbers
    InsertedCustom2 = Table.AddColumn(InsertedCustom1, "Week", each Date.WeekOfYear([Date]))
in
    InsertedCustom2
in
    DateFunction
```

How Long Was a Stock Price Above a Given Value?
Objective

Figure 8-51 shows a table containing the stock price of a company at one-minute intervals over the course of an hour.

Time	Stock Price
09:00	50.01
09:01	48.36
09:02	49.01
09:03	49.02
09:04	49.01
09:05	49.54
09:06	49.9
09:07	50.01
09:08	50.11
09:09	50.12
09:10	50.13
09:11	50.09
09:12	50.02
09:13	49.99
09:14	49.98
09:15	49.56
09:16	49.88
09:17	49.75
09:18	49.74
09:19	49.73

Figure 8-51. *Stock price data*

As you can see from this data the price hovers around $50. The objective for this query is to find out the maximum length of time in minutes that the price was greater than or equal to $50 in this period.

Steps

1. Click inside the table in the Excel worksheet, then click the From Table button on the Power Query tab in Excel to create a new Power Query query. The Query Editor window will open.

2. Select the Time column, and in the Data Type drop-down box on the Home tab of the Query Editor toolbar, set the data type for this column to be Time. Then select the Stock Price column and set the data type for this column to be Number.

3. Next, click the Insert Custom Column button to add a new custom column to your table. Call the new column Above50 and use the following expression for it:

```
[Stock Price]>=50
```

The output should be as shown in Figure 8-52 – the new column returns the value TRUE when the stock price is greater than or equal to 50, and FALSE otherwise.

	Time	Stock Price	Above50
1	09:00:00	50.01	TRUE
2	09:01:00	48.36	FALSE
3	09:02:00	49.01	FALSE
4	09:03:00	49.02	FALSE
5	09:04:00	49.01	FALSE
6	09:05:00	49.54	FALSE
7	09:06:00	49.9	FALSE
8	09:07:00	50.01	TRUE
9	09:08:00	50.11	TRUE
10	09:09:00	50.12	TRUE
11	09:10:00	50.13	TRUE
12	09:11:00	50.09	TRUE
13	09:12:00	50.02	TRUE
14	09:13:00	49.99	FALSE
15	09:14:00	49.98	FALSE
16	09:15:00	49.56	FALSE
17	09:16:00	49.88	FALSE
18	09:17:00	49.75	FALSE

Figure 8-52. *Custom Column showing whether the stock price is greater than or equal to $50*

4. Select the Above50 column and click the Group By button on the Home tab of the Query Editor toolbar. When the Group By dialog appears, make sure that Above50 is the only column selected in the Group By drop-down box, then create three aggregate columns (you will need to click the + button on the right-hand side of the dialog to add the second and third columns): one to find the minimum value of the Time column, called Start; one to find the maximum value of the Time column, called EndTemp; and one to count the number of rows in the table, called Minutes. The dialog should be configured as in Figure 8-53.

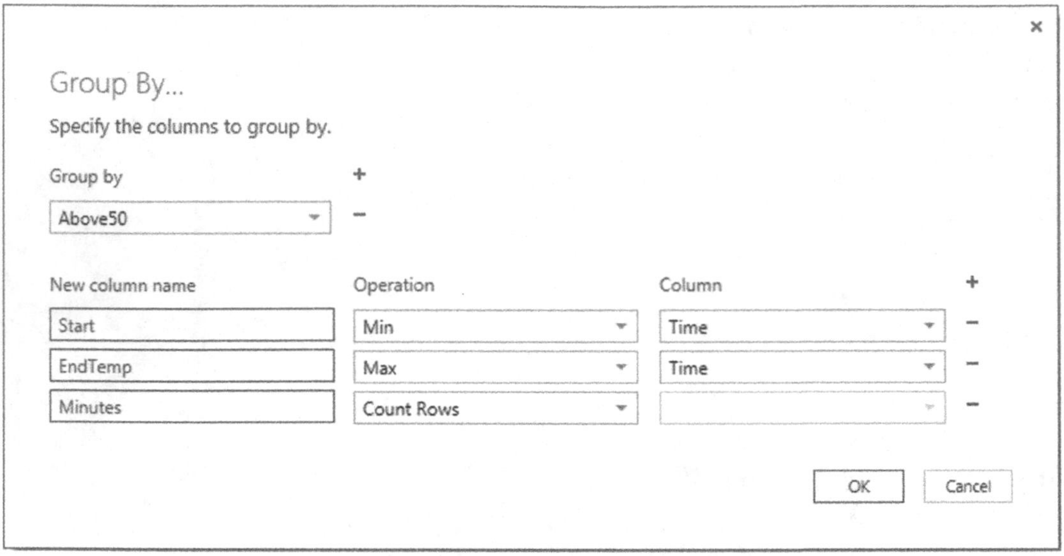

Figure 8-53. *The Group By dialog*

5. When you click OK to close the Group By dialog, you will see the table has been aggregated so that there are only two rows in the output: one for the time periods where the stock price was greater than or equal to 50, and one where it was not. This isn't exactly what you need, though. What you actually want is to find *all* of the time ranges where the stock price was greater than or equal to 50, and to do this you need to perform a local grouping by adding GroupKind.Local as the fourth parameter of the Table.Group() function. To make this change, go to the formula bar and change the code for the current step from this:

```
Table.Group(
InsertedCustom,
{"Above50"},
{{"Start", each List.Min([Time]), type time},
{"EndTemp", each List.Max([Time]), type time},
{"Minutes", each Table.RowCount(_), type number}})
```

to this:

```
Table.Group(
InsertedCustom,
{"Above50"},
{{"Start", each List.Min([Time]), type time},
{"EndTemp", each List.Max([Time]), type time},
{"Minutes", each Table.RowCount(_), type number}},
GroupKind.Local)
```

The output should now be as shown in Figure 8-54.

⊞▾	Above50 ▾	Start ▾	EndTemp ▾	Minutes ▾
1	TRUE	09:00:00	09:00:00	1
2	FALSE	09:01:00	09:06:00	6
3	TRUE	09:07:00	09:12:00	6
4	FALSE	09:13:00	09:34:00	22
5	TRUE	09:35:00	09:36:00	2
6	FALSE	09:37:00	09:38:00	2
7	TRUE	09:39:00	09:42:00	4
8	FALSE	09:43:00	09:44:00	2
9	TRUE	09:45:00	09:48:00	4
10	FALSE	09:49:00	09:54:00	6
11	TRUE	09:55:00	09:55:00	1
12	FALSE	09:56:00	09:59:00	4

Figure 8-54. *Local grouping showing time ranges when stock price was either greater than or equal to, or less than, $50*

6. The times in the EndTemp column are slightly misleading in that they represent the last minute in the time range; to avoid confusion you need to add one minute to these values so that the end of one time range is the same as the beginning of the next one. To do this, click the Insert Custom Column button to create a new custom column, call it End, and use the following expression:

```
[EndTemp] + #duration(0,0,1,0)
```

7. Select the EndTemp column, right-click, and select Remove from the right-click menu to remove the EndTemp column from the table.

8. Select the End column in the Query Editor and drag it in between the Start and Minutes column. The output will be as shown in Figure 8-55.

▦▾	Above50 ▾	Start ▾	End ▾	Minutes ▾
1	TRUE	09:00:00	09:01:00	1
2	FALSE	09:01:00	09:07:00	6
3	TRUE	09:07:00	09:13:00	6
4	FALSE	09:13:00	09:35:00	22
5	TRUE	09:35:00	09:37:00	2
6	FALSE	09:37:00	09:39:00	2
7	TRUE	09:39:00	09:43:00	4
8	FALSE	09:43:00	09:45:00	2
9	TRUE	09:45:00	09:49:00	4
10	FALSE	09:49:00	09:55:00	6
11	TRUE	09:55:00	09:56:00	1
12	FALSE	09:56:00	10:00:00	4

Figure 8-55. *The table with correct End times for time ranges*

9. Since you are only interested in the time ranges when the price was greater than or equal to $50, you can now filter the table so that you only see rows where the Above50 column contains the value TRUE. You can do this by clicking the down arrow button in the column header for the Above50 column and unchecking the FALSE value, then clicking OK, as shown in Figure 8-56.

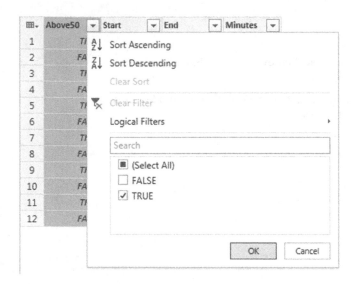

Figure 8-56. *Filtering the Above50 column*

10. Next, sort the table by the Minutes column in descending order by selecting that column and clicking the down arrow in that column's header, then clicking Sort Descending, as shown in Figure 8-57.

Figure 8-57. Sorting by Minutes in descending order

11. Finally, to return only the longest time range (i.e., the time range with the largest value in the Minutes column), click the Remove Rows drop-down on the Home tab in the Query Editor toolbar and select Keep Top Rows. When the Keep Top Rows dialog appears, enter the value **1** in the Number of rows box as shown in Figure 8-58 and click OK.

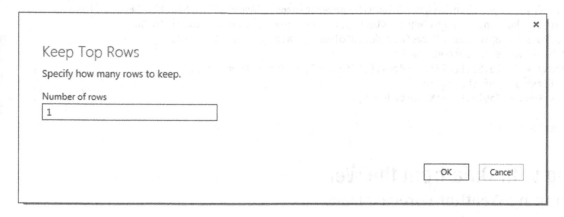

Figure 8-58. The Keep Top Rows dialog

12. The final output of the query will be as shown in Figure 8-59.

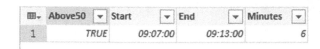

⊞▾	Above50 ▾	Start ▾	End ▾	Minutes ▾
1	TRUE	09:07:00	09:13:00	6

Figure 8-59. Final output of the query

Code

The M code for the entire query is given in Listing 8-9.

Listing 8-9.

```
let
    //Load data from Excel
    Source = Excel.CurrentWorkbook(){[Name="StockPrice"]}[Content],
    //Set column data types
    ChangedType = Table.TransformColumnTypes(
                    Source,
                    {{"Time", type time},
                    {"Stock Price", type number}}),
    //Is Stock Price greater than or equal to 50?
    InsertedCustom = Table.AddColumn(ChangedType, "Above50", each [Stock Price]>=50),
    //Aggregate time ranges
    GroupedRows = Table.Group(
                    InsertedCustom,
                    {"Above50"},
                    {{"Start", each List.Min([Time]), type time},
                    {"EndTemp", each List.Max([Time]), type time},
                    {"Minutes", each Table.RowCount(_), type number}},GroupKind.Local),
    //Add one minute to the values in the EndTemp column
    InsertedCustom1 = Table.AddColumn(GroupedRows, "End", each [EndTemp] + #duration(0,0,1,0)),
    //Remove the EndTemp column
    RemovedColumns = Table.RemoveColumns(InsertedCustom1,{"EndTemp"}),
    //Move the End column in between Start and Minutes
    ReorderedColumns = Table.ReorderColumns(RemovedColumns,{"Above50", "Start", "End", "Minutes"}),
    //Filter to show only ranges where stock price is greater than or equal to 50
    FilteredRows = Table.SelectRows(ReorderedColumns, each ([Above50] = true)),
    //Sort by Minutes in descending order
    SortedRows = Table.Sort(FilteredRows,{{"Minutes", Order.Descending}}),
    //Keep first row of the table
    KeptFirstRows = Table.FirstN(SortedRows,1)
in
    KeptFirstRows
```

Working with Data from the Web
Web-Scraping Weather Forecast Data
Objective

Figure 8-60 shows an Excel table containing a list of some of the royal palaces in the United Kingdom along with their post codes (a post code in the UK is like a zip code in the United States—it identifies a small number of addresses in the same geographic area).

Palace	Postcode
Buckingham Palace	SW1A 1AA
Windsor Castle	SL4 1NJ
Sandringham	PE35 6EH
Holyrood Palace	EH8 8DX

Figure 8-60. *A table containing palaces and their post codes*

You can look up the weather for any post code in the UK on the BBC's weather web site. For example, the weather for the post code HP6 6HF can be found by typing that post code into the Find a Forecast box at www.bbc.co.uk/weather/; the output is as shown in Figure 8-61.

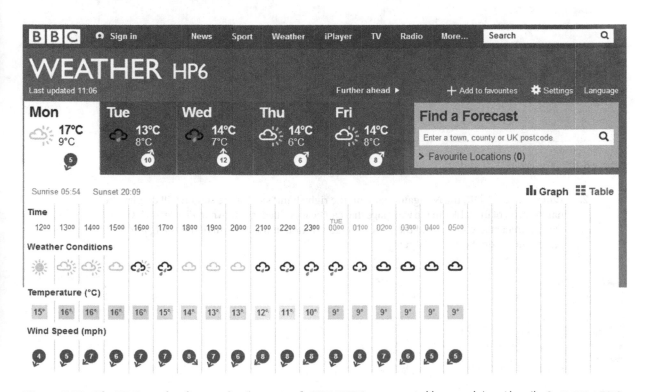

Figure 8-61. *The BBC weather forecast for the post code HP6 6HF Source - www.bbc.co.uk/weather/hp6 - © 2014 BBC*

The URL for this page contains the first part of the post code, before the space, for example www.bbc.co.uk/weather/hp6. The characters after the last slash represent the post code area.

The objective of this exercise is to scrape the weather forecast for all of the palaces shown in Figure 8-60 and combine them into a single table.

■ **Note**   If the format of the web page or the URLs used in this section changes in the future then the query in this section may no longer work.

Steps

1. This exercise will require the creation of two Power Query queries. The first query will be a function that can be used to scrape the weather forecast data from the web page shown in Figure 8-61. Click the From Web button in the Power Query tab in the Excel ribbon and enter the URL http://www.bbc.co.uk/weather/hp6 in the From Web dialog, as shown in Figure 8-62.

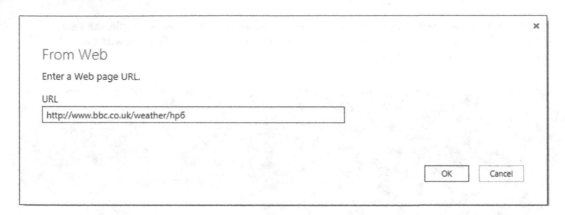

Figure 8-62. *The From Web dialog*

2. When you click OK, the Navigator pane on the right-hand side of the screen will display the names of all of the tables in the web page that can be identified, as shown in Figure 8-63. Click Daily Forecast to select it and then click the Edit button at the bottom of the Navigator pane. The Query Editor will open.

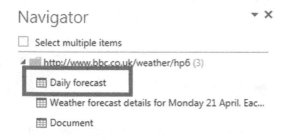

Figure 8-63. *Tables on a web page*

3. When the Query Editor opens, it will display the forecast for the next five days for the HP6 post code area, as shown in Figure 8-64.

⊞▾	Day	▾	Weather	▾	Maximum Day Temperat...	▾	Minimum Night Temperatu...	▾	Wind Direction and Speed	▾
1	Monday		Light Cloud		17°C 63°F		9°C 48°F		North North Easterly 8km/h 5mph	
2	Tuesday		Light Rain		13°C 55°F		7°C 45°F		South South Westerly 16km/h 10mph	
3	Wednesday		Light Rain		14°C 57°F		7°C 45°F		Southerly 19km/h 12mph	
4	Thursday		Sunny Intervals		14°C 57°F		6°C 43°F		West South Westerly 10km/h 6mph	
5	Friday		Sunny Intervals		14°C 57°F		7°C 45°F		South South Westerly 11km/h 7mph	

Figure 8-64. *Five-day forecast for the HP6 post code area*

4. You now need to convert this query into a function that can return the forecast for any post code area. To do this, click the Advanced Editor button on the View tab in the Query Editor toolbar to open the Advanced Editor. At this point the M code for the query will be as shown in Listing 8-10.

Listing 8-10.

```
let
    Source = Web.Page(Web.Contents("http://www.bbc.co.uk/weather/hp6")),
    Data0 = Source{0}[Data],
    ChangedType = Table.TransformColumnTypes(
                    Data0,
                    {{"Day", type text},
                    {"Weather", type text},
                    {"Maximum Day Temperature", type text},
                    {"Minimum Night Temperature", type text},
                    {"Wind Direction and Speed", type text}})
in
    ChangedType
```

5. Edit the code as shown in Listing 8-11 (the changes to the original code are in bold type).

Listing 8-11.

```
let
    GetWeather = (Postcode1 as text) as table =>
let
    Source = Web.Page(Web.Contents("http://www.bbc.co.uk/weather/" & Postcode1)),
    Data0 = Source{0}[Data],
    ChangedType = Table.TransformColumnTypes(
                    Data0,
                    {{"Day", type text},
                    {"Weather", type text},
                    {"Maximum Day Temperature", type text},
                    {"Minimum Night Temperature", type text},
                    {"Wind Direction and Speed", type text}})
in
    ChangedType
in
    GetWeather
```

6. At this point the Query Editor should show the name of the new function and its parameters, as shown in Figure 8-65. Rename the query GetWeather.

Figure 8-65. *Function details shown in the Query Editor*

7. Uncheck the Load to Worksheet box and the Load to Data Model boxes in Load Settings, then click the Apply & Close button on the Query Editor toolbar to close the Query Editor.

8. In the Power Query tab in the Excel ribbon, click the Fast Combine button and then, in the Fast Combine dialog, click the Enable button. This will stop Power Query from prompting you for data privacy settings later on.

9. Now click inside the table containing the information on the palaces inside the Excel worksheet and click the From Table button on the Power Query tab in the ribbon. The Query Editor will open and a new query will be created showing the data from that table.

10. Right-click the Postcode column in the table, and from the right-click menu select Split Column ➤ By Delimiter..., as shown in Figure 8-66.

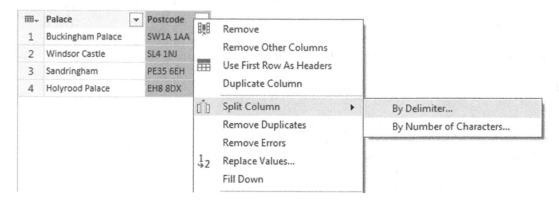

Figure 8-66. *The Split Column ➤ By Delimter... right-click menu option*

11. In the Split a column by delimiter dialog, select Space in the drop-down menu, as shown in Figure 8-67, then click OK. The Postcode column will be split into two columns called Postcode.1 and Postcode.2; the Postcode.1 column will contain the post code area.

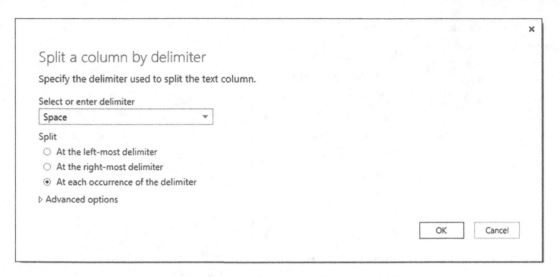

Figure 8-67. *The* `Split a column by delimiter` *dialog*

12. Right-click the Postcode.2 column and select Remove from the right-click menu to remove this column from the table. The output will be as shown in Figure 8-68.

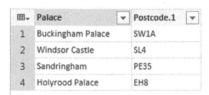

Figure 8-68. *The table with the Postcode.1 column showing post code areas*

13. The post code areas now need to be transformed to lowercase. To do this, right-click the Postcode.1 column and select Transform ➤ lowercase from the right-click menu as shown in Figure 8-69.

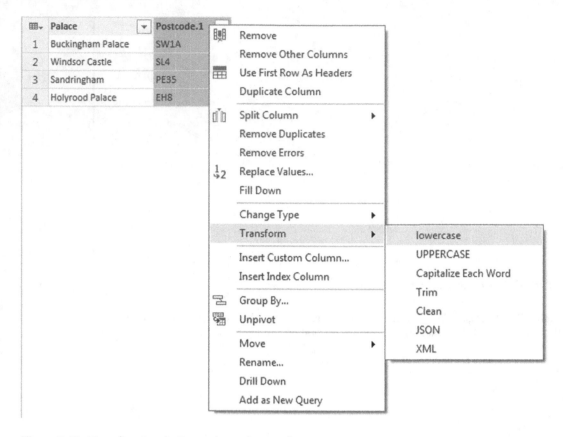

Figure 8-69. *Transforming the Postcode.1 column to lowercase*

14. You now need to call the function you created earlier for each row in this table. Click the Insert Custom Column button on the Insert tab of the Query Editor toolbar, call your new custom column Forecast, and use the following expression:

```
GetWeather([Postcode.1])
```

Click OK to close the Insert Custom Column dialog. The output will be as shown in Figure 8-70.

⊞▾	Palace	▾	Postcode.1	▾	Forecast	⁴ᵖ
1	Buckingham Palace		sw1a		Table	
2	Windsor Castle		sl4		Table	
3	Sandringham		pe35		Table	
4	Holyrood Palace		eh8		Table	

Figure 8-70. *The Forecast custom column containing table values*

15. Click the Expand icon in the header of the Forecast column and then, in the fly-out menu, click OK to expand all the columns in the table values in that column (as shown in Figure 8-71).

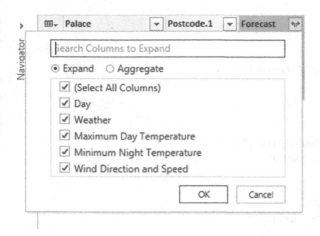

Figure 8-71. *Expanding the table values in the Forecast column*

16. Once you have done this, you will see the weather forecast data for each palace shown in the table. The final output of the query will be as shown in Figure 8-72.

	Palace	Postcode.1	Forecast.Day	Forecast.Weather	Forecast.Maximum Day Temperat...	Forecast.Minimum Night Temperatu...	Forecast.Wind Direction and Speed
1	Buckingham Palace	sw1a	Monday	Heavy Rain	19°C 66°F	10°C 50°F	East North Easterly 8km/h 5mph
2	Buckingham Palace	sw1a	Tuesday	Light Rain Shower	16°C 61°F	9°C 48°F	South Westerly 13km/h 8mph
3	Buckingham Palace	sw1a	Wednesday	Light Cloud	16°C 61°F	9°C 48°F	Southerly 16km/h 10mph
4	Buckingham Palace	sw1a	Thursday	Light Rain Shower	16°C 61°F	8°C 46°F	West South Westerly 6km/h 4mph
5	Buckingham Palace	sw1a	Friday	Light Cloud	16°C 61°F	9°C 48°F	West North Westerly 11km/h 7mph
6	Windsor Castle	sl4	Monday	Heavy Rain	17°C 63°F	9°C 48°F	North Easterly 10km/h 6mph
7	Windsor Castle	sl4	Tuesday	Light Rain Shower	14°C 57°F	8°C 46°F	South Westerly 16km/h 10mph
8	Windsor Castle	sl4	Wednesday	Light Cloud	15°C 59°F	7°C 45°F	Southerly 18km/h 11mph
9	Windsor Castle	sl4	Thursday	Sunny Intervals	15°C 59°F	6°C 43°F	West South Westerly 8km/h 5mph
10	Windsor Castle	sl4	Friday	Light Cloud	15°C 59°F	8°C 46°F	West North Westerly 11km/h 7mph
11	Sandringham	pe35	Monday	Thick Cloud	17°C 63°F	9°C 48°F	North Easterly 16km/h 10mph
12	Sandringham	pe35	Tuesday	Light Cloud	15°C 59°F	8°C 46°F	South South Easterly 16km/h 10mph
13	Sandringham	pe35	Wednesday	Light Rain Shower	16°C 61°F	9°C 48°F	South South Easterly 16km/h 10mph
14	Sandringham	pe35	Thursday	Light Rain Shower	15°C 59°F	7°C 45°F	Westerly 8km/h 5mph
15	Sandringham	pe35	Friday	Light Cloud	13°C 55°F	8°C 46°F	North Westerly 14km/h 9mph
16	Holyrood Palace	eh8	Monday	Light Cloud	13°C 55°F	8°C 46°F	North Easterly 26km/h 16mph
17	Holyrood Palace	eh8	Tuesday	Heavy Rain	9°C 48°F	8°C 46°F	East North Easterly 27km/h 17mph
18	Holyrood Palace	eh8	Wednesday	Light Cloud	12°C 54°F	8°C 46°F	East South Easterly 18km/h 11mph
19	Holyrood Palace	eh8	Thursday	Light Rain	11°C 52°F	6°C 43°F	South Easterly 10km/h 6mph
20	Holyrood Palace	eh8	Friday	Light Rain	11°C 52°F	7°C 45°F	East North Easterly 11km/h 7mph

Figure 8-72. *The final output of the weather forecast query*

Code

Listing 8-11 already gives the full M code for the GetWeather() function. Listing 8-12 gives the M code for the query that calls this function for each of the palaces in the Excel table.

Listing 8-12.

```
let
    //Load data from Excel worksheet
    Source = Excel.CurrentWorkbook(){[Name="Palaces"]}[Content],
    //Split post codes by space into two columns
    SplitColumnDelimiter = Table.SplitColumn(
                            Source,
                            "Postcode",
                            Splitter.SplitTextByDelimiter(" "),
                            {"Postcode.1", "Postcode.2"}),
    //Set the type of each column to text
    ChangedType = Table.TransformColumnTypes(
                            SplitColumnDelimiter,
                            {{"Postcode.1", type text},
                            {"Postcode.2", type text}}),
    //Remove the Postcode.2 column
    RemovedColumns = Table.RemoveColumns(ChangedType,{"Postcode.2"}),
    //Change the values in Postcode.1 to lowercase
    TransformedColumn = Table.TransformColumns(RemovedColumns,{{"Postcode.1", Text.Lower}}),
    //Call the GetWeather() function for each row
    InsertedCustom = Table.AddColumn(
                            TransformedColumn,
                            "Forecast",
                            each GetWeather([Postcode.1])),
    //Expand the table values returned by the GetWeather() function
    #"Expand Forecast" = Table.ExpandTableColumn(
                            InsertedCustom,
                            "Forecast",
                            {"Day", "Weather", "Maximum Day Temperature",
                            "Minimum Night Temperature", "Wind Direction and Speed"},
                            {"Forecast.Day", "Forecast.Weather",
                            "Forecast.Maximum Day Temperature",
                            "Forecast.Minimum Night Temperature",
                            "Forecast.Wind Direction and Speed"})
in
    #"Expand Forecast"
```

Finding the Driving Distance Between Two Locations Using the Bing Maps Route Web Service
Objective

Figure 8-73 shows a table in a worksheet containing two addresses. The aim in this section is to find the length (in kilometers) of the shortest driving route between these two addresses by calling the Bing Maps route web service.

Start	End
Buckingham Palace, London, SW1A1AA, UK	Windsor Castle, Windsor, Berkshire, SL4 1NJ, UK

Figure 8-73. Table containing the two addresses to find the distance between

■ **Note**   The Bing Maps web service used in this section is free to use for 90 days for evaluation purposes; for most other commercial uses you will need to buy a license. The full terms and conditions for this service can be found at www.microsoft.com/maps/product/terms.html.

Steps

1. To use any of the Bing Maps web services, you need to obtain a key. You can get one for free by going to https://www.bingmapsportal.com.

2. In the Power Query tab in the Excel ribbon, click the Fast Combine button; then, in the Fast Combine dialog, click the Enable button. This will stop Power Query from prompting you for data privacy settings later on.

3. Click inside the table shown in Figure 8-73 and then click the From Table button on the Power Query tab in the ribbon. The Query Editor will open and a new query will be created.

4. Click the *fx* button next to the Formula Bar in the Query Editor to add a new step to the query. Delete everything in the Formula Bar after the equals sign and copy in the following expression:

    ```
    Web.Contents(
    "http://dev.virtualearth.net/REST/V1/Routes/Driving",
    [Query=
    [#"wp.0"=Source{0}[Start],
    #"wp.1"=Source{0}[End],
    #"key"="InsertYourBingMapsKeyHere"]])
    ```

    Insert your own Bing Maps key where indicated. This expression uses the Web.Contents() function to call the Bing Maps routes web service.

5. Once you have done this, the Query Editor will display a document icon as seen in Figure 8-74. This is the JSON document that the web service returns containing the information you need. Double-click it.

Figure 8-74. *The JSON document returned by the web service*

6. Once you have double-clicked on the document, you will see the data inside it (as shown in Figure 8-75). Click the value List in the resourceSets row where indicated.

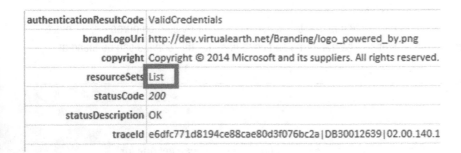

authenticationResultCode	ValidCredentials
brandLogoUri	http://dev.virtualearth.net/Branding/logo_powered_by.png
copyright	Copyright © 2014 Microsoft and its suppliers. All rights reserved.
resourceSets	List
statusCode	200
statusDescription	OK
traceId	e6dfc771d8194ce88cae80d3f076bc2a	DB30012639	02.00.140.1

Figure 8-75. *Contents of the JSON document*

7. Clicking the value List will display a list with a single value, Record. Click the value Record where indicated in Figure 8-76.

Figure 8-76. *Navigating through the JSON document*

8. The contents of yet another Record will appear, and you need to click the List value in the resources row where indicated in Figure 8-77.

Figure 8-77. *Still navigating through the JSON document*

9. Another list containing a single Record value will appear, exactly the same as shown in Figure 8-76. Once again, click the Record value.

10. You will now, at last, have reached the data you need, as shown in Figure 8-78. Right-click the travelDistance row and select Drill Down from the right-click menu.

__type	Route:http://schemas.microsoft.com/search/local/ws/rest/v1
bbox	List
id	v64,h966024641,i0,a0,cen-US,dAAAAAAAAAAA1,y0,s1,m1,o1,t4,wLu-TBB_H_P81~A5
distanceUnit	Kilometer
durationUnit	Second
routeLegs	List
travelDistance	39.176
travelDuration	2682
travelDurationTraffic	2829

Into Table
Drill Down
Add as New Query

Figure 8-78. *Isolating the travel distance value*

11. The final output of the query will be as shown in Figure 8-79. The value shown is the distance in kilometers between the two addresses in the source table.

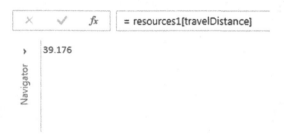

× ✓ *fx* = resources1[travelDistance]

39.176

Figure 8-79. *The final output of the query*

Code

The M code for the query is given in Listing 8-13.

Listing 8-13.

```
let
    //Load source data from Excel worksheet
    Source = Excel.CurrentWorkbook(){[Name="RouteData"]}[Content],
    //Call Bing Maps route web service
    Custom1 = Web.Contents(
                    "http://dev.virtualearth.net/REST/V1/Routes/Driving",
                    [Query=
                    [#"wp.0"=Source{0}[Start],
                    #"wp.1"=Source{0}[End],
                    #"key"=" InsertYourBingMapsKeyHere "]]),
    //Treat response as JSON document
    ImportedJSON = Json.Document(Custom1),
```

241

```
    //Navigate through JSON document to find the distance value
    resourceSets = ImportedJSON[resourceSets],
    resourceSets1 = resourceSets{0},
    resources = resourceSets1[resources],
    resources1 = resources{0},
    travelDistance = resources1[travelDistance]
in
    travelDistance
```

Summary

In this chapter you have seen a number of examples of how to solve problems with Power Query. Hopefully you will now be able to take these examples, learn from them, and be able to use Power Query to load your own data in Excel. As you will have realized by now, Power Query is an incredibly flexible and powerful tool that is central to Microsoft's new vision of Business Intelligence and Analytics. Have fun with it!

Index

▪ A, B, C

Calculations, Power Query
  distinct customers
    code implementations, 205
    duplicate date
      and customer, 204
    group by dialog
      configuration, 204
    objective, 202
    output, 205
    Query Editor toolbar, 203
    remove duplicates button, 203
    steps, 203
  grand total
    code implementations, 193
    custom column dialog, 192
    final output, 193
    group by dialog configuration, 190
    objective, 189
    query editor, 191
    source data, 191
  growth in sales
    code implementations, 198
    custom column definition, 197
    insert custom column dialog, 194
    merge dialog, 195
    merge operation, 196
    objective, 193
    PreviousDateSales column, 197
    sales column, 196
    sales growth figures, 198
    steps, 194
  tied ranks
    code implementations, 202
    final output table, 201
    input data, 199
    objective, 199

    Rank() function, 200–201
    steps, 199
Cloud services, 2
Comma-separated value (CSV), 27

▪ D

Data destinations
  Excel Data Model
    advantages, 106–107
    breaking changes, 110
    definition, 103
    Existing Connections dialog, 104
    Existing Workbook data model, 104
    Power Pivot Window, 105–106
  Excel worksheet
    data dialog, 103
    data tab, 102
    Existing Connections dialog, 102
    table creation, 101
  query editor
    Excel ribbon, 100
    load setting, 99
    options dialog, 100
  refresh button
    connection properties dialog, 113
    Excel workbook connections dialog, 111
    Query Editor toolbar, 112
    workbook queries pane, 111
  table relationships (*see* Table relationships)
Data retrieving, 189
  Bing Maps route web service
    code implementations, 241
    final output, 241
    JSON document, 239–240
    objective, 238
    steps, 239
    travel distance value, 241

Data retrieving (*cont.*)
    web-scraping weather forecast data
        code implementations, 237
        delimiter dialog, 235
        forecast column, 237
        HP6 post code, 233
        objective, 230
        post codes, 231, 235
        query Editor, 234
        split column, 234
        steps, 232
        table values, 236
        web dialog, 232
        web page, 232
Data sources
    active directory data, 53
    comma-separated value (CSV) files
        and code pages, 60–61
        definition, 27
        query editor, 28
        text buttons, 27
    data using power query
        online search, 38
    dialog setup, 58
    duplicating queries, 45
        Excel files working
        navigator pane, 32
        sales data, 31
    Excel workbook
        Excel table, 34
        Excel Web App, 47
        OData feed, 48
        query editor, 35
        salestable, 34
    Facebook
        connection dialog, 54
        table and record links, 54
    filters, 43
    folders and multiple files, 32
    HDFS and HDInsight working, 52
    importance of locale, 58
        drop-down box, 59
        English locale, 60
        French (France) locale, 60
        testing different locales, 59
    individual values from queries, 45
    JSON files working
        query editor, 31
    using web services, 30
    managing credentials, 57
    Microsoft Exchange
        navigator pane, 53
        query editor, 54
    multiple text files, 33
    new query option, 45

OData data sources
    OData entity, 47
    web service, 46
    working principle, 46
public data searching, 38–39
referencing entire queries, 43
    query tab, 45
    workbook button, 44
    workbook queries pane, 44
relational databases
    connecting to SQL server, 17
    database button, 18
    DimDate table, 23
    DW table, 22
    expand/aggregate dialog, 24–25
    expand icon, 23
    FactInternetSales table, 25
    Microsoft SQL database connection, 19
    navigator pane, 21
    query editor navigation pane, 23
    record object, 26
    scalar functions/table-valued functions, 21
    SQL Server authentication dialog, 20
    types, 26
RESTful web services, 38
reusing recent data sources, 56
    drop-down box, 57
    sources dialog, 57
SAP businessobjects
    modifying query editor, 56
    navigator pane, 55
    universe, 55
search tab, 42
shared queries and organizational data
    online search results, 41
    shared button, 41
    shared queries pane, 42
    sign in button, 40
sharepoint lists
    navigator pane, 49
    query editor, 49
    working, 48
text files working, 28
web page, 35
    navigator pane, 37
    query editor, 38
    table of data, 36
Windows azure blob storage and table
    storage working, 52
windows azure marketplace
    datasets, 50–51
    datasets in navigator pane, 52
    Windows Azure Marketplace
        account key, 51
    working, 49

XML files
  drilled-down employee data, 30
  expanded employee data, 30
  query editor, 29
  typical XML file, 29
Data transformation, 63
  aggregating values
    drop-down box, 89
    group by dialog, 88
    Query Editor, 89–90
  built-in custom columns
    statistics drop-down box, 96
    values across columns, 96
  change type, 72
  creating custom columns, 94
  custom columns with
      M calculations, 97
  date/time/duration transforms, 84
  drop-down box, 83
  Fill drop-down box
    country values, 86
    empty text values, 87
    ship to city and ship to country, 87
  filtering out rows with errors, 79
  filtering rows
    auto-filter box, 72–73
    filter rows dialog, 74
    icon menu, 77
    number filters, 73
    number filters menu, 74
    query editor toolbar, 77
    by range, 76
    remove alternate rows dialog, 78
    text filters, 74
  Locale option, 72
  merge columns
    dialog, 70
    option and button, 69
    Query Editor toolbar, 70
  moving columns, 66
  naming columns
    columns buttons, 66
    source step, 65
  number transforms, 83
  queries and steps, 63
    ChangedType, 64
    FirstRowAsHeader, 65
    Source step, 64
  removing columns, 66
  removing duplicate values, 78
  replace values button, 80
  replace values dialog, 81
  setting data type column, 70
    data types, 71

shipping cost column, 98
sort a table, 79
split columns
  delimiter button, 67
  delimiter dialog, 67
  position dialog, 68
  split and merged, 66
table transposing, 93
text transforms, 81
unpivoting columns to rows, 91
  sales person, 93
  unpivot button, 92
  unpivoted data, 92
word transform, 82
XML data stored in table cells, 82

■ E

Excel.CurrentWorkbook(), 119
Excel Data Model, 21
  advantages, 106–107
  definition, 103
  Existing Connections dialog, 104
  Existing Workbook data model, 104
  Power Pivot Window, 105–106

■ F, G

FactInternetSales table, 25
Formula Bar, 8
Functions
  definition, 138
  expressions, 139, 142
  MultiplyThenAddOne() function, 141
  parameter value, 139
  queries function, 140
  recursive function, 143
  Table.TransformColumns(), 140

■ H, I, J, K

Hadoop Distributed File System (HDFS), 52

■ L

Lists, records, and tables
  aggregate table data, 127
    sales table, 130
      Table.Group() output, 129, 131
      Table.RowCount(), 128
  aggregate value list, 125
  definition, 124
  DimDate table, 135
  filtering lists, 125

Lists, records, and tables (*cont.*)
    filtering tables, 132
    functional list, 124
    pivoting and unpivoting tables, 133
    primary and foreign keys, 135
    records lists, 126
    referencing fields records, 137
    referencing items lists, 136
    referencing row tables, 136
    referencing value tables, 137
    sorting list, 125
    sort tables, 131
    Table.Column() function, 134
    tables creation, 127
    working, 124

M

M language
    advanced editor window, 116
    blank query creation, 117
    concepts of, 118
    expressions, values, and let statements, 118
    formula bar, 115
    functions (*see* Functions)
    HTTP header, 144
    lists, records, and tables (*see* Lists, records, and tables)
    query folding (*see* Query folding)
    standard library, 119
    table.selectrows() function, 120
    types, 120
        comments, 121
        conditional logic, 123
        date, datetime, datetimezone, or duration, 121
        trapping errors, 122
    web services working, 143
Mobile BI app, 4
Multiple queries
    appending queries
        dialog, 159–160
        output, 160
        Query Editor window, 159
        ribbon, 158
        Table.Combine() function, 160–161
        user interface, 158
    data privacy settings
        DimDate table, 152
        levels dialog, 153
        Organizational, 154
        Private, 154
        Public, 154
        Query Editor, 153

    Excel worksheet, 149
    fast combine option, 156
    Formula Firewall
        edit permission, 155
        error, 156
        native database query prompt, 155
        SELECT statement, 154
    merge button
        ApplesProfit table, 162–163
        dialog, 162
        non-matching rows, 164
        Query Editor toolbar, 164
        ribbon, 161
        Table.AddJoinColumn() function, 165
        Table.Join() function, 165
        Table.NestedJoin() function, 164–165
    parameterized query
        data sources, 150
        filters, 150–152
        ProductQuery, 151

N, O

Navigator pane, 8

P

Power BI
    cloud services, 2
    Excel add-ins, 1
    Mobile BI app, 4
    Power Map, 3
    Power Pivot and Excel 2013 Data Model, 2–3
    Power Query, 2
    Power View, 3
    SharePoint, 3
    working process, 4–5
Power BI Data Catalog, 167
    data sources
        data sources tab, 175
        metadata, 176–177
    Data Steward
        calculation/transformation, 180
        certified queries, 178–179
        functions, 180
        tasks, 177–178
    Excel workbooks
        Admin Center, 181, 185
        configuration, 184
        connections dialog, 182
        data refresh option, 186–187
        data sources, 180
        data source wizard, 183
        enabling, 181

sharing queries
Active Directory Security Groups, 171
analytics tab, 174
Excel workbooks, 171
My Power BI site, 173–174
Power BI site link, 173
Power Query tab, 168
Share Query dialog, 170
Sign In dialog, 168
updation, 172
URL, 170
Workbook Queries pane, 169
Power Map, 3
Power query, 1
aggregation/filter, 14
automate data loads, 14
CSV button, 7
data sources, 14
editing an existing query
fly-out menu, 11
result, 13
top rows dialog box, 12
Workbook Queries pane, 10
Excel's ribbon menu, 7
Excel workbooks, 15
installation, 6
licensing model, 5–6
Microsoft Excel, 13
Power BI (*see* Power BI)
Query Editor window, 8
query. unfortunately, 6
transformations and
calculations creation, 14
worksheet, 9
Power View, 3

Q

Query Editor toolbar, 8
Query folding
monitoring query in SQL server, 145
operations
advanced features, 148
custom SQL statements, 147
remove rows with errors, 147
prevent code, 146
Query Settings pane, 8

R, S

Results pane, 8

T, U, V, W, X, Y, Z

Table.Distinct() function, 135
Table relationships
data sources, 110
foreign key, 108
Navigator pane, 109
Power Pivot window, 110
Table.UnPivotOtherColumns(), 133
Transformation table, 189
date table
code implementations, 222
custom column expression, 221
dates to years conversion, 220
dialog table, 219
List.Dates() function, 218
objective, 217
output, 222
steps, 218
new, lost, and returning customers
append operation, 211
code implementations, 216
custom column expression, 215
distinct customers, 212
final output, 216
LastYear column, 215
merged table, 212
merging, 213
non-blank rows, 214
objective, 210
steps, 211
Year column, 214
single-column table to a multiple-column table
code implementations, 210
customerID column, 209
index column added, 207
objective, 205
pivoted table, 209
row type identification, 208
steps, 206
stock price
code implementations, 230
data, 224
filtering, 228
final output, 229
group by dialog, 226
keep top rows dialog, 229
local grouping, 227
objective, 223
sorting descending order, 229
steps, 224

Get the eBook for only $10!

> Now you can take the weightless companion with you anywhere, anytime. Your purchase of this book entitles you to 3 electronic versions for only $10.

This Apress title will prove so indispensible that you'll want to carry it with you everywhere, which is why we are offering the eBook in 3 formats for only $10 if you have already purchased the print book.

Convenient and fully searchable, the PDF version enables you to easily find and copy code—or perform examples by quickly toggling between instructions and applications. The MOBI format is ideal for your Kindle, while the ePUB can be utilized on a variety of mobile devices.

Go to www.apress.com/promo/tendollars to purchase your companion eBook.

Apress®
THE EXPERT'S VOICE™